You Can
If You Think
You Can

NORMAN VINCENT PEALE

PRENTICE
HALL
PRESS

New York   London   Toronto   Sydney   Tokyo   Singapore

PRENTICE HALL PRESS
15 Columbus Circle
New York, NY 10023

Published in 1986 by Prentice Hall Press
A Division of Simon & Schuster, Inc.
Previously published by Prentice-Hall, Inc.

PRENTICE HALL PRESS and colophons are registered
trademarks of Simon & Schuster, Inc.

ISBN 0-13-976879-3

Manufactured in the United States of America

18   17   16   15   14

Dedicated to
RUTH STAFFORD PEALE
my beloved wife
and
constant partner
in all our many activities
with love and gratitude

A special word of appreciation to my secretaries, Miss Grace M. Blythe, for her splendid assistance in the preparation of this manuscript, and Mrs. Alice Olivet, for her helpfulness in research.

ACKNOWLEDGMENTS

Permission to reprint excerpts is gratefully acknowledged: Guideposts Associates, Inc., to quote from *Guideposts* Magazine, copyright by Guideposts Associates, Inc., Carmel, New York 10512: "Back from Happy Town," copyright 1968; "I Fought the River for My Child," copyright 1961; "What the Mountain Did to Me," copyright 1972. Curtis Brown Ltd., *Why Some Men Live Longer* by Mary McSherry with Frederick J. Stare, M.D., published in *Woman's Day* Magazine, copyright © 1971 by Fawcett Publications, Inc. *Success Unlimited*, 6355 Broadway, Chicago, Illinois 60660, copyright 1973, "Six Secrets to Double Your Idea Power" from the April 1973 issue. Pantheon Books, a Division of Random House, Inc., *The Wild Wheel*, by Garet Garrett, copyright 1952. *Science of Mind* Magazine, February 1971, article by Dr. Krimsky, "A Doctor Looks at Religion." *The National Observer*, copyright Dow Jones & Company, 1972, "The Boredom Epidemic," by Peter T. Chew.

Also excerpted: "Two Words to Avoid, Two to Remember," copyright 1967 by the Reader's Digest Association, Inc. "Michigan's Giant Stride," *The Story of the Mackinac Bridge*, by Walker L. Cisler, copyright 1967. Printed for the Newcomen Society in North America by Princeton University Press.

Dear Reader—

If you are an old friend, welcome to another book. If you are a new friend, welcome to you, too. One of the chief delights in life is to keep old friends and make new ones.

But why another book when we have already written seventeen and collaborated on others? Well, perhaps it is strange, but one seems to keep on feeling that he has something more to say, or that he would like to repeat in a different way some things he has already said, or perhaps he hopefully wants to express in a more persuasive manner those principles which he knows to be effective.

A long time ago I developed what might be called an obsession. The obsession is to try to help people get the best from life and learn how to live with its hard experiences in a creative manner.

Personally, I have always been fascinated by the tremendous qualities in the individual and by the amazing things human beings can do with themselves. To me this is so exciting, so fabulous, that I just cannot help coming forward once again with more inspiring stories of turned-on people who have really done something remarkable, especially in releasing their own potential. And these are stories of the plain people, just like ourselves. At least, like me.

Having known many men and women and having had opportunity to watch them overcome problems and come up with real values, I have become aware that certain specific principles are always involved in creative outcomes. This book is written to outline those dynamic and workable principles and to encourage my readers to put them into operation for themselves. Its purpose is to persuade you, the reader, that you can if you think you can.

This book is produced out of an enthusiastic belief in people and a desire to encourage them to take charge of their lives by fully realizing the amazing possibilities inherent in the mind.

If you are not experiencing the best and most exciting values, this book is designed to offer workable suggestions for reaching your objectives. If difficulties and problems are ganging up on you and your confidence is shaky, it is hoped that this book may make you realize that you can indeed handle whatever comes and handle it well. Practical suggestions are offered that can help you as they have helped others.

After you have read this book, if your belief in the powers of your own mind is enhanced, if you have a more workable thought pattern, and if you know for a fact that you can successfully deal with any problem, I shall feel that my sincere purpose in writing it has been achieved.

Of course I believe in everything said and reported in the book, in every idea and principle advanced. I believe in them because they work. Our hope is that the book says something to you and does something for you.

JUST ONE WORD MORE

Did you ever stop to think what a book can do? A book written from a positive and inspirational point of view? I wish it were possible to reproduce here many

of the letters received which tell of the marvelous results such books have had in people's experience. Let
me give you just one, a letter that came just as I was
finishing this manuscript. It tells what a book did for a
young woman, Loan Eng Tjioe, Ph.D. She writes:

Dear Doctor Peale:
   Your books guided me through difficult phases
of my life even before I came to the United States.
I was still in my home country in Indonesia, when
I came across your book, *Stay Alive All Your Life*.
At that time I was an unhappy, frustrated college
student. I wanted to go abroad badly to receive a
better education and to see what the world outside
my country looked like.
   Many friends of mine had gone to Europe for
study, and I accompanied them one by one to the
airport, where I said goodbye to them. I always
came home in tears asking when it would be my
turn to go too. However, my father was a small
businessman and had five children to take care of.
It was impossible for him to finance study in
Europe.
   I knew a miracle had to happen if I were ever
to go abroad. Then I found your book and learned
that I could get what I wanted, if I but *believed!*
Your book also said that I had to act as if I were sure
I would get what I wanted. Well, I thought I had
nothing to lose by trying it.
   I told myself that I would get a scholarship to
Germany, the country where I wanted to study,
because Psychology, the subject I majored in, origi-
nated there. I started taking German lessons intensively. I wrote to German universities asking about
the possibilities of a scholarship. They all replied
in the negative. No one could give me a scholarship

unless I was already studying in Germany and proving my abilities there. But I kept on believing. My parents thought I had gone out of my mind to fight such a hopeless struggle. I let them talk and one day I received a letter from the University of Bonn that they were willing to consider my application.

I was excited and nervous. Now I had to go a step further in my positive thinking. I had to believe that I was going to study at the University of Bonn in Germany. I found a picture of this university and pasted it on the wall of my bedroom. I kept looking at it and told myself: "That is where you are going to study!" I learned the German language even more intensively. Then, after an agony of nearly a year, I received the letter that I had indeed won a scholarship. Three months later I left for Germany.

This happened about eight years ago. It was the first but not the last time in my life, which showed me that God is willing to give you everything you ask for, if you but believe.

I always thought that I would like to see you in person one day. Now this wish has been fulfilled, since my husband and I are living in New York at present. On coming Sunday our first son will be baptized by you. Who would have thought that long ago as I was still in Indonesia, clinging to your book as my only source of hope? Thank you so very, very much!

May God bless you!

Sincerely yours,

Perhaps this book may do something comparable for you. The principles it teaches are packed with power;

so why not draw on that power? The book tells how. And remember, always remember: You can if you think you can.

NORMAN VINCENT PEALE

CONTENTS

ONE

❀

THE PERSISTENCE PRINCIPLE:
IT'S ALWAYS TOO SOON TO QUIT

When you have a problem, one that is especially difficult and baffling, perhaps terribly discouraging, there is one basic principle to apply and keep on applying. It is simply this—never quit.

To give up is to invite complete defeat. And not only in connection with the matter at hand. Giving up contributes to an ultimate defeat of the personality. It tends to develop a defeat psychology.

Come at the problem a different way if the methodology you are using is not working. And if the new approach fails to go well, then come at it still another way until you do find the key to the situation. For there is a key, there always is, and continual, thoughtful, undeviating search and attack will produce it.

At luncheon I noted that a friend of mine had the habit of drawing diagrams on the white tablecloth to illustrate points he was making. He was talking about a man who had it tough but who was tougher than his problems and who, because he wouldn't quit, came through finally to a spectacular outcome.

The diagram was of a man facing an enormous mountain. "How is he going to get on the other side of that mountain?" my luncheon companion asked.

1

"Go around it," I replied.

"It's too wide."

"O.K., burrow under it," I offered.

"No; it's too deep. Here's the way. He rises above it mentally. If man can devise a mechanism that can fly forty thousand feet high—above mountains—he can come up with a type of thinking that can lift him above any mountainous difficulty."

"Bill, that is pretty ingenious, but I read that concept a long while ago. 'Whosoever shall say unto this mountain, Be thou removed, and be thou cast into the sea; and shall not doubt in his heart . . . .' " *

"Yes, that's the idea," he agreed enthusiastically. "Just think, don't get emotional, and hold to the basic principle that it's always too soon to quit."

Recently I received an upbeat letter from a man who utilized this principle successfully. He told me that a few years ago he developed a prefabricated wall system for mobile homes. He organized a company and put all his money into it, but it didn't take hold, failed to move. The firm ran into one difficulty after another, so much so that his associates pleaded with him to "bury the corpse." But he would not let go.

This man is a positive thinker. He is also an individual who demonstrates the "hold on" type of faith, actually an invincible character, you might say. He believed that this difficulty need not defeat or destroy him. He said, "I refused even to entertain the thought of quitting." So he did some rational, in-depth thinking and got an idea. And you'll always get an idea if you think and don't panic. He decided to establish a line of prefabricated floor systems to go with the prefabricated

——* Mark 11:23.

wall systems. And with this he "hit the jackpot." A big company manufacturing mobile homes bought him out. Writing to tell about it, he gave me this terrific phrase: "It's always too soon to quit!"

You and I have seen repeated again and again a real tragedy. We've seen people with goals and objectives. They worked . . . they struggled . . . they thought . . . they prayed. But because the going was hard, they grew tired and discouraged and finally they quit. And afterward it was often discovered that had they persevered just a little longer, had they been able to see just ahead of them, they would have found the result they sought.

NEVER TALK DEFEAT

How can you develop this nonquitting, undefeatable attitude? Well, for one thing, never talk defeat, for if you do you can actually talk yourself into acceptance of defeat. One time when I personally was having some hard going, a man on the West Coast, whom I did not know, called me on the telephone. All he said was this: "Don't you be worried and don't you give up. I am saying the Good Word for you." Before I could ask him what the Good Word was, he hung up. And I still don't know what he meant by the Good Word. But I suddenly realized I had not been saying good, hopeful words; I had been talking "down." And by that action I was actually talking myself into a defeatist attitude and therefore into defeat itself. So I began saying good words, words like hope—belief—faith—victory. I used the powerful affirmation, "I can if I think I can." I began to act and think and work on that basis. Try that and your whole personality will begin reaching for the good things; and get them, too.

In an article Phyllis Simolke discussed this idea of "the good word," and how dangerous it is to use negative words. She suggested, for example, consideration of the word "no." That word "no" denotes a shutting of the door. It means failure, defeat, delay. But spell it backwards and take new hope, for backwards it spells "on." Get really activated; push "on" unremittingly toward your goal until your problem is solved, your difficulty dealt with.

She also drew attention to the word "teem." Everything seems to be "teeming" in your life, teeming with difficulty, teeming with regret, teeming with ineffectiveness. So she advises turning it around to form the word "meet." Meet each problem as it arises. You will no longer be teeming with defeat and hopelessness, but will become productive and creative by vigorously meeting each challenge as it arises. Turn "no" into "on" and "teem" into "meet."

Change your thinking to meet problems in a positive, constructive way. And remember the persistence principle: It's always too soon to quit.

Indeed, your chances of really getting where you want to go in life often hinge on your reaction to some shattering setback. Will you give up or will you keep on trying? It's as simple as that. And what you decide, decides your future.

CALL ON YOUR GRIT

Ever hear of the thrilling career of Hayes Jones? Back in 1960 this man was the phenomenon of the year in high hurdles racing. He won race after race. He broke records. He was, in fact, sensational. Naturally he was picked for the Olympic Games held that year at Rome. There he ran in the 110-meter high hurdles amid worldwide expectations that he would carry off the gold medal.

But surprisingly he didn't. He finished third. It was, of course, a keen disappointment. His first thought was: "So what! I might as well quit running." There would be no more Olympic Games for four long years. Besides, he had already won all the other coveted high hurdles championships. Why subject himself to four more strenuous years of keeping in top form? The only sensible thing was to forget it and get started in a business career.

This was plain logic, for sure. But Hayes Jones couldn't settle for that. "You can't be logical," he says, "about something you've wanted all your life." So he started training again, three hours a day, seven days a week. And in the next couple of years made some new records in the 60-yard and 70-yard high hurdles.

Came the night of February 22, 1964 at Madison Square Garden. Jones was competing in the 60-yard high hurdles. He had announced that this would be his last indoor race. Tension ran high; every eye was on him. And he won, tying his own previous all-time record. Then a strange thing happened. In those days in the old Garden, when runners had crossed the finish line they disappeared under a ramp before they could slow down and stop. Walking back onto the track, Jones stood for a moment with head bowed, acknowledging the applause. Then seventeen thousand people packing the Garden stood in tribute. Jones wept. Many spectators wept, too, because a once-defeated man had still hung in there. He wouldn't quit, and the fans loved him for that

He entered the 1964 Olympics at Tokyo and ran the 110-meter high hurdles in 13.6 seconds, finishing first—winning his gold medal.

After that he went to work for an airline as a sales representative.

Later he offered to help as a volunteer in his city's physical fitness program. His activities got spectacular results.

In a speech to a crowd of young men he quoted some lines which anyone would do well to tuck into his mind and live by: *

> *It's the plugging away that will win you the day,*
> *So don't be a piker, old pard!*
> *Just draw on your grit; it's so easy to quit:*
> *It's the keeping-your-chin-up that's hard.*
> *It's easy to cry that you're beaten—and die;*
> *It's easy to crawfish and crawl;*
> *But to fight and to fight when hope's out of sight—*
> *Why, that's the best game of them all!*
> *And though you come out of each grueling bout,*
> *All broken and beaten and scarred,*
> *Just have one more try—it's dead easy to die,*
> *It's the keeping-on-living that's hard.*

Hayes Jones's story brings to mind a line from Goethe: "Austere perseverance, harsh and continuous, may be employed by the smallest of us and rarely fails of its purpose, for its silent power grows irresistibly greater with time." That is to say, just keep on trying—that will do it.

This refusal to quit is called the persistence principle.

———* "The Quitter," by Robert W. Service, from *Collected Poems of Robert Service* (New York: Dodd, Mead & Co., 1966).

Sadly enough, we hear little about persistence in this soft, permissive era. But as America historically produced strong men, the importance of persistence was constantly driven into the consciousness of youth. They were told to fight the good fight and never let anything throw them, and if it did, get right back up and attack the difficulty, hit it hard and then some, and keep on no matter what. Perseverance—that was the key word then, and it still remains the basic principle for anyone who wants success. You cannot creatively get anywhere in this life without sturdy application of the persistence principle.

KEEPING AT IT GETS RESULTS

The thinkers of the world, those who know the score, always ring the changes on persistence. Mohammed said, "God is with those who persevere." Mohammed, it appears, knew his stuff, and so did Shakespeare, who told us that "Much rain wears the marble." Well, marble is hard, very hard, but little raindrops constantly keeping at it can wear it down. Seventeen centuries before the Bard of Avon came up with the foregoing wise observation, Lucretius made the same point: "The fall of dropping water wears away the stone."

Edmund Burke, the great British statesman, gave us a man-sized bit of advice. He, too, believed in the power of the persistence principle. He said, "Never despair, but if you do, *work on in despair.*"

May I refer to another person, perhaps not so famous but certainly just as wise as those previously mentioned? The lady is my own mother. She practiced the never-quit persistence principle all her life and she had plenty to contend with—very little money and all the ordinary human problems. But she was never about to fold and give up. She was made of sterner stuff. She was strong, always and inevitably.

I remember two things in my boyhood that I hated: spinach and algebra. And I do not really care for either of them today, although I must admit they now doctor up the spinach so it is more palatable. I would come home from school and inform my mother glumly that I just couldn't get algebra. I recall one especially gloomy day when it really had me on the ropes and I complained, "I can't get it. That's all there is to it. I just can't get it. I can't, I can't."

She looked at me and, believe me, it was no soft "mama" look that she leveled my way. Her voice was sharp and crisp. She has been gone from this earth physically a good many years, but I can still hear those dynamic words as she quoted a familiar line from a man named William Edward Hickson: "If at first you don't succeed, try, try again." And she would add, "You can if you think you can." She made me believe that I could. The affirmation of strong perseverance, of keeping at it, of continuous, undeviating effort, is bound to pay off ultimately if you have the inner compulsion to visualize and keep at it.

THE PERCEPTION PRINCIPLE

To be effective, the persistence principle must be supported by another vital principle—the perception principle and the power that derives from it.

What do we mean by the perception principle? When a person is defeated in his mind or is over-

whelmed by a self-defeating situation, he needs perception. He must have the insight to perceive the inner
cause of his defeat. He must see the situation not only
on the outside, but on the inside as well. He must have
an intuitive insight and understanding concerning himself—who and what he is. He must perceive and cultivate his inner powers. Then he can go on to a successful
outcome.

It is a fact that most people who mess up their lives
and fail do so, in part at least, because they are not
organized inwardly; they are lacking in insight as to
who and what they are. It has often been said, "He is
his own worst enemy." People can have goals and objectives and work hard and still fail. A person may wish
to accomplish something creative and yet he cannot
seem to do it; he fails at it. Why? Perhaps the trouble
is something amiss within himself.

Actually, the hardest person in the world to know is
oneself. We have a built-in, self-protecting mechanism
that always tries to do what we want. It seeks to make
the irrational appear rational. Many people simply do
not want to know themselves. They will talk about
other people and their problems, but they hide from
themselves and will not face reality. Actually, one of the
greatest moments in anybody's developing experience
is when he no longer tries to hide from himself but
determines to get acquainted with himself as he really
is.

People who fail usually do so not because they are
unable to handle an outward situation—it is the inner
or mental conflict that defeats them. You must see yourself as you really are and deal with yourself on that
honest basis. That is the perception principle, and it is
based on self-examination. Stand in front of a mirror

and say to yourself, "Now, look, I want the truth about you." Right away your mind may tell you, "Why, you're all right. Don't make so much of it." But the normal, healthy-minded individual will realize that true self-knowledge is always the beginning of self-development.

I spoke at a meeting in Washington, D.C. There were many distinguished government officials present and not a few so-called celebrities. I did not know many of them personally, but one man came to me afterward and introduced himself. I recognized him immediately as an outstanding person, a man of distinction and ability, and proceeded to tell him how much I admired his leadership.

"Isn't that something!" he remarked. "I thank you very much. But if it is justified, there is a good reason why."

"Oh?" I replied.

"Yes," said he. "It is a talk you gave one night about fifteen years ago right here in Washington. I attended that meeting and heard you speak. I was ambitious and well trained," he continued. "Everybody told me I had ability. But much that I did went wrong. I was strangely mixed up in my thinking and reactions and did a lot of dumb things. But that night, as I listened to your speech, all of a sudden something dramatic happened to me. It was like being in the country on a very black night," he reflected, "when suddenly comes a flash of lightning and you see the entire landscape clearly revealed.

"I had a flashing view of my inner self. And I could see that I was disorganized, and that was the reason I was being defeated. Right then and there I decided that I would get with it. So the first thing I did was to ask the good Lord to organize me, to bring all my shattered parts together inwardly. And my request was granted. In succeeding days," he concluded, "I began increasingly to have a marvelous, actually unbelievable sense of capacity, unity and power. Of course, everything wasn't suddenly rosy, but it got better, lots better."

This creative change happened because the man was able to apply the principle of perception. He got a good look inside himself and then corrected what he saw that was amiss. Result: He got a power that projected him to success.

When one begins to realize the potential within himself through the application of the perception principle, power takes over to release it, develop it, and actualize it into successful performance. By power is meant a sense of new strength, a feeling of adequacy. But before creativity can become operative, the individual must not only learn to know and believe in himself but must also have a power-releasing experience so conclusive that he will be able to carry on despite all odds.

Persistence motivated by perception releases new power and is the valid formula that leads to successful achievement, hard though the process may be.

NUDGED BY HIS INNER POTENTIAL

Take the career of Bob Pettit, for example. Bob became one of the greatest professional stars of his generation, one of the highest-scoring men in basketball history.

At fourteen years of age, when Bob was a freshman in high school, he was 5 feet 7 inches and weighed 118 pounds. As he put it, he had "the coordination of a broomstick." He was a weak, frail little fellow. But he had a strong motivational urge to be an athlete. Instinctively he employed the perception principle. He alone felt, rather than saw, his potential.

He went out for football but didn't make the team. However, they did put him on as a third-string tackle. One day, when nobody else was available, he was put in a game, and the opposing quarterback poured a play over him for a 65-yard touchdown. That was the end of Bob as a football player!

Then he went out for baseball. And finally one day he was put in to substitute at second base. A player hit a fast ground ball to him and it zoomed right through his legs and two runs came in. So that was the end of his baseball career.

Next, Bob went out for basketball. They needed twelve boys for the high school team; seventeen applied. When the list was posted, Bob's name wasn't on it. Small, frail, and weak, it seemed he just couldn't make it in sports. But he wanted so much to be an athlete—with giants!

So Bob went to his church and talked with the minister, who saw at once what was in this young boy. He told him that the Lord would make him great. Bob became a believer. Furthermore, the minister had an idea. "We'll organize a church team," he said. "And we'll get several other churches to organize teams, too!" These teams were made up of boys who couldn't get on the high school team. Bob was finally on a team!

For the first time in his life Bob felt important. He practiced constantly. He took a wire coat hanger and bent it in such a way that it resembled a basket and nailed it against the garage. Hour after hour he threw tennis balls through this improvised basket. His father, impressed by his persistence, got him a regulation basketball and backboard.

Every afternoon after school Bob would throw baskets until dinner time. Then he would go in and have dinner, do his homework and go back out and shoot baskets until dark. Every time he saw any kind of open trash can along the street he would throw something into it, constantly throwing things into baskets. He became the leading scorer on the church team. He was determined to excel in basketball. His inner potential nudged him on.

He did not have natural strength, so Bob began daily exercises to build up his legs and arms. He did these exercises faithfully each day and because of his determination, it is said, he grew five inches in his sophomore year! By the time he was a junior in high school, he had made the school basketball team. The coach couldn't get over the change in Bob, who "wasn't good enough to make junior varsity last year"!

The team became state high school champion in Bob's senior year, and Bob went on to become the highest scorer at Louisiana State University and later with the St. Louis Hawks. He became a magnificent physical and spiritual specimen, one of the greatest athletes of his generation. Why? Because he practiced two principles—perception and persistence. Sensing the potential power within him, he simply would not give up.

But we do not have to be great athletes to make use of the perception and persistence principles. In day-to-day activities we are often confronted by situations where our ability to think positively and never give up is called upon.

KEEP ON KEEPING ON

The story of a problem I suddenly had to deal with illustrates that often a situation which may seem completely hopeless will work out if you just keep hoping and, better still, keep trying! Unexpected obstacles gave me quite a demonstration of this.

After speaking at a meeting in Holland, Michigan, where I stayed overnight, I had an engagement the following night in Phoenix, Arizona. Under normal travel conditions it appeared to be no problem getting there. I was scheduled to take an early plane from Grand Rapids to Chicago and connect with a plane to Phoenix, which would get me there in plenty of time. It seemed like an easy travel setup.

But that morning in Holland, Michigan, you could hardly see the car parked right outside the motel room window. That is how foggy it was. I telephoned to the Grand Rapids airport and found it was fogged in. No planes going out.

I called Detroit. It too was fogged in. They advised that Chicago's O'Hare Airport was also at a below-minimum overcast and did not expect any planes to be getting out that morning. I called Minneapolis. Fogged in. In short, I was fogged in—hundreds of miles from Phoenix and my evening engagement.

What could I do? Well, I sat down and had a positive-thinking session, practicing the persistence principle. The people in Phoenix had booked me eight months before. To call now and tell them I couldn't make it was the last thing to consider. I might have given up and said, "Well, there's nothing I can do about it. I just can't get there." Had I admitted that, I'm sure I would not have gotten there. But instead, I definitely practiced a positive mental attitude, rented a car, and set out for Chicago, visualizing the fog as lifting by arrival time.

After going about sixty of the two hundred miles to Chicago, the engine started sputtering and missing. The prospects of my travel program were not brightened by this mechanical difficulty. I forced my mind to take a positive view. At this point I came to a service station where, believe it or not, they had one of the best mechanics I have ever met. In a jiffy he had the engine half apart. He cleaned and scraped a lot of things and ended by putting in eight new spark plugs. "Now," he said, "it will go."

From a pay phone I called Chicago again. "Your plane's been cancelled," I was told. But the young lady added, "There's one going at four o'clock this afternoon." That would get me to Phoenix in just the nick of time for my speaking engagement.

Getting back in the car, what do you know? It wouldn't start. The battery was dead. The man recharged the battery. However, he told me, "You can get to O'Hare all right, but don't turn the engine off on the way, no matter what!"

With new spark plugs and all, the car ran beautifully. When I pulled up at O'Hare Field, I had to turn the motor off to get my bag out of the trunk, and then the car would not start again. The battery was really dead. So I simply turned the ailing vehicle over to an unappreciative policeman.

In the terminal thousands of people were milling around. While I stood hesitating, suddenly out of the crowd walked an airline official who recognized me and asked, "What's your trouble?" I explained. "Our planes are all grounded," he told me, "but another airline is going to try to get a plane out. If you can get on it, you'll make your meeting. Let's practice positive thinking— 'never give up.' Wait here for me."

He was gone a good half hour; then came back and said, "That plane is going out, all right, but there's no space on it. But I'll tell you what; we'll go down to the gate and we'll hold the thought that there will be a cancellation." Well, when the plane was just about to take off, my friend informed me with a broad grin that I had a seat. Someone had failed to show. I arrived in Phoenix forty-five minutes before I was scheduled to speak.

When everything seems to be going wrong, that is the time to practice the positive mental belief that you can still achieve your objective provided you persist, trying everything. If you start thinking it's hopeless, your state of mind will actually attract further trouble to defeat you. Instead, hold the thought that conditions will shift in your favor—and get going.

The glib excuse about circumstances being beyond our control is too often used to rationalize a feeble giving up too soon. The people who get on in this world are the people who get up and look for the circumstances they want, and if they can't find them, make them. That is the attitude that works wonders in handling problems. It is always too soon to quit—so don't quit. You can if you think you can.

Well, now, let's pull together a few ideas on the important principles in this chapter:

1.   When tackling a problem the number-one thing is, never quit attacking it. Always use the persistence principle.

2. *Remember—you can get over those big mountains of difficulties by thinking over them.*

3. *Adopt the motto, "It's always too soon to quit." Keep it going.*

4. *Use upbeat words. Never talk down. Speak the Good Word.*

5. *Plugging away will win the day.*

6. *Master the perception principle. Learn to know yourself. Know the real person deep within you.*

7. *If at first you don't succeed, try, try again.*

8. *Do not let circumstances defeat you. With your mind, control circumstances. You can if you think you can.*

9. *Just keep on keeping on—just keep trying—for that will do it. Keep going. It can turn out O.K.*

10. *And God bless you all the way.*

TWO

SO WHAT'S YOUR PROBLEM?
YOU CAN HANDLE IT

"Every problem contains the seeds of its own solution."
That significant statement by Stanley Arnold, one of
America's outstanding idea men, underscores the important fact that the solution is built into every problem. This chapter will tell how to find that solution. It
will show how you can handle your problems. Here
again, you can if you think you can.

Almost invariably people assume that a problem is
inherently bad. Whereas on the contrary, a problem
may be, and usually is, inherently good.

When the Lord wishes to give you a great value, how
does He go about it? Does He wrap it up in a glamorous
and sophisticated package and hand it to you on a silver
platter? No. He is too subtle for that. More than likely
He buries it at the heart of a great big, tough problem
and watches with anticipation to see whether you have
what it takes to break the problem apart and find at its
center what might be called the pearl of great price.

Some people seem to feel, "Wouldn't life be simply
wonderful if we had easier problems, or fewer problems, or better still, no problems at all!" But is that
necessarily true? Would we be better off if such were
the case? Let me answer this question by telling you
of an incident.

18

Walking on Fifth Avenue, I saw approaching a friend named George. It was apparent from George's melancholy and disconsolate demeanor that he wasn't filled to overflowing with the ecstasy and exuberance of human existence. This is a high-class way of saying that George was "dragging bottom." He was really low.

This excited my natural sympathy; so I asked him, "How are you, George?" That was only a routine inquiry, but it represented an enormous mistake on my part, for George took me literally and for fifteen minutes enlightened me meticulously on how badly he felt. And the more he talked, the worse I felt.

So I asked him, "George, what is disturbing you? What is eating at you? What is bothering you?" This really set him off. "Oh," he replied forcefully, "it's these problems, problems . . . nothing but problems! I am fed up with problems and I don't mean maybe. All I want is to get rid of these everlasting problems." He became so exercised about the matter that he quite forgot whom he was talking to and began to castigate these problems vitriolically, using in the process a good many theological terms. But he did not put them together in a theological manner, I regret to say.

WANTED: NO MORE PROBLEMS

"Norman," he continued, "get me rid of these blankety-blank problems and here is what I'll do. I will give you one thousand dollars cash money, no strings attached, for your work." Well, I am not one to turn a deaf ear to such an offer; so I ruminated, cogitated, and meditated upon the proposition and came up with a solution that seemed to me not bad; at least it was realistic. But apparently George didn't go for it, as I have yet to receive the aforementioned one thousand dollars.

"Well, George," I said, "I certainly would like to help you. But let's get the matter straight. Am I to understand that you want to get rid of all your problems, every last one of them? Is that it?"

"You said it," he replied. "I want to get through with every last problem I've got. Believe me, I've had it—and then some. I'm through. I want no more problems—ever."

"O.K., George, I have the solution, but I doubt you will like it. Anyway, here it is: The other day I was in a certain place on professional business, if I may thus characterize it, where the head man told me that there are a hundred thousand people; and not a single, solitary one of them has a problem." The first enthusiasm I saw in George suffused his countenance and flashed up in his eyes as with considerable eagerness he exclaimed, "Boy, that's for me! Lead me to this place!"

"O.K.," I replied. "It's the cemetery."

And that is a fact—nobody in the cemetery has a problem. For them life's fitful fever is over; they rest from their labors. They couldn't care less what you and I read in the daily paper or hear on radio or TV. They have no problems at all—nary a one. But they are *dead.*

PROBLEMS, A SIGN OF LIFE

It follows, then, in logical sequence that problems constitute a sign of *life.* Indeed, I would go so far as to suggest that the more problems you have, the more alive you are. The person who has, let us say, ten good old tough, man-sized problems is, on this basis, twice as alive as the poor, miserable, apathetic character who has only five problems. And if you have no problems at all, I warn you: You are in great jeopardy. You are on the way out and don't know it. Perhaps what you had better do is immediately go to your room and shut the door and get down on your knees and pray to the Lord, "Lord, please; look, don't you trust me anymore? Give me some problems!"

One wonders what has come over this great, free country. We are the descendants of a once great breed of men who had problems and had them aplenty. But did they whine and whimper and crawl through life on their hands and knees piteously demanding of some so-called benevolent government that they be taken care of? Not on your life! They stood solidly on their feet and they took care of themselves. And they built the greatest economy in the history of the world—one that has made available more goods and services to more people than any other in the long life of mankind on earth.

Could it be that the breed has run out? Have we come to a time when we are so superficial in our thinking as actually to believe that we are being mistreated by some cruel fate in having to deal with problems?

Our forefathers were philosophers. They knew that problems are inherent in the structure of the universe. That is the way it is made. They realized that the purpose of the Creator is to make men, strong men, tall men who have what it takes to stand up to the vicissitudes of human existence, to the harsh facts of life on earth, and not to back away and supinely fold up, but instead to deal with all of it creatively and forthrightly.

Our forefathers knew, because they were philosophical thinkers, that the only way to make strong people is through struggle. One grows tough mentally and spiritually by putting up a strong resistance to hardship, to obstacles, to suffering. This is the disciplinary value of a problem in the development of a person. It enhances his insights, his strengths and his general capability to live constructively. The late Charles F. ("Boss") Kettering, famed research scientist, recognized these facts when he placed a sign on his laboratory wall at General Motors worded for the benefit of his aides as well as for himself: "Do not bring me your successes; they weaken me. Bring me your problems; they strengthen me."

Actually, one may learn a great deal about the state of his normal mental health by noting his reaction to problems. If it is to whine and turn bitter and complain of his "unfair" treatment, a "Why me?" attitude, maybe the need for help is evident. However, if he calmly accepts a problem as part of the pattern of life and thinks that possibly it might be turned to his advantage; and if at the same time he confidently believes he is equal to it, then a healthy mental condition would seem indicated. Hence our emphasis on the principle—you can if you think you can.

At one time I was connected with a clinic in which psychiatrists, psychologists, and clergymen of all faiths collaborated in counseling and treating persons facing problems. Indeed, with the well-known psychiatrist, Dr. Smiley Blanton, I founded this organization over twenty-five years ago. Accordingly I have a warm feeling for psychiatrists and esteem them highly as professionals in their field. They are, as a group, dedicated men and women highly sensitive toward human need and creative in their helpfulness in personal problems.

Because of my high regard for psychiatrists, I may be forgiven for retelling an amusing story which appeared in a New York newspaper. The American Association of Psychiatrists, it appears, held a four-day convention at a hotel on Seventh Avenue in New York City. The hotel was packed with psychiatrists; they filled the lobby to overflowing.

Across the street from the hotel is the Penn Central Railroad Station, around which, from time immemorial, huge flocks of pigeons have made their headquarters. As far as anyone could ascertain, these were well-organized, emotionally contained, soundly integrated pigeons going about the daily function of being pigeons. But apparently the emotional instability of the multitudes thronging in and out of the station transmitted itself to one of the pigeons, and it, so to speak, got off the beam. By some process never accounted for, this pigeon found itself in the lobby of the hotel flying around among these psychiatrists. Indeed, it is reliably reported that this pigeon flew around the lobby for two whole days before any psychiatrist would admit to another that he saw a pigeon.

In this clinic we had practically every known human problem. You name it and we had it. There was the problem of worry. (And it is significant that the English word "worry" is apparently derived from an old Anglo-Saxon word which meant to strangle or to choke. If someone were to grasp you tightly about the neck, cutting off your air supply, he would be doing to you dramatically what you do to yourself if over a long period of time you are a victim of worry.)

THE CHIEF PROBLEM IS HOW TO COPE

Among other problems were fear and anxiety, the latter being a haunting apprehension that something awful is going to happen. The late Dr. Blanton used to call anxiety "the great modern plague." There were also the problems of guilt and resentment, together with drug problems, alcohol problems, marital and youth problems. All of these we had and more. But again, according to Dr. Blanton, one of the chief problems was a deep inner conflict, a sense of inadequacy and inferiority, the individual feeling that he just did not possess the ability to cope with the ordinary problems of human existence.

As a result of my earlier association with this counseling activity, I became aware that at least three procedures were vital to the successful handling of problems: (1) knowledge, (2) thought, and (3) belief; or to put it another way, know, think, believe. This has been confirmed by later and more comprehensive experience with people.

When you become aware of the roots of your problem you have taken a long step toward handling it. Almost any problem will yield to know-how, to knowledge and understanding. The problem, however, assumes difficulty out of all proportion to the facts when you have failed to examine it. Human intelligence is a powerful factor when it studies and analyzes every facet of a problem until it is laid out in orderly fashion for scrutiny and decision. Then it is usually discovered that the problem which appeared to be not only complex but also potentially destructive may contain remarkably creative possibilities for solution.

HAVE A PROBLEM? CONGRATULATIONS!

I recall a conversation with W. Clement Stone * when we were jointly involved in a project which had developed a real problem. I telephoned Mr. Stone and

_____* Chairman, Combined Insurance Co. of America

said, "We have a problem," to which he made the astonishing reply, "Congratulations!"

"But," I declared, "no fooling, this is a very tough problem."

But Mr. Stone was unimpressed. "In that case," he said cheerily, "double congratulations!" Then he added, "Always remember that to every disadvantage there is a corresponding advantage."

He went on to ask if a complete and thorough study and analysis of the problem had been made. Had we tackled it scientifically? Had we sought competent advice? In short, did we know all about the problem, or were we simply appalled by it because on the surface it seemed to present unusual difficulties? "Let's really get down to this problem," he said. "Let's take it apart, see what is wrong, then put it together again in the proper manner."

We applied knowledge to the situation until we were on top of it, and the final outcome of the matter, which at first seemed all but hopeless, proved highly desirable. Indeed, the problem when taken apart yielded values that would not otherwise have been obtained. So get to know your problem; more than likely it's your friend—not your enemy.

I have been fortunate over the years in knowing successful men who had become so, in part at least, because they learned to probe for knowledge of problems. They did not allow themselves to be overwhelmed by problems and certainly not to be frightened by them. Instead, they coolly and factually studied the situation in depth from all angles. They got advice from experts and from others who had faced similar problems. They probed and examined and minutely took the problem apart until there was nothing they didn't know about it. They mastered it by the strict use of intelligence, and that always produces understanding. And understanding can overcome any situation, however mysterious or insurmountable it may appear to be.

An unforgettable friend was Harlow B. Andrews of Syracuse, New York, a businessman of outstanding capacity. Mr. Andrews was an extraordinarily wise man with a very acute and subtle mind. His knowledge of men was sharp and intuitive. As a young man when I needed advice about problems, I knew exactly where to go for the kind of insight that resulted in answers that really answered. He had missed nothing in the learning process of life, though his formal education was limited. A university professor in my hearing once congratulated him on never going to college. "I'm afraid we might have educated that amazing native wisdom out of you and made you just like our standardized graduates," he asserted with a grin, and maybe more than half-believing what he said. At any rate, Harlow Andrews had what it took to handle problems.

This was demonstrated when I went to see him once with a problem that had me pretty well baffled. He listened carefully as I outlined the situation, his keen mind concentrating on and sorting the material as I spoke. He grasped the essence of the problem at once and proceeded to deal with it expertly as his questions indicated. (1) "Have you made a complete and detailed study of all factors involved? Do you honestly feel you are knowledgable?" Whereupon he put some searching questions designed to test my knowledge of the material with which we were working. (2) "Is the organization of your material as clear and concise as it should be?" he asked. And he added, "Let's regroup it."

He then engaged in a strange procedure, the effectiveness of which I have recalled many times and have used creatively on many problems. He walked around the table making a kind of heaping motion with his hands as though to bring all elements of the problem together.

Then he started poking at the accumulated problem with a long, gnarled forefinger. Mr. Andrews had some arthritis which had curved the finger and caused knobs to develop on the joints. But he could point straighter with that crooked finger than most people with a straight finger.

Finally he said, "Come here. There's a soft spot in every problem. All you've got to do is to keep looking until you find it. I've found the soft spot in this problem." He then "worked his finger" into that problem, sort of the way a dog works its teeth into a bone, until he broke it into pieces. But there was now an orderly pattern in those pieces. And he found the answer. It proved to be a good solution, too.

"Just use your head, son, when a problem comes along," he advised. "Study it until you are completely knowledgable. Then find that weak spot, break the problem apart, and the rest will be easy."

YOU CAN THINK YOUR WAY THROUGH ANYTHING

And the second technique is thought. Think; just think. You can, if you exercise will and persistence and mental calmness, think your way through anything. Your great tool is mind. With mind you have power over all conditions and circumstances and over any problem however difficult. You can if you think you can and if you think straight.

Thomas A. Edison said the only reason we need the

body is to carry the brain around. The brain is domi-
nant. Perhaps that is why it was placed at the very top
of the body in the skull. What Edison was saying, of
course, is that all things—our daily existence, our success, our happiness, our future—are determined in the
mind—in that function which operates within the
brain. There we remember; there we understand, and
dream, and think. Poetically we have ascribed these
functions to the heart, but since that is an instrument
the function of which is the pumping of blood, it is in
the mind, with its ability to think, that is found the real
essence of man. The mind actually is you, and in it is
resident that part of man known as soul or spirit.

Usually, however, when a problem strikes, the tendency is to react emotionally rather than to think. The
mind that is not under cool and logical control sends
emotional stimuli to the nerves, even to the stomach,
which, in a panic reaction, feels sick. One becomes
nervous, waking in the middle of the night feeling hot
and cold all over, mouth dry, heart palpitating. "Why
me?" he cries. "Why should I be called upon to face this
situation? I just don't know where to turn."

The answer, of course, is to turn to your good, sound
mind—to think. Just think. All the answers to your
problems are resident in your mind, but they are being
blocked off because of your strong emotional reactions,
even panic. One thing is sure; the human mind will not
function creatively when it is hot. Only when it is cool
—absolutely cool—will it deliver those factual, rational,
intellectual insights which produce solutions that solve.

All the time, deeply buried in the unconscious, a
process of problem-solving is going on. In normal
course, ideas to meet the situation are trying to float to
the surface. Remember that your mind always wants

to help you, and will, if you permit it to do so. But panic, hysteria, even relatively mild emotions keep the surface of the mind in a state of disturbance, making it impossible for the great insights to rise from the deeper levels of consciousness.

So the first step when a problem hits you is to achieve calmness. This may require the exercise of discipline, but what is wrong with discipline? It's an all-too-little-used aspect of personality development nowadays. Take yourself resolutely in hand and insist upon reacting calmly. Achieve emotional balance and firmly maintain it.

COOL IT WHEN A PROBLEM COMES

In the rather astonishing language forms of some young people today is a phrase that is so wise and subtle that it deserves to become immortal. If it were more widely practiced, everyone, including the nation itself, would benefit immeasurably. The phrase is two words—cool it. So when a tough problem enters your life and you tend to become tense and uptight about it, just practice becoming as cold mentally as you can. Then say to yourself, "O.K., this is the problem. Let's examine it and carefully study its component factors. Let's calmly consider its implications. Let's think, really think and only think. In no case shall I react emotionally."

When you approach a problem in this manner, your mind will immediately go into action. All your mental and, yes, your spiritual power will be released. Your mind will take hold of the problem and literally shake ideas out of it. In addition to your own cool, rational thinking, I suggest that you also make use of prayer. What is prayer but a form of thought transmission? By means of it you can draw upon the power of the Divine Mind where all wisdom reposes. Prayer is actually a line of communication along which come insights, intuitions, fresh understandings. With two calm minds working on a problem—God's mind and your mind— you're in. What else?

Remember this: You can if you think you can, because all the ideas you need to handle any problem are all about you, both within and without your mind. Cool reactions will open up the lines of communication by which ideas will flow to you.

One of the greatest idea geniuses of recent American history was the first Henry Ford, one of the basic creators of the motor car. A biographer,* writing of Mr. Ford as a thinker, says: "I once asked Ford where ideas come from. There was something like a saucer on the desk in front of him. He flipped it upside down, tapped the bottom with his fingers and said: 'You know that atmospheric pressure is hitting this object at fourteen pounds per square inch. You can't see it or feel it, but you know it is happening. It's that way with ideas. The air is full of them. They are knocking you on the head. You only have to know what you want, then forget it and go about your business. Suddenly the idea you want will come through. It was there all the time.'

"One day I saw this work. At lunch, Ford was talking to me and William J. Cameron, who did the company's radio broadcasts, when his tall body stiffened; the expression of his face, which had been lively, changed

_____* Garet Garrett, in *Reader's Digest 50th Anniversary Treasury* (Pleasantville, N.Y.: Reader's Digest Association, Inc., 1972).

to that of a sleepwalker, and he said to no one in particular, 'Ah-h! I'm not really thinking about that at all!'

"With no other word he rose and walked rapidly away. An idea he had been wanting had come through, and he had gone to do something about it. Cameron said, 'That happens often. We may not see him again for a week.'"

Henry Ford was a cool-thinking machine, although a warm human being as well. It was said in Detroit of Mr. and Mrs. Ford that they were a rare partnership— she the believer, he the thinker. What a combination— think and believe. And it is unbeatable, provided you cool it, cool it, and think and think.

FREDDIE THE THINKER

That you can successfully deal with problems by rational thinking was illustrated by Freddie, a friend of mine aged sixteen. When the summer vacation came, Freddie said to his father, "Dad, I don't want to sponge on you all summer. I want to get a job."

After the father had recovered from shock, he said, "O.K., Freddie, I'll try to get you a job; but it may be impossible, for jobs are pretty scarce just now."

"You misunderstand me, Dad. I don't want you to get me a job. I'm going to get one on my own. And besides, don't be so negative. I can get a job even if they are scarce. There's a type who can always get a job."

"And what type is that?" the father asked doubtfully.

"It's the thinking type," replied the son. "All you have to do is think—really think. Don't get upset or negative, just think; and think positively."

Quite a boy, if you ask me.

Freddie searched the want ads and found a job that suited his specifications. Applicants were directed to show up at an address on 42nd Street next morning at eight o'clock. Freddie was there not at eight but at a quarter to eight, only to find twenty boys lined up leading to the secretary of the man doing the hiring. So here he was, the twenty-first kid in line.

Freddie looked his competitors over and had to admit they were a prepossessing group of boys. "If I were the boss," he said to himself, "I would hire any one of them." But he did not want one of them to get the job; he wanted that job for himself. He was a competitor. But how could he get the attention necessary to compete successfully?

There was his problem; how should he handle it? According to Freddie there was only one thing to do: that was to think. So he entered into that most painful but exhilarating process. He thought. When you really think, you will always get an idea. And Freddie got one. Taking a slip of paper, he wrote something on it. Folding it neatly, he walked up to the secretary, bowed respectfully and said, "Miss, it is very important that your boss receive this note immediately."

Now she was an old hand, and had he been an ordinary boy she would have said, "Forget it, sonny. Get back there in line in the twenty-first position." But he was not an ordinary boy, as she instinctively perceived. Already an emanation of executive quality proceeded from him and she picked it up.

"O.K.," she said, "let me read the note." And when she did she smiled. She at once arose from her chair, went into the office of the boss and put the note on his desk. When the boss read it he laughed out loud, for this is what it said: "Dear Sir: I am the twenty-first kid in line. Don't do anything until you see me."

Did he or did he not get the job? Will he or will he not meet the problems he will have to face in life? Of course he did and of course he will, because early in his career he learned to think. A thinker can always get on top of a problem. He can either solve it, or eliminate it, or develop an idea pattern that will enable him to live with it.

So the simple principle is, don't react emotionally— think and think and think. And along with that, pray and pray and pray. For when you pray Almighty God is thinking with you. And He, of course, is quite a thinker.

But you, the reader, may object that this is all very well, but "you don't know my problem. Mine is really tough and there is just no way out, no answer, no solution. No amount of thinking will get me anywhere, and I ought to know for I've thought and prayed until I'm blue in the face, and no result."

Well, now, this author hasn't been working with human beings all these years without knowing something about the harsh, painful, and discouraging problems people face. They are indeed deep, dark, grievous problems. There are inevitabilities in life for which, seemingly, no alternatives exist, and there are some things we must live with and endure.

The great psychiatrist, Sigmund Freud, said: "The chief duty of a human being is to endure life." At first sight that statement sounds heroic, and it is. And furthermore, it is not without profound truth. But if that were the whole story, life would be bleak indeed. I would rather take the position that the chief duty of a human being is to master life. And with all its pain and difficulty, one can do just that if he will pray and think and work and study and believe. That for a fact is true —absolutely true.

FREE ICE WATER

So the positive thinker, the positive believer knows that there is always available to him an idea which will lead to a solution of his problem. And he determines to find that dynamic and creative idea. This is our third point: belief. Like Ted and Dorothy Hustead, for example. Back in December of 1931 Ted, a pharmacist, and his wife, Dorothy, a former teacher, bought a little drugstore in the town of Wall, South Dakota, population then three hundred. They had been looking to settle in a town with a school and a Catholic church where they could attend daily Mass. Wall filled those requirements. In addition, it boasted its own doctor.

However, there were other aspects of Wall, South Dakota, at that time that would dismay all but the most intrepid souls as a place in which to establish roots, a place to call "home." Tourists traveling between the Black Hills and the Badlands found themselves in Wall only accidentally, referring to it as the "geographical center of nowhere." An agricultural economy, the area had sustained all manner of natural catastrophes— drought, grasshopper plagues, crop failures, and the like—before the Great Depression worsened matters considerably.

The year 1932 was not, you might say, the most propitious time to begin a commercial enterprise. But if you always wait for a propitious time you may have a long wait.

The dust lay inches thick on the parched ground in the intense heat that summer. The winds sweeping and sighing down over the Badlands scooped up tons of dust, hurling it into the sky, almost blotting out the sun. What few tourists drove through town along dusty roads in nonair-conditioned cars suffered from searing heat and choking dust, throats parched, tongues hanging out. Practically nobody entered the drugstore, so Ted and Dorothy Hustead had plenty of time to think and pray. And that was good, for otherwise they might have missed the tremendous idea that brought them spectacular success.

The problem was how to get those disconsolate passing tourists off the main highways into town and into the store; so these two people thought, seeking an idea. They prayed, asking for insight. And when you do that, an idea will come. And it did. It was in the form of a question. What would those tired, dusty, hot tourists rather have at this moment than anything in the world? Answer—a tall, cold, frosty glass of ice water! Free ice water at Wall Drugstore!

So they went outside of town and put up some cleverly worded signs—just a few at first—and things began happening. Potential customers were finding their way to Wall Drugstore! Encouraged, they put up more and more signs each week, and before that summer was over they extended fifteen to twenty miles along the highway in each direction. Free Ice Water, Wall Drugstore, Wall, South Dakota.

Ultimately, through Hustead enterprise and the enthusiasm of friends and tourists alike, Wall Drug signs blanketed the country. They found their way to the capitals of Europe and to remote places all over the world. The walls of the store are covered with photographs of the signs in such unlikely places as the Great Pyramid, the North Pole, the thirty-eighth parallel in Korea. The picture taken in front of the Taj Mahal in India shows a sign reading, "Ted Hustead's Wall Drug Store, 10,728 miles," with an arrow indicating the direction.

Now druggists had been handing out free ice water for years, but Ted and Dorothy Hustead were the first to advertise it. Result—every day from four to six thousand customers from everywhere crowd their store in this little town, making of it one of the most famous and successful of all drugstores. And what accomplished this remarkable result? Simply two people who did not react emotionally to a tough problem, who did not get discouraged and give up. Instead, they thought and prayed and believed, and the great idea came that solved their problem. So in addition to know-how, you need thought, and to that add belief.

Believe that problems do have answers. Believe that they can be overcome. Believe that they can be handled. And finally, believe that you can solve them. Belief is an extraordinarily powerful force. Send out positive belief thoughts and they will strongly tend to bring back belief results. Even as unbelief thoughts will turn off success, so real belief thinking leads to successful achievement.

A SUCCESS FORMULA THAT WORKS

In Hong Kong I met a successful Chinese businessman who lives in a nice home and is active in creative enterprises for the common good in the community. But it was not always so with him. Some twenty years ago, with his wife and two small children, he walked several hundred miles out of Red China into Hong Kong, "voting with our feet for freedom," as he described it.

But hundreds of thousands of others were doing the same, and soon Hong Kong was swamped by a couple of million refugees. This taxed the resources of the Crown Colony even to feed them, let alone house this multitude of freedom-lovers. Those of us who visited Hong Kong back in those days recall the harsh living conditions of the refugees. Anything would do for a place to live; old packing crates, scraps of tin, even paper cartons, were put together to protect from the elements. Later the government embarked on a splendid housing program, and the shacks on my most recent visit seemed a thing of the past.

This man used to sit dejectedly in his lean-to shack after having futilely tramped the streets for work. The family went daily to the soup kitchen. Through it all he sadly wondered what life held for his wife, his children, and himself. Could there possibly be a real future in his future? How could he ever improve his family's condition? That was his problem, and a problem it was, for sure.

Escaping from Red China with only the clothes on his back, he had nevertheless brought along a small New Testament. This he read daily, and one day he came upon this statement: "I can do all things through Christ which strengtheneth me." * That struck him like a bolt of lightning. "All things" seemed incredible, but in that flashing moment he actually became a believer. He could—he knew he could—move up to better things.

But the problem was so overpowering! How could he

_____* Philippians 4:13.

start? Where could he begin? He prayed, he thought, he studied, he believed. "Then," said he, "I found my formula, the formula that led me to self-support and some success. One day I just decided to believe that I could. Aloud, I said, 'Why not?' But it all seemed so audacious. But even so, why not?

"I began to look for opportunities, but with a new belief that I would find them. Now I had the motivation to keep going, keep thinking, keep looking. And when the first job came, I worked at it like it was the most important job in the world. Then I added some other astounding words: 'I can—I will.' And finally that affirmation, 'I can—I will' equalled 'I did!' That is the formula by which my problem was solved, and it's workable for anyone: 'Why not?' equals 'I can, I will' equals 'I did!'"

There you have it—knowledge, thought, belief. So what's your problem? You can handle it. You can if you think you can.

And now a recapitulation. What are the successful problem-handling principles stated in this chapter?

1. *A problem is inherently good, not inherently bad as is commonly supposed.*
2. *Only alive people have problems. And the more you have, the more alive you are. So be glad you have problems.*
3. *Get all the possible know-how about your problem. Knowledge of the problem is a key to successful solution.*
4. *When a problem comes, do not react emotionally—cool it.*
5. *The mind will not function when it is hot, only when it is cool and factual.*

6. *Think—the successful idea is always in your mind. Think it out.*
7. *Believe you can. Believe it is possible to solve your problem. Tremendous things happen to the believer. So believe the answer will come. It will.*

THREE

❧

UPTIGHT? TENSE?
HOW TO COOL IT AND RELAX

Uptight! That word is heard everywhere. And it seems potently descriptive of many individuals today.

Perhaps the present time is one of the tensest eras any of us has known. Indeed, it is not too farfetched to call ours the uptight generation. A friend who works for a brokerage house on Wall Street showed me a few lines from his company's newsletter, lines that point up the prevailing tension:

> *The age of the half-read page*
> *And the quick hash and the mad dash*
> *The bright night with the nerves tight*
> *The plane hop—the brief stop*
> *The brain strain and the heartpain*
> *The cat naps till the spring snaps*
> *And the fun's done.**

Can this be an accurate characterization of our time? Well, maybe things are not quite that bad, but who can deny that there is stress and tension everywhere? And what are people doing about it? For one thing, they are

——* *Time of the Mad Atom* by Virginia Brasier.

popping more pills into their mouths than ever before. Somewhere I read that an estimated eight billion amphetamine pills are produced in our country every year. There are pills to relieve our weariness, pills to put us to sleep, pills to keep us awake, pills to assist in weight reduction.

It used to be that people took simple aspirin. Now there is the stronger stuff—pills to which you can become addicted. Such pills easily become a crutch so that you escape temporarily from having to deal with your problems or struggle to overcome them. Pills help to forget for a while. And people keep on taking them, hoping their problems will go away, and all this instead of facing up to problems rationally with calm, keen minds and solving them creatively.

WHY ARE WE UPTIGHT?

What has brought about all this tension? According to my recollection, things did not used to be this way. The fact that "uptight" is a relatively new term indicates that the disease itself is of fairly recent origin, beginning perhaps within the last three or four decades. It is true that the American has always been a restless, aggressive type, which accounts for his amazing achievements in every field. But if memory serves us correctly, we began losing quiet power control and became emotionally uptight to the present level only within the recent past.

What, then, brought about this deterioration of emotional control on so wide a scale? Immediately we begin to add up reasons, among which are several wars—World Wars I and II, the Korean and the Vietnam Conflicts. Add to that the Great Depression of the thirties, the widespread tumult of social change, the decline of religion as a personal practice, and do not forget the vast increase of noise—just plain, unceasing noise everywhere. Almost never are you out of hearing of a motor or a television set or a blaring radio. The noise level is bound to be a factor in the rising incidence of tense uptightness.

Indeed, noise has been termed a pollutant! It is definitely a health hazard in addition to being an annoyance. In an interview in *U.S. News & World Report*, the chairman of the President's Council on Environmental Quality called attention to the fact that prolonged exposure to noise can cause severe stress symptoms. Some medical authorities believe it can lead to chronic effects such as hypertension or ulcers. Efforts are being made looking toward legislation on the increasing noise problem. The federal government is concerned with the setting of noise standards with respect to certain equipment and facilities.

One trouble about noise in today's world is that it is invariably rasping, shrill, and stridently mechanical. I read of a woman who one day became aware that every machine in her house was turned on. Suddenly she was conscious of the cacophony of deafening noise bombarding her. The dishwasher was swishing, the washing machine growling, the kitchen radio was blaring. In the living room the television was blasting as bullets ricocheted off canyon walls, and her three young sons shouted above the din! The dog began to bark when the doorbell started ringing, and outside a jet airliner shrieked overhead, a motorcycle roared by, and the lawnmower set up a clatter! Since noise is such a con-

stant factor, it probably has lodged in our deep unconscious with irritant effect both emotionally and physically.

A LAND OF HAPPY PEOPLE

Well, enough of the problem. We require no convinc-
ing that uptightness is something with which we must
deal unless we are to end up breaking apart. How may
it be dropped from our life-style? That is the question.
How may we live in effective control of tension? And
this can be done if at the start you think that it can.

Of course, we could all go to the famed island of Bali
in the blue Java sea. I mention Bali for I was there not
long ago and it struck me as one of the most peaceful
and untense places on this turbulent earth.

What a place! Soft white sands, blue coral-enclosed
lagoons, and tall, graceful palm trees. Amidst all this
peace and quiet, uptightness fades away.

Sometime—some happy sometime—I'm going to
take six months off (I hope) and spend most of it in Bali,
for though it has experienced troubles, still in my book
it's perhaps the number-one happy land I've found on
earth. The Balinese people seem happy and relaxed. I
tried to find out why and generally got five answers: (1)
"We have nothing," (2)"Our life is simple," (3) "We like
each other," (4) "We have enough to eat," (5) "We live
on a beautiful island." Well, it must be so, for as one
strolls through the soft, balmy night, the sound of
happy, modulated laughter floats on the evening air.

Chief entertainment is in the form of folklore dances
in which large numbers of the villagers participate.

Dances are performed in the courtyard of the village temple. Everything is over and finished by nine o'clock, and soon the fabled island is wrapped in slumber while the ancient sea breaks softly on coral reefs and the moon fills the silvery night with radiance.

This is one of the few places I've found on earth where the blight of "civilization" is not too apparent. There is one deluxe hotel, but Bali is no Miami Beach; far from it. Just a bit of heaven on earth, that's all, where as yet uptightness does not intrude.

But since we cannot all move to Bali (and heaven help us and Bali if we did, for we would take our tensions along and make it just like New York or Los Angeles or wherever), we must figure ways to live where we are on a non-uptight basis. And let's begin by reminding ourselves that we can so live if we think we can.

One thing I could suggest is just to accept all the noise and upset and learn to live with it. Others do, so why not you or I? But that would scarcely be meeting the problem intelligently and in depth. As a matter of fact I tried this suggestion only recently on a tensed-up man who lives on the approach paths of airplanes into Kennedy Airport.

"I've tried every put-off type of mental device to shut out this insufferable noise," he told me, "but just when I try to go to sleep a big plane seems to scream right over my bed. I try to follow your ideas about cultivating peace of mind, but how can I do it under these conditions?"

Well, in trying to help him I told him about Queen Elizabeth II, thinking it would at least enlighten him and maybe give him a sense of having company in his misery. Not long ago I flew from Amsterdam to London on a huge jet. The plane was descending lower and lower for a landing at London's Heathrow Airport when suddenly, looking out the window, I saw directly below the historic towers and turrets of Windsor Castle, the long-time seat of English monarchs.

We were very low over the castle. I wondered how old Henry the Eighth would have felt about these huge things coming in overhead. He seems to have been a tense gentleman, from what I've read of history. There were no planes then, but he had plenty of trouble of another kind! Then I asked myself, "Wonder if Queen Elizabeth is bothered by the noise of this plane?" So I told my friend, "You're not the only one. When Queen Elizabeth sleeps in Windsor, she too has descending jets zooming directly above her." He expressed interest, but seemed uncomforted by this example!

UPTIGHTNESS NOT NECESSARY

Despite everything, you do not need to be tense. This I feel free to assert because I have met some people who found how to live in the midst of super-tension and not be uptight. Their experience indicates that you can eliminate uptightness if you think you can.

I was in the oval office of the President of the United States, President Nixon. It was a day when a demonstration was going on outside the White House. People were carrying the most uncomplimentary kinds of signs and shouting all kinds of ribaldry. The word nowadays, I believe, is *obscenity*, but I prefer the word *ribaldry*. They were carrying coffins and calling the President a murderer. This could be heard faintly in the innermost sanctum of the White House, the oval office.

I sat watching the President. It was four-thirty in the afternoon, and he had been dealing throughout the day with all kinds of international affairs. I happened to notice his hands. You can tell a lot from a hand. There was absolutely no perceptible movement of his hands. They were perfectly quiet. And his voice was low and calm; his demeanor relaxed. I was interested in this phenomenon and asked him, "Mr. President, with all the problems of the world plus what is going on outside your office, how can you act so calm?"

"Why, because I *am* calm," he answered.

"But how do you keep from becoming tense?" I asked.

"Well," he said, "look. They've got a right to march and shout out there, saying anything they want. It's a free country and they are American citizens. And I'm just doing what I think is right. If you do what you think is right, you don't need to be tense."

Let me tell you about a visit with the late President Harry Truman in the same office! I always liked Mr. Truman because he was a natural human being. Despite his great distinction, he did not take himself too seriously; he just did the job as best he knew how, and he did it well. I was in his office one day at a time when there were a lot of troubling things going on in the country and the world. From the media I gathered that civilization was about to fall. It's always supposedly falling, and everybody gets tensed up about it. Strangely, it never seems to fall.

"Mr. President," I asked, "don't you ever get tense? You always seem very calm."

"Why not?" President Truman replied. "I'm no epical figure of history. I got elected to this job and intend to do my best. I come to this office each morning and

I stay for long hours doing what has to be done to the best of my ability. And when you've done the best you can, you can't do any better. So when I go to bed at night I turn it all over to the Lord and forget it. I say, 'Lord, I did my best today. Now You please take over from here.' And then I go to sleep. Of course," he added with a grin, "after the Lord gets through, the voters still blame me. That I know." So President Truman also maintained that you don't need to be tense.

I walked out of the White House on both those occasions saying to myself, "If the President of the United States, with all that furor constantly coming at him, can say that you don't need to be tense, then why should I be uptight about the many lesser things that come at me?"

PRESCRIPTION FOR TENSENESS

So the fact is, you do not need to be uptight, or nervous, or tense. But if you are in that state, take heart, for there is a cure available; an effective medicine for tension and uptightness. You can go to the drugstore and buy every kind of pill they have in stock—and it's doubtful if all of them together will cure tension as will that healing factor which I am about to suggest. This medicine is not taken by mouth but, rather, by mind. And it is this: "Peace I leave with you, my peace I give unto you: not as the world giveth, give I unto you. . . ." * The natural world can induce peace at times. You watch a sunset, or moonlight on water, and a feeling of peace comes. But when the sunset or moonlight fades and is gone and you turn back to your

——* John 14:27.

problems, then the sense of peace often ends. The peace of the world passes away. But God's peace remains. It has staying quality in depth.

This Scripture is not only beautiful but it is therapeutic as well. I believe that anyone who will commit it to memory and say it over and over again until it sinks into his deep unconscious can, in due course, find effective healing of any uptight condition. There is a remarkable therapy in words, especially in such words as the foregoing. With this certain cure available, it is little less than pathetic to permit ourselves to be dominated by tension; to be victimized by uptightness.

The Twenty-third Psalm has doubtless been of help in subduing uptightness for many. Someone gave me a modernized version of that Psalm * which seems to have a healing effect on fevered mental processes. Here is how it goes:

> *The Lord is my Pace-setter, I shall not rush;*
> *He makes me stop and rest for quiet intervals,*
> *He provides me with images of stillness,*
> *which restore my serenity.*
> *He leads me in the ways of efficiency through*
> *calmness of mind,*
> *And His guidance is peace.*
> *Even though I have a great many things*
> *to accomplish each day,*
> *I will not fret for His presence is here,*
> *His timelessness, His all importance, will*
> *keep me in balance,*
> *He prepares refreshment and renewal in*
> *the midst of my activity,*

_____* A translation of the Japanese version by Toki Miyashina from *Psalm 23: Several Versions Collected* by K. H. Strange (Edinburgh: The Saint Andrew Press).

By anointing my mind with His oils of tranquillity.
My cup of joyous energy overflows,
Surely harmony and effectiveness shall be
the fruits of my hours,
For I shall walk, in the pace of my Lord
and dwell in His house forever.

But perhaps that poem is too religious for you, and the foregoing ideas as well. Like a woman who wrote me saying, "I like your books, they do me good, but I skip all that religious stuff." But then she adds, "I'm trying to practice positive thinking about myself and my situation, but I'm as uptight as hell. What can you suggest?"

YOU CAN RELAX

Well, what we might suggest to the lady is to read the following letter which I received from another equally uptight woman, one who didn't skip the religious stuff. Here is what she has to say:

Until the time I read your booklet entitled "You Can Relax," I had never been able to do that. I would have a physical check-up and the doctor would tell me to "relax, relax, you're braced like you're going to hit a brick wall." I would say, "I can't!" Of course I started taking nerve pills every now and then.

The climax of my life was a crucial time. I had to have a complete hysterectomy. After this, I started taking nerve pills, two sleeping pills at night; just a nervous wreck, wanting to cry if anyone looked at me, just plainly—a stinker! I didn't want to talk to anyone outside the family, I devoured nerve pills, one kind or another, anything to relax, but to no avail. I had everything to live for—an understanding husband and three children. I was visiting the doctor's office quite frequently. I was on so much medication I was just like a zombie. This resulted in another stay at the hospital for a week—too much medication and a near nervous breakdown.

Our doctor told me if I hadn't pulled out of it when I did, shock treatments were next, but, praise the Lord—I didn't need them! During my stay in the hospital I had 40 nerve shots (I counted them), 4 nerve pills daily. Then when I came home, shots twice a day, 4 nerve pills, 2 sleeping pills; then I graduated from the shots to just nerve pills.

I was home a week, lying on the couch, trying to rest, something hit me—I had to get up and move, move—what horrible thoughts went through my mind. I remember I said, "Oh, my God, not again!" I knew the next time I would probably take my life. I had enough medication to stock a drugstore. I was miserable. But that very day my son-in-law's mother sent me your booklet! Dr. Peale, that was when I began to live again. It took weeks and weeks of fighting, but, thank God, today I am without nerve pills.

Sure, I get uptight every now and then, but the best thing about it all—I CAN RELAX!! I have tried to tell others of your suggestions, but they say they've tried but it didn't work. All I can say is, they didn't try hard enough. And what do you know! The doctor had his nurse call later when he could see it was working—he wanted the name of your booklet to help his other patients in the same condition!

It could just be that it isn't too smart to "skip that religious stuff" if you are serious about wanting to eliminate uptightness and learn to relax.

A prominent New York City heart specialist would, I believe, share that assumption. He showed me the X-rays of three patients (no names, of course) and said, "These are pictures of the hearts of two men and a woman, all of whom were in their fifties when these were taken." And he pointed out the damaged condition.

"They must be dead by now," I commented.

"Not on your life. They are in their late sixties now, living full, active lives."

"You must be a wizard doctor," I said admiringly.

"Not at all," he said. "I simply told them they had better practice their religion. One was Jewish, the other two Christians. They followed the prescription and in time eliminated mental and emotional stress from their lives. They got well and have remained so." And so can you, too, if you think you can and follow the prescription used by these people.

LEARN TO MANAGE YOURSELF

Still another case of an uptightness cure based on revitalized, emotionally controlled thinking was related by the head of a firm of management engineers. He writes:

A most amazing transformation came over one of our men, a man very valuable to our industry, through your book, "The Power of Positive Thinking." This man, Phil, is supervisor of a large labor

force in one of our utilities. For years his whole
approach to getting things done was pressure,
pressure, push, push, without the slightest thought
of what was happening to his men or to his own
nervous system. It was the only way Phil knew.

Then the company sent him to a new area to
straighten out some ragged practices. In his efforts
to control the situation he came close to a nervous
breakdown. What he was trying to do was entirely
correct, but you cannot shout people into acceptance of new ideas. Continuous headaches were the
penalty Phil was paying for his frantic efforts.

My son gave him three books in the last-ditch
hope that he might look at one of them. One was
yours. At three o'clock one morning Phil woke up
with his head aching fit to split apart. This was a
nightly occurrence. For weeks he had not been
able to sleep the night through. He sat up in bed.
For a moment he thought he would go out and get
drunk, throw up his job and start over somewhere
else. This had been a repeating pattern of his in
earlier years.

But as he sat there in a muddle, he saw those
books. He grabbed one, looked at it, hurled it
across the room. He grabbed the second one,
threw it after the first. Then he grabbed yours,
started to throw it, but for some reason checked
himself, maybe because it was the only one left. He
opened it blindly and started to read. He read on
to the conclusion of the chapter and found himself
repeating the relaxing formula which it taught. He
lay down and before he knew it was sound asleep.

Next morning Phil woke up refreshed. But he
still hadn't learned his lesson. How could he in one
night? Back to the job he went with the same old
murderous drive and the same old results: mount-

ing tension and more headache. The following morning he again awoke at three o'clock with anvil hammers in his head. He sat up in bed and immediately thought of that book. His wife, a meticulous housekeeper, had straightened up the room. The book was nowhere to be seen. So he proceeded to tear the house apart until he found it. Leafing through it until he came to the chapter of the night before, he sat down and read, this time with expectancy. When he had finished the chapter sleep came to him naturally and easily.

Well, it seems that after this second experience it dawned on Phil that he needed a new angle on himself and his problems. Then he began reading and thinking in real earnest. It had a great effect on him. Now he has turned the corner and begun the climb toward a reasonable degree of maturity. He has become a successful manager of men because he is himself managed.

Still another important secret of tension control is to become aware of all possible causes and sources of uptightness. Stevenson and Milt,* of the National Association for Mental Health, write that "pure tension, that is, the feeling of being keyed up and taut as a bowstring, is hardly ever experienced by itself. It is almost always felt as part of an over-all emotional upset. You may say: 'I feel tense,' but if you were to look into that feeling a little more closely, you would find that you really mean: 'I feel unhappy, miserable, blue, worried, touchy, irritable,' or some similar combination of upset-

____* "Tensions and How to Master Them," Public Affairs Pamphlet No. 305, condensed from book by George S. Stevenson, M.D. and Harry Milt, *Master Your Tensions and Enjoy Living Again* (Prentice-Hall, Inc., 1959).

ting emotions and tension. Therefore a practical examination of your tensions should cover the different types of emotional upsets of which tension is an important part."

LOOK INSIDE

Carefully consider your mental attitudes, your lifestyle setup. Do you fear new situations? Do you feel inadequate? Do you get depressed without knowing why? Are you able to enjoy life's simple pleasures or must you always have "exciting" people around and do crazy things to feel alive? Look inside yourself more deeply. Perhaps there is something you would like to forget and can't.

One day in my office an extremely uptight man picked up a rubber band and stretched it as far as it would extend. "That's me," he said, "I'm tense and uptight, just like that."

"That rubber band has only so much elasticity," I replied. "It can stand only so much of that kind of tension, and that goes for you, too. Just how did you get this way?"

"Oh, the complexities of modern living," he sighed.

"I know, but what else specifically?" I prodded.

"There's a guy in my office who did me out of a promotion. I can't stand him," he admitted. "I hate the so-and-so."

"My wife doesn't understand me, either," he offered.

"And the other woman does?" I suggested, taking a shot at random.

"How did you know about that?" he asked, startled.

"Just a long shot," I told him.

Suddenly, to my astonishment, tears showed on his face and he really started blurting out everything. "I'm a mess," he said. "I can't stand living this way. I'm going nuts."

"You don't have to, you know," I answered. "Two things you can do right off: Stop hating that guy in the office, and check off the other woman. You are so wound up, you don't even know how to relax. You must so organize yourself that you do not let tension-producing problems pile up. Take one thing at a time. Talk things out calmly and objectively. And give your wife a chance to understand you. Another thing you might do," I concluded, "is to try finding spiritual peace."

He sat in silence. A sense of calmness visibly seemed to come over him. He picked up that rubber band, letting it hang limply over his finger. Later, believe it or not, he actually framed it and put it up in his office. Beneath he printed these words: "Thou wilt keep him in perfect peace, whose mind is stayed on thee." *

UNHURRY YOURSELF

A further tension-reducing method that has proved effective is the "unhurry-yourself" technique. Never allow anyone or anything to push you. Get into a go-ahead, rhythmic, and unhurried pace. Keep impatience down, and consistently practice the "easy does it" psychology.

Rabbi Sam Silver of Stamford, Connecticut, develops this unhurry-yourself procedure in a story about star baseball player Ron Blomberg of the New York Yan-

_____* Isaiah 26:3.

kees. It seems that this method saved Blomberg's career.

"He almost lost that career when he grew tired of being held in the minor leagues," writes Rabbi Silver. "Blomberg says that he had virtually given up baseball because he was fretful over the fact that the Yankees didn't put him on their roster. Straining to prove how good he could be, Blomberg did poorly for the minor league outfit he played for.

"Then what happened? He went back to his home city of Atlanta and chatted with his rabbi, Dr. Harry Epstein. 'Ron,' said the rabbi, 'unhurry yourself. Be calm. Take it easy. Don't be so impatient.' Blomberg took the advice. He changed his pace. He relaxed. The result? He was called up to the Yankees. He blossomed into a formidable hitter and may some day fill the bill as 'the Jewish Babe Ruth.' "

The ability to unhurry yourself is vital in the cure of uptightness and it can be cultivated by mental practice, by getting yourself into the "easy does it" tempo mentally and physically.

To become expert in that unhurry-yourself procedure, it helps to induce into the mind some profound philosophical thoughts about life and man. Personally, I have found many such thoughts in the classical writings of Emerson, Marcus Aurelius, and others who had a wise and urbane understanding of human nature. I like to call this procedure the "getting of tranquillity," and it may be practiced, for example, by meditating on the following statements from the great Roman thinker, Marcus Aurelius:

> The first rule is to keep an untroubled spirit. The second is to look things in the face and know them for what they are.

Vex not thy spirit at the course of things; they heed not thy vexation.

How ludicrous and outlandish is astonishment at anything that may happen in life.

There is also Emerson's subtle observation, "Keep cool: it will be all one a hundred years hence."

In Hong Kong, I ran across an old Chinese proverb that has often helped me to siphon off uptightness, especially in a crisis or when a sudden emergency develops, the usual response to which is tense excitement. Ponder it thoughtfully. It reads: "Take an emergency leisurely." That is to say, let nothing make you hot and bothered. Cool it, always cool it. Think and react slowly and in leisurely fashion. Quick reaction can often lead to ill-conceived action. Leisurely procedure gives time for emotion to cool and rational insight to take over.

There is also Thomas Carlyle's wonderful statement, "Silence is the element in which great things fashion themselves together." Reflection upon that profound thought can lead you into the essence of creative quietness.

Poetic writings have the same power to touch the mind with in-depth peace in which uptightness recedes. Such a verse as the following from Robert W. Service * has served this purpose for me over the years:

> *I've stood in some mighty-mouthed hollow*
> *That's plumb full of hush to the brim;*
> *I've watched the big, husky sun wallow*
> *In crimson and gold, and grow dim,*
> *Till the moon set the pearly peaks gleaming,*

_____* "The Spell of the Yukon," from *Collected Poems of Robert Service* (New York: Dodd, Mead & Co., 1966).

And the stars tumbled out, neck and crop;
And I thought that I surely was dreaming,
With the peace o' the world piled on top.

Actually, the ability to relax and not be uptight and
tense, the great capacity to cool it under any and all
circumstances no matter how critical, depends upon
long practice and determined cultivation. Proficiency
may not and, indeed, usually does not come easily, but
it comes if subjected to perseverance. Avoid the notion
that you can achieve strong emotional control simply
by reading this book or by ten easy lessons. The emotions, especially if they have been treated permissively,
are not easily brought under control. But the fact is that
the human being can develop any desired thought pattern if he strongly wills to do so and assiduously culti-
vates it.

CULTIVATE CALMNESS

From an admiral in the United States Navy I picked
up a little gem of wisdom along this line that illustrates
what it takes to keep emotionally calm. After speaking
to eighteen hundred young men in training at the naval
aviation station at Pensacola, Florida, I attended a dinner party on the post. Another officer present related
an interesting episode from the career of an admiral
who had been in command of an aircraft carrier in
World War II.

During the war the carrier under this admiral's command (he then being a captain) had proceeded from
San Francisco to Pearl Harbor loaded with planes
gassed to capacity and ready for action. She also carried

on the hangar deck large quantities of reserve gasoline. As the captain was bringing his huge vessel through the roadstead toward the inner harbor, a merchant ship started through the same rather narrow channel on its way out.

For two sizable ships to pass one another safely under these circumstances required considerable navigational skill and care. Not only did the tide and wind have to be right; things had to be done just so. The captain was bringing the carrier in slowly, concentrating all his attention to catch the slightest miscalculation or unexpected move, when the executive officer dashed up to the bridge and shouted excitedly, "Captain, there's a fire on the hangar deck!"

Now there is perhaps nothing more serious on an aircraft carrier than fire on the hangar deck. If it got out of control there could be a holocaust. But the captain kept his eye on that merchant ship coming out on the tide, giving it his whole attention. The executive officer, thinking the captain hadn't heard him, shouted even louder, "Captain! There's a fire on the hangar deck!"

Without raising his voice or turning his head the captain said, "I heard you the first time. Put it out," and continued easing his vessel into the harbor.

After hearing about this incident and being much interested, I asked the admiral, "Tell me, how were you able to be that calm? Such a situation would agitate anybody—a fire on the hangar deck! Even I can appreciate that. How could you take it so calmly?"

The admiral replied, "You see, I *had* to get the carrier past that merchant ship and safely into the harbor. Besides, I knew that my executive officer was perfectly competent to get that fire out. So I made him handle it. There are men who won't take responsibility unless you make them. So I made him take it."

"But how," I persisted, "did you come by the inner calm you showed?"

"How?" was his rejoinder, "I cultivated it. That's how. How else? When I became an officer I knew that nobody could ever be a good commander of men if he did not keep his head in a crisis. So I cultivated that ability. That's all there was to it."

Finally, the non-uptight person is a sound and sensible type of individual who has an objective in life, who knows what he wants to do and just goes on doing it. He lets nothing agitate or disturb him unduly. Thoroughly in control of himself mentally and emotionally, he goes along at an unhurried, orderly pace, on his way all the way.

The late Pearl Buck will long be remembered as one of our greatest writers, one who was truly loved by the American people. And she was a philosopher, too.

In an interview shortly before her death, she was asked the secret of her extraordinarily constructive life. Her answer was surprising, but certainly on the wisdom beam. She replied in the form of a little family anecdote.

It seems that when her father was a missionary in China he received a sum of money from back home to build a chapel. But being of a practical mind, Dr. Buck decided that the need for a riverboat to transport food to the poor was more pressing than a chapel. This raised a furor back home, and a storm of criticism. "But," said Miss Buck, "that didn't bother my father at all. He just went calmly on his way. And," she added, "that's what I have done all my life. So what? I've just gone calmly on my way."

Uptight? Tense? Well, then, cool it and relax; just go calmly on your way. You can if you think you can.

To conclude this chapter, here are a few reminders for those who want to drop tension from their life-style and live relaxed:

1. *You do not have to be uptight. You can control tension if you think you can.*

2. *Remember that the relaxed though power-driven life is not easily attained. It must be cultivated. So start to work at it now. Practice and continue practicing.*

3. *Practice the getting of tranquillity by passing peaceful words and thoughts through your mind daily and nightly. They have a strange healing quality.*

4. *Reduce as many of the noise decibels from your environment as possible.*

5. *Seek within your religion for peace of mind. It is there for you.*

6. *Look inside and get at the deeper cause of your nervous tension.*

7. *Eradicate any unhealthy attitude pattern which is keeping you stirred up in your deep unconscious.*

8. *Unhurry yourself.*

9. *Put your trust in God and just go calmly on your way.*

FOUR

❦

MOTIVATION THAT REALLY
MOTIVATES

"I'm going to fire that guy," growled an irate employer. He was talking about a salesman in his organization. "The fellow is just too slow. He isn't interested—couldn't care less. He's listless and dull; in fact, he's downright sleepy."

I responded with a thought that did the trick: "Instead of firing him out of your business, why don't you fire him into it?"

"What do you mean, fire him into the business?" he demanded. "You mean build a fire under him?"

"No," I said, "build a fire *in* him. Get him excited about his job. Give him motivation, some real go-ahead attitude."

It turned out to be sound advice, and my friend now says admiringly of the formerly lackluster salesman: "This guy is really changed. He is a terrific ball of fire. I just wouldn't have believed it; no, sir, for a fact I wouldn't have believed he had it in him."

Well, the plain fact is you never know what a person has in him until you apply dynamic and creative motivation to him. Every human being can be triggered. Indeed, every person can be opened up to more effective performance when the combination is found that swings wide the door to let the real personality emerge.

The method of inner fire-building mentioned above, while severe, proved to be sound psychologically. The employer called the salesman into his office. "Sit down, Jim," he said, "I want to study you. Now I hope you can take it, for I'm going to give it to you straight. I hate to say it, but you are just about the lousiest salesman I've ever known. You're lazy; no ambition; no energy; no imagination. You just don't care; you're totally without interest. You expect me to hand you out a drawing account and you hardly bring in enough orders to cover it.

"But the real lowdown, the real reason you aren't deserving of respect, is that you have the makings of a stellar salesman, you can do it, you've got what it takes, but you're selling your own ability short. Guess you're not much good for anything."

The salesman flushed angrily, his eyes flashing. He leaped to his feet, slammed his fist hard on the boss's desk. "Damn it," he shouted, "you can't talk to me like that! You just don't know me at all!" He started for the door. "Take your job! To hell with it!"

The astonished employer jumped up, grabbed the young man and flung his arms around him. "Boy, that's great—really great! You've got it; you've got it. There's a man in that big, hulking frame of yours. I always knew you could be a tremendous guy—if you once got motivated. Just keep on being that way—the way you are this minute—and let's get going. You're fired, all right, not out, but in—really in."

Of course, that is not the whole story. The boss began feeding Jim self-help inspirational books. He sent him to sales rallies, took him to the annual industry convention where he was exposed to the best producers in the business.

He got the young man interested in a church where they had an on-the-ball, dynamically dedicated minister. This put more fuel on his inner fire. Another thing the boss did was interesting and unusual. He made the young man join his golf club by telling him it would bring him in contact with important business people. And he made him pay his own membership fee, too.

Of course the real reason for this action was that the boss wanted his erstwhile sleepy salesman to get the feel of competition. The salesman was not a good golfer, but the boss felt that he had potential and saw to it that he played with some of the best golfers in the club. "Show those guys up," he demanded. Thus challenged and spurred on, the young fellow finished the season well up on the club roster.

The strategy worked. He got the keen and exciting feel of the competitive spirit; and that feeling will activate anyone into new life. He began to sense qualities within himself never before released—actually, qualities he never realized he possessed. Growing interest turned into excitement. He really got with it—with himself, with his job, with people. He went forward on the power of a motivation that really motivates. He got the message that you can if you think you can.

Such an experience stimulates an enthusiastic belief in human potential. Never write anyone off. There is always the hopeful possibility that any person may be reached and may have one of the greatest of all human experiences—to know and find himself. And further, he may become a changed individual, a new man, a new woman, in whom old things have passed away, all things have become new and vital.

BE AN ALL-OUT, NOT A HOLD-OUT

And no human being should ever under any circumstances give up on himself, ever assume a defeatist attitude with respect to his own capacity. Always that inner successful quality inherent in his personality awaits its consummation under the impact óf the motivation that really motivates.

But why is it that some people never seem to get going even though their ability is readily apparent? Could be that they are *hold-outs* rather than *all-outs*. That is to say, they never fully give themselves but always hold back some portion of their capacity, as if they feared to let themselves go and wholeheartedly give it all they've got. Those who really make it in life, in any phase of human existence, are the enthusiastic all-outs, not the hold-outs.

I have often told about an inspiring human drama in which one such hold-out really got going under a powerful motivation. It was in the form of an awakened desire to reach for a big goal, one greater than he had ever conceived remotely possible.

And it came about in this way. I met Charlie when I gave a talk to a business convention in Chicago. Back in my hotel room after the speech the phone rang and a woman's voice rather peremptorily announced, "I am bringing my husband up to see you."

"But I have to leave in a few minutes to catch a plane," I protested.

"A few minutes will be long enough," she countered firmly. "We heard your speech. I am bringing him to see you." And with that she hung up.

Soon appeared a determined-looking little woman flanked by a burly fellow with a faint, embarrassed smile on his face. "I'm Mabel," said the woman. "This is my husband Charlie. And the problem is Charlie."

"He looks like a nice fellow," I remarked.

"He is," she said, "and that's the trouble. He's too nice! Has no force, no get-up-and-go. So talk to him," she ordered. Whereupon they sat down.

"How are you, Charlie?" I asked.

"Guess Mabel is right," he answered. "Maybe I do need some help."

"He's a good man," his wife interposed. "He has brains and ability. But he can't seem to get himself organized. He lives in a dream world. He just isn't getting ahead. I've tried and tried to get him motivated, but nothing happens. As I listened to your speech I thought maybe you could straighten him out."

Well, I took a liking to Charlie. And I liked Mabel, too. Her aggressive bossiness was because she loved her husband. She believed in him and wanted him to make something of himself. I agreed to work with him at intervals and try to help. In the months that followed we had several talks.

Presently I noticed that every now and then he would mention something he had thought of for increasing his job productivity. For example, he would say, "I have half a mind to do that," or "I have a half a mind to try this." Asked later how his latest idea had worked out, it was always the same: "Oh, that; well, I had second thoughts about it and dropped it." But then he would exclaim: "But now I have a really great idea! Let me tell you about it . . . I have half a mind to give this one a go."

Once the repetitiveness of this pattern was evident I became aware of his difficulty. I said, "Charlie, the trouble with you is you're a half-a-minder." He stared, visibly startled. "Yes," I repeated, "that is why you are missing out on success. You're a half-a-minder."

"I don't get you," replied Charlie, puzzled.

CHARLIE, THE HALF-A-MINDER

"O.K., let me explain. You see, a lot of people have this trouble. Actually, it is the problem of a divided self. Once you understand the divisiveness of personality, then you can proceed to correct it. In your case, part of your personality is outgoing and enterprising, it has ambition, comes up with dynamic ideas. But another part timorously holds you back from taking bold initiatives. Subconsciously you expect to make a mess of anything new you might undertake. You lack self-confidence, you're afraid to take a chance. And to go ahead in this world you have to take chances. So you never get further than having half a mind to do it. Therefore you do not do it.

"That part of you that produces creative ideas, Charlie," I told him, "is your real self; your strong self. The part that shrinks from acting is your defeatist self. And in inner conflict of this nature the defeatist self tends to rationalize failure and finds convenient reasons for not acting on your ideas.

"It just isn't the right timing, you persuade yourself; or maybe there will be bugs in it—or something—and so forth. But the real reason is that your motivation just isn't motivated.

"Now," I continued, "the cure for your difficulty, as I see it, is to check off that half-a-minder attitude and start acting with all your mind on the ideas you get." Reminding him of one interesting project he had been talking about intermittently, I said, "All this time you've stymied yourself by that half-a-mind attitude. O.K., try that project and do it now! Sure, it will take courage and faith. But nothing ventured, nothing gained. Break the grip of this endless hesitating. Now! And I mean now. Pronto. If you don't, you'll be second-rate for life. But you don't need to be second-rate. Stop being that way. Ask God to help you get organized and get going."

Thus admonished and pushed, Charlie ventured. And things worked out much better than he ever imagined they could. That was his big turning point. He soon went into action with another creative idea. Before long Charlie's irresoluteness was a thing of the past. Today he is a successfully motivated man. His aimless life was changed by the dynamic principle, you can if you think you can.

"There is no more miserable human being," wrote psychologist William James, "than one in whom nothing is habitual but indecision." So don't be a half-a-minder. Implement your creative ideas with your whole mind. Go all out and watch things really work out.

A powerful motivational experience, one that really reaches you away down deep, one with the power to thrill and drive to the inner center of your personality reaction mechanism, can have the most determinative and lasting effect upon your future.

For this reason one should keep ever alertly open to possible motivational experience. Indeed, it is vital constantly to expose oneself to inspiration of the kind that lifts the spirit and the mind to upper-level emotional and intellectual response. To accomplish this creative end it is most important to read material of an upbeat nature, such as the biographies of men and women who developed their own talents to maximum effectiveness, who solved problems, and whose careers demonstrate the principles of successful achievement. Books that put muscle into the intellectual process, enabling you to grow in the ability to think, really think, are very important. Get acquainted with people who have demonstrated successful achievement. Talk with them. Listen carefully to their ideas. Study their method and experience. And do not neglect development of the spiritual quality, for it is in this area that motivation receives perhaps its profoundest impulse.

To use a personal example, I well recall that in my college days I had no real goal, no definitive objective. I considered many lines of activity. Perhaps the most compelling was to go into newspaper work. But this had not grabbed me with any real motivation.

Then one day I went as a delegate to a big meeting in Memorial Hall at Columbus, Ohio, of a then widely respected youth organization called the Student Volunteers. It was a spiritually oriented movement and was composed of some pretty dedicated and enthusiastic young college people. Student leaders of the time were involved. Indeed, this movement had swept the college campuses of America with a strong religious impulse.

The great hall was packed to capacity. The atmosphere was charged with powerful emotional feeling. As I entered the hall I stopped short in my tracks, for, stretched across the stage high enough for the enormous audience to see was a huge sign which read, "The Evangelization of the World in This Generation."

Something about the audacity, the consummate nerve of that slogan, hit my mind with a powerful impulse. At that moment I experienced an inner response so deep in content that I knew what I had to do in life, what down deep I wanted to do. I had my goal instantly formed, which was to do all that I could by whatever means to persuade and persuade and persuade people that they have built within them God-given and fantastic powers that, when released, can and will revamp them into significant personalities.

Thereafter I have used every possible means—books, articles, newspaper columns, television, radio, the platform, the pulpit, before large audiences and one-to-one—to plead with people to be what they really can be. That is, to get motivated by a motivation that really motivates.

Anyone who earnestly wants to do something of value in this world should get himself some truly vital, up-thrusting experiences of the kind that will change him from a desultory to a vibrantly alive person.

Well, you may object, "Why push this at me? I'm just an ordinary person." (O.K., listen; so am I.) "Besides," you may continue, "I have just an ordinary job . . . I don't see anything in it to get worked up about . . . ." Now, that is where you need to change your thinking about yourself and your job. Get going! Get worked up about your job and you will work your job up. Get fired up about it and you will put fire into it. And it will grow as you grow. Any occupation, any job has excitement in it if you have some excitement in you.

MOUNTAINTOP MOTIVATION

I talked with a young woman whose job is selling inspirational self-help books by direct mail. She said, "I sure have gotten steamed up. Boy, am I motivated. I discovered what mountaintops can do for you!"

"What do you mean, mountaintops?"

She filled me in. "Here I am in the business of selling books by direct mail. And I believe in these books. They've got something to say and I am eager to see them widely read. My boss sent me to a one-week conference on direct mail selling . . . ."

You wouldn't expect a person to come back from a direct marketing conference so thoroughly inspired and revitalized as was this girl. But it isn't so strange when you consider the terrific enthusiasm in some business groups. This girl, by attending the conference, had been made aware of the vast possibilities of direct mail selling—how you can do it more effectively, how you can get through to people and really communicate, how you can motivate them, indeed, how you can make the whole selling process creative.

"I came back to the job walking on air," she said. "Look what life can be! Look what I can make out of selling!" Her face was aglow. Talk about a fire being built inside someone—she was afire and then some.

"Mountaintops!" she repeated. "You can't live without mountaintops. But the thing is, you can't be on the mountaintop all the time, either. You've got to come down and do the humdrum things. And down below in the daily routine it is easy to lose sight of the upper-level experience. So when I begin to feel negative and dull again, I go back in my mind to the mountaintop motivation that showed me what I really am and what I can really do."

"You are a smart girl," I said admiringly. "Before you ever thought of that, the Bible said it in one of the most glorious statements ever formulated."

And I quoted: "They that wait upon the Lord shall renew their strength; they shall mount up with wings as eagles . . . ." That is a mountaintop. But that is not the end. It comes down a little: ". . . they shall run, and not be weary . . . ." Even that isn't the end; it comes down a little more: ". . . they shall walk, and not faint." *

The reason you can walk through the humdrum of this world and not faint is because you have been on the mountaintop of motivational experience.

That is why a person should get an inspirational rejuvenation regularly. The fire of enthusiasm won't burn forever unless you throw some fresh logs on it. Your motivation can sag and leave you drained of driving impetus unless you have a definite program of renewal. And how is that accomplished? As I said earlier, read inspirational books. Go to inspirational meetings. Get to know men and women who are doing inspiring things. Above all, run as hard as you can from the cynics and the gripers and the negativists. They are not going anywhere. You are.

And then there is the time when a magic word may bring motivation. You can never tell when it is going to come. Therefore it is smart to keep your eyes, your ears and, supremely, your mind, open. For that magic word may indeed change you, and in doing so, change your life.

Like Steve Carlton, for example. Carlton was the top pitcher in the National League in the baseball season of 1972. And with a last-place team at that, the Phillies.

It seems that two years earlier Carlton was pitching for the St. Louis Cardinals and usually losing. Then it came, the magic word of motivation. He received a letter from a fan and that letter produced the spark which gave an ordinary pitcher a great season. It was

—— * Isaiah 40:31.

so simple. The fan told the pitcher that he sure had the stuff but he certainly was not thinking positively out there on the mound.

"It was beautiful," said Steve Carlton. "It changed my entire outlook on things." That letter must have really motivated this hitherto lackadaisical pitcher, for after receiving it he won four of his last five games that year and went on to post a twenty and nine record the following season.

"Defeat? I never even consider it now," he says.

Of course, along with positive thinking, what kept Mr. Carlton winning that season was a fast ball that rushes by the batter, a curve ball that turns a batter around, and a slider that skips all over on its way to home plate! Willie Stargell, first baseman for the Pittsburgh Pirates, ruefully observed that "hitting Carlton's pitching is like drinking coffee with a fork." And Carlton should maintain his pace as long as he keeps, in depth, his new thought pattern.

All the time Carlton was losing he possessed the technical qualifications of a champion pitcher. He just hadn't gotten the motivation that really motivates. But when suddenly he saw his real self he went on to spectacular success that season. When you get the motivation that really motivates, so will you take on new power.

THE MAGIC WORD THAT MOTIVATES

The magic word that motivates is a mysterious and powerful phenomenon. The person who keeps his mind open to it is on the way to fabulous life experiences. And how do you keep your mind open to it? The

answer is: Keep thinking, keep interested, keep praying, keep dreaming. Be mentally sensitive at all times
so that the magic word may one day speak to your deep
inner self. And when it does, you want your lines of
communication to be open.

Take the case of Mary B. Crowe, a young girl whose
daily job was to wash her father's grimy overalls. Mary's
father was a miner and his overalls were dirty, indeed.
And in those days and as poor as the family was, she had
only a tub and an old-fashioned scrubbing board—no
modern clothes washer and dryer. It was hard scrubbing.

Well anyway, one day while Mary was sloshing these
dirty clothes, the tremendous thing happened. Something astonishing took place in her mind, that fabulous
place where astonishing things happen. The magic
word was spoken. Her keen mind and believing spirit,
sensitized to the higher world, heard it. Immediately
it formed an idea; an inspired image flashed up. While
scrubbing away, a breathtaking picture formed in her
mind, sharp and clearly defined. College!

Where did that magic word come from? That is an
interesting question. Out of the air, from the deep unconscious, from God? Who knows? But come it did, a
thought never before held, but now there it was, the
motivation that really motivates.

Mary Crowe saw herself in cap and gown coming to
the platform to accept her diploma. A college degree?
But how silly can you get? No money, no help, no pull,
no chance at all. No member of her family had ever
gone to college. It was inconceivable. Forget it! But she
couldn't forget it, for a creative image had come; enthusiasm had been born, and with it the kind of motivation that makes things happen.

So she kept on washing overalls every day and meanwhile went to high school. Came commencement day, Mary graduated with honors. The parish priest called her into his office and pulled out an envelope from his desk, one which he had held there for four years. It contained a scholarship to St. Mary's of the Springs College. He had been waiting for someone to earn this coveted scholarship. The image was working—a scholarship for a girl who had imaged, dreamed, worked, and practiced positive thinking and studied diligently, while washing the inevitable overalls.

Enthusiastically she went to college; she worked as waitress, housemaid, cook—anything to get funds. She graduated, then took a course in insurance. One day she went to an insurance office and asked for assignment as an agent. But the manager snorted, "What do you know about life insurance, or about selling? You don't know anyone. Besides," and this was the clincher, "you're a woman. The answer is no!" This man turned her down time after time as she continued to ask for a chance. But she sat daily in his office waiting room until finally, in desperation and to get rid of her, he snapped, "O.K., here's a rate book and a desk, but no drawing account and no help. Starve yourself to death if you want to." She failed to oblige, and a few days later came in with her first policy sale.

Twenty-five years after being grudgingly hired, her associates gathered at a dinner honoring her as one of the outstanding insurance sales producers of the country. Her formula for success? It was a process of imaging, praying, having faith and positive thinking, plus enthusiasm and always inspired motivation. Taken together, that power-packed formula made incredible things happen. This woman demonstrated a powerful motivational force, backed by faith, that activates top job performance, overcomes every potential defeat and makes big things happen. Since it was not in her plan to take defeat, she became a winner.

CHANGED THINKING CAN CHANGE YOUR LIFE

"You can change your thinking and thereby change your life," says Mary Crowe. "You can do this by deliberately imaging into your subconscious vital ideas, positive images, instead of negative ones. You are constantly in a state of becoming. And you do become what you think! This philosophy does not mean, of course, that your life will be without problems. What it means is that you will be able to meet any problem full of confidence that you have the courage and the strength and the know-how to face it. You need only ask—and believe! Image and believe; work and believe."

Miss Crowe and her partner, Miss Gladys Bowen, are among the most successful practitioners of the technique of imaging. It has brought outstanding success to these positive and motivated women. In a recent letter Miss Crowe further develops the process:

Dear Dr. Peale,
"Miracles" have happened in our lives in the past ten years as a result of the daily practice of your philosophy that "believing is seeing."

Perhaps I should review our technique. First, we form an "image" or "idea" of what we need or want. Next we put it on paper, in a place where we'll see it every day. Then we "turn it over to the Spirit"—that is, we start believing—or acting as if it is already accomplished. We also try to get excited about the whole thing—to "keep our vibes up" as the kids say today. Having done all these things, we then *go to work* ourselves, doing everything we can logically think of that *we* should be doing to achieve our goal.

Our health has improved steadily each year as we've grown older. Considering that we've both passed the three score mark, this fact alone deserves the attention of the Medicare folks at H.E.W.! We image perfect health every day (in a sign on the refrigerator door!). We're also natural food enthusiasts and we attribute our glowing health and vitality to the fact that we police rigidly what we allow to enter our mouths and our minds.

In 1957 when I was disabled with a mysterious inflammation in the muscles of my rib cage which caused excruciating pain whenever I used my arms, I stumbled on an article by you, Dr. Peale, in *Look* magazine, which offered a free copy of *Thought Conditioners* * for a 3¢ post card!

I was practically penniless at the time and the outlook was totally bleak! I was unable to work. There were several persons who had been dependent on me, and no one on whom I felt I had any right to become dependent.

That 3¢ post card was to become one of the best investments in history! *Thought Conditioners* not only saved me from the psychiatric hospital; the positive "imaging" it taught me to do led me to a clinic which diagnosed my problem, and cured it.

The use of "imaging" in our insurance business —and the daily blessing of every person on our

_____* If you would like regular monthly mailings of such inspirational material, write: Foundation for Christian Living, Pawling, New York 12564.

prospect list (as well as blessing "all the ones we don't know about yet"), augmented by a highly honed and kept-always-current expertise in estate planning, has led us to a rather amazing record. In the past twelve years we have negotiated more policies for $100,000 or over (including the only $600,000, $700,000 and $1,000,000 policies ever sold in our agency) than have all the men, *combined,* in the entire 50 year history of our agency. Not bad for a couple of "little old ladies without even any tennis shoes" whom two ex-football coaches in management tried their best not to hire because they were sure we'd never survive the first six months!

The other half of "we," of course, is my business partner, Gladys Bowen, a former teacher. I feel extremely fortunate to have found a business partner who was also "attuned to the power within."

I'll never be able to express my gratitude to you, because by showing me how to change my mind you have helped me change the whole world in which I live and move and have my being!

Mary Crowe's story proves once again that faith and enthusiasm constitute the powerful motivation that makes things happen. And, of course, if this can happen to one person, it can happen to others; it can happen to you. Listen for the magic word of motivation and you will hear it. And then? Well, the sky is the limit!

WHEN THE GOING GETS TOUGH

Sometimes motivation comes in the form of hard knocks, hard blows. You face roadblocks and some really tough experiences. This causes some to fold up and give up. But to others trouble is an incentive that motivates to harder thinking and harder working. William A. Ward says it well: "Adversity causes some men to break; others to break records." Perhaps that is why the wise Shakespeare told us that "Sweet are the uses of adversity," because he knew it to be a motivational force that lifts strong people to higher levels. I once asked J. C. Penney the secret of his success. Without hesitation he replied, "Adversity," adding, "I would never have amounted to anything had I not been forced to come up the hard way."

Some time ago, walking on Nathan Road in Kowloon, Hong Kong, I saw in a window the famous statue-like figure of an old and dear friend of mine. It was a replica of Colonel Harland Sanders dominating a Kentucky Fried Chicken shop.

"You've come a long way, Colonel," I ruminated, "not only in geographical distance but also from that day of failure back in Corbin, Kentucky, some years ago. What a romance of motivation that really motivates; a failure at sixty-five; world-famous and a beloved and outstanding American at eighty."

His father was a miner, back in the days when miners didn't make much money. His mother worked in a shirt factory. There were several young children and Harland was assigned the job of cooking for the family, which later paid off with the fried chicken business. He worked hard always. He had to leave school at the end of the sixth grade, experiencing the kind of poverty that in those days existed in the Kentucky mountains and in the Tennessee poverty pockets. He was very poor. Finally he opened a little restaurant. Folks have to eat, he reasoned. He put several years of back-breaking work into it. It was doing well. Then the highway was rerouted and he lost everything. He was sixty-five years old at the time.

COLONEL SANDERS AND KENTUCKY FRIED CHICKEN

As Colonel Sanders was sitting on his porch in Corbin, Kentucky, one morning, the mailman came up the walk and handed him his first social security check. Sixty-five years old, broke and defeated, he looked at the check and said, "My government is going to give me a hundred and five dollars a month so I can eke out an existence. Surely there is something I can do for myself and other people." Motivation was working on him. He began to think, and thinking always produces results.

The thought of his mother's special recipe for fried chicken came to him. It was a particular formula which he considered something special. He decided to try to sell franchises for marketing his fried chicken formula.

After being turned down by scores of restaurants, he sold his first franchise in Salt Lake City. It was an instantaneous hit. Ten years later at age seventy-five, he sold his rights in the company and was employed as a good-will ambassador for the new organization. It is not the financial success that Colonel Sanders achieved that makes his life story significant. His experience primarily underscores the fact that no person need be defeated unless he wills it so. And it also illustrates that life is full of possibilities if one gets motivated and works and thinks. Then you find that you can if you think you can.

At Notre Dame when Frank Leahy was turning out his marvelous football teams, I noticed on the locker room wall a fascinating legend. It was seen by players as they trotted out to the football field. It read, "When the going gets tough, let the tough get going." Hold that thought in consciousness and the tough in you will indeed get going and keep on going when circumstances become difficult. And when things are going hard and even harder, remember this may be just the situation that will open golden opportunities for you. So keep it going, the motivation that really motivates.

Let's recapitulate a bit and put down a few suggestions that point up what motivation can do for you:

1. *It puts the fire within you—the fire that gets the inner power going.*
2. *It reveals your own talents. Do you really know your own potential? Search for it, for it's there. Then release it.*
3. *Don't be a hold-out—be an all-out.*
4. *And whatever you do, never be a half-a-minder.*
5. *Remember that the most powerful motivation is spiritual motivation. So expose yourself to the spiritual.*
6. *Keep alert to the magic motivational word that can reactivate and change you from indifferent to dynamic living.*
7. *Associate with motivational people.*
8. *Cultivate motivational ideas; ideas that pulsate with go power.*
9. *In adversity keep motivated, for often the best comes from difficulty.*
10. *Image your goal. Hold that image in consciousness. Keep that image always before you and your goal will materialize.*

FIVE

❦

KEEP ON BELIEVING IN YOURSELF— HAVE CONFIDENCE

"Men are born to succeed, not to fail," said Henry Thoreau. "Self-trust is the first secret of success," declared Ralph Waldo Emerson.

But how very many persons do not trust themselves! How terribly many are afflicted by that career-crippling mental attitude of self-doubt, self-disbelief!

They must number literally in the millions, men and women who, in effect, write themselves off as lacking adequate capacity and ability. These unhappy individuals, these pathetic "haven't got what it takes" types, are everywhere hampering and defeating themselves.

Like the telephone call I received recently from a foreign country. The voice on the wire belonged to no one whom I knew. It was that of a young man who spoke English but came across in a kind of half-frightened, even apologetic, manner. "I am really up against something that I can't manage. I just know I can't. In fact, I'm absolutely certain that it's too much for me. I can't . . . ." His voice trailed off in a sort of despair.

"Do you think of yourself as a normal person?" I broke in.

"You mean, am I normal mentally? Well, I've never

82

been asked such a question, but I'm not batty or anything like that."

"Good. Are you sick or physically ill?"

"Oh, no. I'm young and in excellent health."

"Wonderful! How about education?"

"Well, I graduated from the university and had a good scholastic record, too."

"O.K., young man, let's look at the situation. You are a normal person mentally and physically, you have a good education. What, then, causes you to spend all this money to telephone across the Atlantic Ocean to tell me in a weak, scared voice that you have a situation you are absolutely sure is too much for you, that you can't handle it?"

"Well, you see, in thinking of all the difficulties involved, suddenly I felt swamped, absolutely swamped. Guess I sort of folded up completely. Then I happened to see one of your books on a shelf. I took it down, read a bit, finally computed the time to be noon in New York, so I just up and telephoned you. In five minutes you were on the wire. Isn't that something?"

"All of which," I responded, "suggests considerable aggressiveness on your part, and dynamic action. Also I note rather unusual executive capacity. You didn't say to yourself, 'Should I telephone? Maybe he won't be available. And if I get through, what will I say to him? Maybe he will think I'm off the beam, flighty and all that.' No indeed, you had no such negative, self-doubting thoughts. Your good mind decided on a course of action and you proceeded forthwith to put it into effect.

"That tells me the real truth about you. Your opening remark that some problem is too big for you, that you can't, you can't, you can't, indicates a spurious, false you. Now I won't say that it isn't difficult. Indeed, it may be very tough and probably will take all you've got, but get this straight: Whatever it takes, you've got it.

"And one more question. Do you believe in God?"

"Dr. Peale," he answered, "if I didn't believe in God I wouldn't have telephoned you, a minister!"

"Great," I said. "Then tell you what let's do; let's pray right now over the telephone. This will probably be the most expensive prayer you've ever heard, but here goes!" And I prayed that he would put his good health of body and mind confidently up against his problem; that his hesitant, frightened spirit would be reactivated. I also gave thanks for his aggressive, action-motivated ability and expressed the positive thought that his attitude was already changed.

"Well, drop me a note sometime and tell me how you licked that problem. Just remember that you can if you think you can. And I'll be sending positive thoughts to you across the water."

It's gratifying that later he came through with a report which indicated progress. At least his new attitude showed through. "When you got me started believing in myself," he wrote, "confidence began to flow back. I'll keep on thinking the way you said and I believe the ability to keep on top of things will come."

Of course it will. Anyone can handle his difficulties when he really learns to trust himself. Then he has the first secret of success. So keep on believing in yourself. Have confidence.

People become really quite remarkable when they start thinking that they can do things. And those who have learned to have a realistic, nonegotistical belief in themselves, who possess a deep and sound self-confidence, are assets to mankind, too, for they transmit their dynamic quality to those lacking it.

TACKLE LIFE WITH ABANDON

Whenever I think about this matter of confidence, my mind goes back to Vince Lombardi, one of the greatest football coaches in American athletic history. I knew him well, and what a man he was! He "turned me on" just as he inspired everyone—players and fans alike. I had been a long-time admirer of Vince Lombardi and knew of his reputation as a hard driver, very tough with his players. Before I met him I had pictured him as a man of gruff personality. Instead I found him affable, friendly, and very good company. Later I communicated my impression of this genial affability to one of his players. He grunted, "Heck, you're not on his team!"

"One thing I always want above all else," Lombardi told me, "is to win. There is no sense playing a game unless you aim to win it. All your playing, working, thinking—everything—should be geared to winning." Referring to the job of a coach, he said, "The big thing is to make men—men who want to win and are willing to give all they've got to roll up a victory. It's to make men who believe in themselves, in their team, and who always think confidently. Believers sweep everything before them."

Vince Lombardi believed that the application of strong rules governing dedication would assist in the process of making strong men and outstanding players. "When you work for me," he told his men firmly, "you are to think of only three things—your God, your families and the Green Bay Packers—in that order."

Jerry Kramer, Green Bay Packers guard, wrote a book called *Instant Replay: The Green Bay Diary of Jerry Kramer.* He remembers Lombardi telling the backs one day: "This is a game of abandon. You run with complete abandon. You care nothing for anybody or anything, and when you get close to the goal line your abandon is intensified. Nothing, not a tank, nor a wall, no eleven shall stop you from getting across that goal line!"

No wonder the Green Bay Packers under Lombardi's inspired leadership became one of the most astonishing teams in football history! And when you think about it, isn't that how you make something of your job also? You don't fool around with it doubtfully. You don't dabble hesitantly. You go at it with abandon. You go all out, holding nothing back. You make up your mind to win, nothing less. You believe in yourself. You have self-confidence. And remember—confidence draws results. It has a powerful magnetism.

A man whom I met when speaking at a sales convention said the biggest thing that ever happened to him was when he grasped this one dynamic idea about abandonment—going all out and running with it and winning. Today he is a top producer on the sales force of a big company. This, he assured me, is a complete reversal of how things used to be.

"For years," he said, "I was almost a total flop. And I was bitter and complaining, too. I felt life wasn't treating me right and I moped around hoping for better breaks. But those breaks didn't come. I had lost all faith in myself. I knew that I had no future. Then I happened to hear a fellow say it was no use waiting for life to do more for you—for it wouldn't until you got busy and put more into life. Life can give back only what you give it. The big question life asks of every one of us is: Are you with it? Do you really believe in yourself? Only the believers pick up the prizes in this life.

"Now that was exactly what I had not been doing at all. I was anything but a self-believer and certainly I wasn't winning any prizes. But suddenly I got a whole new slant on myself. Saw what a failure I'd been. And the solution, though it wasn't all that easy, wasn't at all complex. I just made up my mind that I was going to give my job of selling everything I had. I was going to believe in it and in myself. 'Belief and action' became my slogan.

BELIEF AND ACTION, A WINNING FORMULA

"Belief is no good without action. So the next morning I decided to act, and I got up an hour earlier. 'This is the day I give the job a real treatment,' I said aloud. Looking at the list of customers I was going to sell that day, I started out. I got to the first store before it was even open; actually helped the man open up. What's more, I enjoyed doing it. And I showed a lot of enthusiasm for his business—not mine, but his. As a result I made my first sale before I would normally have been out of bed, and without any effort. In fact, all my talking was about him and his business.

"And that's how things went all through the day. My whole world seemed different. I was amazed. Oh, I've got to admit I've had to fight against slumping back into the old dopey-Joe attitude at times. But somehow it doesn't grab me anymore. The present pace is too exciting. And it pays off, too. I now know what was wrong with me all those mixed-up years; I was a self-disbeliever. Now that I've discovered what I can do I'm positively thrilled. Everything is so different. Maybe," he added thoughtfully, "it's because I'm different."

And how right he is. If you want things to be different, perhaps the answer is to become different yourself. Become a self-believer. Reactivate the dynamic quality of confidence based on the realistic fact that you have the knowledge and the ability to do what needs doing. And furthermore, you know how to do it competently.

In arriving at such expertise and warranty of confidence in yourself, a working knowledge of the laws of mind control is important. It has been said that mind is everything. Whether you are willing to assign such totality of power to mind, it does indeed follow that mental processes are significantly determinative in forming future outcomes.

The case of a man about whom I had some knowledge at one time illustrates the power function of mind in the creative achievement process.

He had just about lost all faith in himself. Self-confidence had drained off. And not without reason. Already he had accumulated several years of failure, job after job. But then he changed and in due course reversed his self-defeating mental attitude so that ultimately he became quite successful both as a person and in business. The dramatic turning point came when he learned to practice an important law of mind action.

The father of this young man wanted to know: "What can be done about my son? I put him through college. Then I used my influence to get him a good job. He lost it. I got him another. He lost that one. He has been handed half a dozen excellent opportunities, but the sad story is always the same. He fails at everything and he is now almost thirty years old." So said the father somewhat despairingly.

We arranged for him to have a comprehensive aptitude test. The results showed he was qualified for personnel work. This surprised him, for this type of work had never been suggested, but he was willing to give it a try. At least he was cooperative. The psychologist said, "In my opinion the requirement for success in this case is for something more basic than a different line of work. This man needs to learn the law of creative anticipation. Otherwise his failure pattern may continue."

PRACTICE CREATIVE ANTICIPATION

Creative anticipation . . . it was the first time I had heard the phrase. The psychologist explained, "The trouble with this young man is that subconsciously he always expects the worst to happen, so that his mind tends to image and then to create a failure situation. He must be taught confidently to image and expect the best. The practice of creative anticipation should teach him to believe in his own potential."

It is of course a fact that what you deeply expect, you tend to get. Habitual expectations attract corresponding circumstances and events.

When the young man started practicing this creative anticipation technique, creative things started happening. For all too long he had lived from day to day grimly assuming that he would "mess things up." Since he expected that result, he got it. Then came this new idea: creative anticipation. There was a period of trial and error, but he learned to think confidently, he began expecting good results to happen. And gradually this became the pattern. When he learned the truth that you can if you think you can, he became an altogether different person.

A number of years have passed since this man made the vital change. He is today one of the most successful men in his line in his area and heads a large work force. "That law of creative anticipation is really something," he declared. "It saved my business life, that's for sure. It got me on the beam. The practice of creative anticipation changed me from constantly expecting failure to a belief that, after all, I could handle myself effectively."

In all thinking and in all action, just as in the precise laws of mathematics and physics, all things are governed by cause and effect. Do a certain thing in a certain way and you get a certain result. Everything in this world proceeds according to law, including thought itself. We can improve ourselves by the use of applicable laws, one of which is the law of creative anticipation, or self-belief.

"The greatest discovery of my generation," said psychologist William James, "is that human beings can alter their lives by altering their attitudes of mind."

THE POWER OF "IMAGING"

The individual who mentally visualizes himself achieving rather than failing and, importantly, who is willing to pay the price of intensive study and sustained effort, advances toward his goal. That mental vision is vital, for what we become is closely related to our basic self-image. What we think, what we visualize, what we image is to a large degree what we are bound to become.

Everyone has been motivated by some incident or story which at one time or another has made a lasting impression upon his thinking. Years ago I heard a story which stayed with me because it confirms both the power of the self-image and the creative anticipation principle. At the risk of repetition I give it here.

It seems that a famous trapeze performer had a group of students—young people who were ambitious to become performing stars. The class went through all the lesser stunts. Now the time came for each to perform on the high trapeze bar. All but one got through this test satisfactorily. But the last young aspirant looked up at the bar and at once a negative self-image took over and he visualized the worst: One slip and he would plunge to the ground. He froze. He could not move a muscle. Imagination was effectively blocking off employment of the knowledge he had gained of the procedure.

Terrified, the boy stammered, "I can't. I cannot do it. I see myself falling. I just cannot do it."

"If I did not know you are capable I would not ask you to do this. Look," said the older man, "I'll tell you how. First throw your heart over that bar up there and your body will follow." He meant, of course, to "throw" faith and confidence and an achievement image over the difficulty—and the material part would follow along naturally. It was very wise advice. The boy's thinking unfroze. The mental image was changed and he was finally able to pass his test without incident.

Everyone faces crises! By anticipating the worst we tend to freeze, unable to function properly. But by substituting the power of imagination, by imaging— "throwing" mind and heart over the obstacle—it can be overcome. The result inevitably follows the thrust of the mind.

People freeze over more than high trapeze bars. For

one thing, let a person make a mistake or two, chalk up a big error, come up with a dumb one, and it can contribute to a devastating lack of faith in himself. Self-reproach, a harsh self-appraisal, an "Oh, why did I do this?" or "Why didn't I do that?" attitude, can diminish if not destroy the self-confidence needed to learn and recoup and go ahead, sadder, maybe, but certainly wiser. Never let a mistake cause you to stop believing in yourself, because everything passes if you let it pass and do not hold onto it mentally.

Let me tell you of one such person. His belief in himself was at an all-time low but he recovered self-faith and rebounded successfully.

He sat in my office, this 29-year-old man, slumped in despondency bordering on despair. "Why did I do it?" he kept asking. "How could I have made such a terrible mistake? How's that for stupidity? I had the opportunity of a lifetime and what did I do? I blew it! My future has cracked up, and I don't mean maybe. I'm just no good . . . no good at all!"

He had been fired from a good position, so he told me, for making a serious mistake. Strange that a company would discharge a man for one mistake; perhaps, I thought, he had made others. In any case the depressed fellow felt that his career was shattered beyond repair. "Sure," I agreed, "it's a tough break. But maybe instead of griping you need to rethink your philosophy of mistakes."

I reminded him that a person learns and grows by trial and error. It just isn't possible that anybody could get by forever without making mistakes and perhaps occasionally some real costly ones. But men who really do things are those who take hold of themselves, derive some new know-how from the error, accept the consequences, pick up the pieces, and get going.

Indeed, over-zealousness to avoid mistakes can actually work against success. I know of one famous employer who had the curious policy of deliberately pushing younger men into situations where they would be forced to handle unfamiliar problems without benefit of instruction from higher up. He wanted to know if the employee had the nerve to risk making a mistake. Lacking that courage, he would not be considered for a higher executive position on the ground that excessive cautiousness marked him as indecisive. His record for developing self-confident and effective men was outstanding.

I pointed out to the dejected young man that some mistakes originate from an error pattern in one's thinking, while others are due to inexperience. When you repeatedly make the same mistakes, then it is a fair assumption that you may be mistake-prone. In that case a psychological study of your attitudes and reactions may be indicated.

The important thing is to profit from mistakes. Just as we may learn from our successes (how to do it) so also can we learn from our mistakes (how not to do it).

"So when you have made a mistake," I told my young friend, "see what know-how it can teach you and then charge it up to experience and try again."

I happened to think of an editorial written years ago by Grove Patterson, an Ohio newspaper editor, entitled "Water Under the Bridge." Having a hunch that it could be helpful, I read it aloud to him. It turned him back on. Here it is, and it's a classic in rebuilding shattered self-esteem:

WATER UNDER THE BRIDGE

A boy a long time ago leaned against the railing of a bridge and watched the current of the river below. A log, a bit of driftwood, a chip floated past. Again the surface of the river was smooth. But always, as it had for a hundred, perhaps a thousand, perhaps even a million years, the water slipped by under the bridge. Sometimes the current went more swiftly and again quite slowly, but always the river flowed on under the bridge.

Watching the river that day, the boy made a discovery. It was not the discovery of a material thing, something he might put his hand upon. He could not even see it. He had discovered an idea. Quite suddenly, and yet quietly, he knew that everything in his life would some day pass under the bridge and be gone like the water.

The boy came to like those words *water under the bridge.* All his life thereafter the idea served him well and carried him through. Although there were days and ways that were dark and not easy, always when he had made a mistake that couldn't be helped, or lost something that could never come again, the boy, now a man, said "It's water under the bridge."

And he didn't worry unduly about his mistakes after that and he certainly didn't let them get him down, because it was *water under the bridge.*

The young man sat without a word. Then he stood up. I had a feeling the editorial had registered. "O.K.," he said, "I get it. It's water under the bridge. I'll try again." And he did all right, because he learned the very great truth that no failure ever need be final. Because you failed, made a mistake, acted stupidly does not indicate lack of brains or ability. It's just that now and then anyone can stumble or even take a bad fall. But that does not mean that you are not all right yourself. Just pick yourself up mentally. Say, "O.K., that happened, but now it has passed. I'll turn my back on all of it and look confidently to the future." Keep on believing in yourself. Have confidence.

Of course, the important thing that happened in the case of the man who had made the costly mistake was that he found himself. You find yourself and then you will begin believing in yourself. And once that occurs, the potential abilities built into your personality, but submerged, will start working creatively to change you. And it follows that such transformation will change everything for you.

A self-realization awakening is a vital and necessary experience; an experience in which an idea explodes in the mind. And such an explosive idea is that when you think you can, then you can. The dawning of self-realization through humble belief in oneself is one of the epochal happenings in the career of a human being.

YOU CAN IF YOU THINK YOU CAN

I was in Australia speaking to the International Rotary Convention once, when Mrs. Peale and I were entertained at dinner by a delightful couple (since become good friends) who own a chain of stores throughout their country.

Their amazingly beautiful and unique home is situated on the shore of Sydney Harbor with an incomparable view of the city and its waterways, one of the most striking panoramas in the world. To reach their home from the roadway level a miniature private funicular, a small ratchet railway, descends through varying scents of exotic flowers. Though it was so-called "winter" in Australia, everything was blooming luxuriantly.

The house, lovely in appointments, opened through wide window-doors onto a terrace which ran down to the harbor, where the owner's small yacht was moored. Our host and hostess, two charming people, were disarmingly humble. They had come to their influential place in life, they said, through a simple success principle. And as the man said, "If that principle worked wonders for me, it will do the same for anyone who will really buy it and work it."

The next day he came to see me at the hotel. "I am a very ordinary fellow," he told me. "I only have a second-class brain. My father put me in one school after another and all I did was fail. I had a most remarkable academic failure record. Finally, by dint of long sufferance of the teachers, I got out of school with a partial, inadequate education. Then in one job after another I managed to keep up my record—failed at every one because I was really very ordinary; had no belief in myself and no confidence.

"I got a job with the National Cash Register Company of Australia," he continued. "But still I was the potential victim of a repetitive and established failure pattern. Then a dynamic leader came out from the main office in the States and made a speech.

"He told us that the basic factor leading to success is positive thinking. This was something I'd never heard before. And he put the new idea in a simple phrase: 'You can if you think you can.' That struck me. It burst in my mind like an exploding bomb. He urged us to form a mental image of what we wanted to be and to believe in our inner power to be that. Then and there I determined to be a successful person and I began seeing myself from a new image point of view."

As part of his training program he came to the United States and while here visited Marble Collegiate Church in New York City. In the church calendar he read about a key ring called a "mustard seed remembrance." It was a plastic ball with a mustard seed embedded in it. He got one of these (he pulled it out of his pocket and showed it to me) and has carried it ever since. I could see that the plastic was very scratched, but the mustard seed was clearly visible.

"I learned that 'If ye have faith as a grain of mustard seed . . . nothing shall be impossible unto you.' * Once I accepted the mustard seed idea I began to follow positive spiritual teachings. I mean I really practiced them. And the most remarkable things happened to me!" (One of those remarkable things was his rise to the position of General Manager of the National Cash Register Company of Australia.)

"I began to set goals for myself and to believe I could realize them. I, a second-rate mind! Later I went into merchandising, and we now have a chain of stores all over this land. We have increased business twenty-one times. It is all because I began to believe in myself as a person. I hadn't amounted to anything before that— and I became a remade individual."

After listening to this remarkable story of a failure pattern being revised into spectacular achievement, I said, "Bert, you have never been an ordinary fellow with a second-class mind. You only thought you were. That was your image of yourself. Actually, all the time

____* Matthew 17:20.

you had buried within your personality an extraordinary person of first-class mind.

"A dynamic experience of new thought occurred when the speaker hurled at you that power-packed phrase, 'You can if you think you can.' Then your equally dynamic religious faith, which you really believed and really practiced, triggered, releasing forces into motion which literally produced a new person."

And evidently even Queen Elizabeth II was impressed, for she knighted our erstwhile "ordinary fellow" who now bears the honored title of "Sir." And "Sir" he deserves to be. And you do, too, sir or madam, when you keep on believing in yourself and have confidence.

Remember the words of Andrew Carnegie: "Tell yourself in your secret reveries, 'I was made to handle affairs.' "

And now a few points from this chapter on which you may wish to focus attention:

1. *Remember that self-trust is the first secret of success. So trust yourself.*

2. *Having learned to believe in yourself, be like Lombardi's football stars: Go at life with abandon; give it all you've got. And life will give all it has to you.*

3. *Practice creative anticipation, the power of positive expectation. Have confidence that you can draw the best, not the worst, to yourself.*

4. *Be sure to image right, for we tend to become as we see ourselves. So see yourself confidently.*

5. *Never let any mistake cause you to stop believing in yourself. Learn from it and go on.*

6. *If you've never really found yourself, do so.*

Then you'll start liking yourself, and with good reason.

7. *You can if you think you can. Engrave those seven words deeply in consciousness. They are packed with power and with truth.*

SIX

❧

YOU CAN
IF YOU THINK YOU CAN

He was a terrific man. And unforgettable. His name was George Reeves, fifth grade teacher in the Williams Avenue School in Norwood, Ohio. I was a member of his class.

Mr. Reeves stood 6 feet 4 inches in height and weighed 240 pounds. His face was rugged, like a granite cliff, and like sunshine on a cliff, his countenance would often light up and then he was tremendous.

His personality was as impressive as his stature. His idea of teaching was simple and uncomplicated. His job, as he conceived it, was to make men out of boys and women out of girls. The strong, undefeatable type.

This teacher had hands as big as hams. I know, for not infrequently he applied them to my posterior anatomy, and in no uncertain manner. He was a practitioner of manual discipline. But he was fair about it, and only when you had it coming to you did that big hand descend upon you. He never spanked the girls; just cowed them with a look.

Once in my newspaper column I told the story of Mr. Reeves and received from all over the country some one hundred letters from his former students boasting that they, too, had been "licked" by this great teacher.

And that he was indeed a great teacher is evidenced by the fact that the ideas and principles which he taught are remembered and practiced after these many years. I mention this for the benefit of any who might disparage the type of pedagogy referred to here.

Occasionally during a class session and for no apparent reason, Mr. Reeves would shout, "Silence!" And when he called for silence he got it and no fooling. Then he would print in large letters on the blackboard the word "CAN'T." Turning to the class he would look at us expectantly. We knew what he wanted and would chant, "Knock the T off the CAN'T." With a sweeping gesture Mr. Reeves erased the T, leaving the word "CAN" standing out clear and strong.

"Let that be a lesson to you," he would say, dusting the chalk off his fingers. "You are meant to grow up into strong, competent people believing in yourselves, in your country and in God. You are not designed to be little weak pygmies. You are to develop into real men and women, and I'm telling you that you can make something of yourselves. And to do that, never forget this principle of successful achievement: 'You can if you think you can.'"

Well, now, who among those kids could ever forget such a point of view, especially when it was consistently hammered into their consciousness by a strong, persuasive man who believed in that action principle, who espoused that dynamic motivation?

In the preceding chapter I told the story of a man in Australia who changed from a consistent failure pattern to one of success by hearing a sales manager say in a speech, "You can if you think you can." This idea brought about a dramatic change in his thinking when it was projected into his mind. As it saturated his

thoughts it started a process through which he finally
found himself as a person. Then he went on to become
a creative and competent individual. In this chapter I
want to pursue in greater depth the motivational factors inherent in that concept, "You can if you think you
can."

EVER ASTOUND YOURSELF?

Obviously, such a principle implies that a person possesses within himself considerable potential. And that
is precisely the assumption we wish to stress; people do
have within them more talent, more ability, more effective functioning than has been apparent. Thomas A.
Edison was an exact scientist and certainly not in the
habit of making loose and unsupportable statements.
And Edison said, "If we did all the things we are capable of doing we would literally astound ourselves." In
the light of this remark, a rather significant question
might be, "Have you ever in your lifetime astounded
yourself?" Well, you can if you think you can.

A dramatic incident I read somewhere told of an
American sailor in the Korean Conflict. This clear-
minded and well-organized young man astounded everyone around him. And no doubt he was himself astounded by qualities that appeared in crisis. Do you
really have any idea of the power inherent in your
personality? It pays to make that discovery, affecting
as it may the future of your life, as in the case of this
sailor.

Well, to get on with our story. It seems that an American destroyer lay at anchor in Wonsan Harbor during
the Korean Conflict. The night was clear, moonlit, and

very still. The quartermaster, making a routine check of the ship, suddenly stopped stockstill. He saw a big, black object floating not far off. Aghast, he realized at once that it was a floating contact mine which had broken loose from a mine field and was slowly drifting with the ebbing tide toward midships.

Grabbing the intercom, the quartermaster summoned the duty officer who came dashing to the scene. Quickly the captain was notified. A general alarm was sounded. The entire ship went into action.

Officers and men stared in consternation at the slowly approaching mine. Feverishly the situation was appraised. Disaster hung trembling in the balance.

Various suggestions were rapidly put forward by the officers. Should they up anchor? No, there wasn't time. Start the engines and shift the position of the ship? No, that wasn't feasible, for the propeller wash would only suck the mine more rapidly inward. Could the mine be exploded with gunfire? No, it was too close to the ship's magazine. What, then, should be done? Launch a boat and push it away with long poles? This wouldn't work, for it was a contact mine and there was no time to disarm it. Tragedy seemed imminent.

ORDINARY SEAMAN COMES THROUGH

Suddenly an ordinary seaman out-thought all his superior officers. "Get the fire hoses," he shouted. Everyone instinctively realized that this suggestion made sense. A stream of water was played into the sea between the ship and the floating mine, creating a current that carried the mine into waters where it was safely exploded by gunfire.

Quite a man, that ordinary seaman. He was certainly no ordinary person—and yet he was. But he had within himself the ability to think cool and straight in a crisis situation. Such abilities are definitely built into each of us, perhaps to a greater extent in some than in others, but no normal human being is lacking in creative potential. It follows, then, that no matter what difficulty or crisis affects your situation, you can handle it if only you think you can. Thinking positively about your ability tends to release positive mental forces that produce effective action.

Take the case of the young foreigner who wanted to go to college, but, having an inferiority complex, he hesitated to try for an American education. He feared difficulties with the English language that might make his classmates laugh at him. He even doubted that he could make it through college. He was motivated by ambition, but hampered by a low opinion of his ability.

A quote by Rudyard Kipling came to mind and I passed it along to him. "We have forty million reasons for failure, but not a single excuse." I told him that of course he need not be defeated by anybody or anything, especially not by himself, that he was an intelligent fellow and certainly could make it if he would start thinking that he could.

"Never think of yourself as failing," I advised. "That is most dangerous, for the mind always tries to complete what it pictures. Instead, stamp indelibly on your mind a mental picture of yourself succeeding. By all means go to college. Laugh at yourself along with your classmates and they will love you for it. Don't let your accent make you feel inadequate. Who knows, perhaps you'll be an English language expert yet! In the meantime, don't be on the defensive about it. Once you change your attitude you will be surprised how friendly your classmates will be, even if they do have some fun with you." We were successful in persuading Hans to go to college. He became very popular with his fellow students and had a creditable scholastic record.

Perhaps nothing so plagues and harasses human beings as the crippling, misery-producing feeling of personal inadequacy. But you can be relieved of this trouble no matter how long you may have suffered from it. And the cure begins when you decide that you really want to change, when you become very determined. You never really know what you can do until you try. And if you keep moving ahead with determination, thinking positively at all times, everlastingly trying, you will not fail.

Whenever a negative thought about yourself comes to mind, deliberately voice a positive thought to cancel it out. And do not build up obstacles in your imagination. Depreciate every so-called obstacle. Minimize them. Of course, difficulties must be studied to be eliminated, but they should be seen realistically only for what they are. Never inflate them by fear-thoughts.

When you become aware of the potential force within yourself, you will realize that you do not need to be defeated simply because you once had feelings of inferiority.

AN EAGLE OR A CHICKEN?

Ever hear the parable about the eagle who thought it was a chicken?

One day, so the story goes, an adventurous young boy climbed high in the mountains near his father's chicken farm and found an eagle's nest. He took an egg out of the nest, brought it back to the farm, and put it with the chicken eggs under a setting hen. The hen sat on the eggs until they hatched and out came a little eaglet along with the chicks. The eaglet was raised among the chickens and never knew it was anything else than a chicken. For a while it was content and lived a normal chicken's life.

But as it began to grow there were strange stirrings within. Every once in a while it would think, "There must be more to me than a chicken!" But it never did anything about it until one day a tremendous eagle flew over the chicken yard. The eaglet felt strange new strength in its wings. It became aware of an enormous heartbeat in its breast. And as it watched the eagle, the thought came, "I'm like that. A chicken yard is not for me. I want to climb the sky and perch on mountain crags."

It had never flown, but the power and instinct were within. It spread its wings and was lifted to the top of a low hill. Exhilarated, it flew to a higher hilltop and finally on into the blue to the summit of a high mountain peak. It had discovered its great self.

Remember that nobody can be you as efficiently as *you* can. But you must discover your truly great self. For then you will know that you can, because you will have learned to think that you can. You will have found yourself. So, to complete our little parable, what do you say we stop being a chicken and be the eagle that is within us! It can be exciting, too!

But of course, someone may say, "That's a pretty parable. But after all, I'm neither a chicken nor an eagle. I'm a human being. Just an ordinary one, at that, and I never expect to do anything much with myself."

Perhaps that is just the trouble; you never expect to do anything much with yourself. It is a fact, a very serious fact, that we peg ourselves at just about the level of our self-expectations.

Refuse right now to believe there are things you cannot do. Some of the greatest things in this world have been accomplished by men and women who never knew what they couldn't do. So, not knowing, they just went right ahead and did it.

ATHLETE WITH ONLY HALF A FOOT

A good example is Tom Dempsey, who kicked that unbelievable 63-yard field goal that electrified the athletic world a few years ago.

Tom was born with only half a right foot and a deformed right hand. He had some really great parents, for never once did they make him uncomfortably aware of his handicap. As a result the boy did everything everybody else did. If the Scouts hiked ten miles, so did Tom. Why not? There was nothing wrong with him. He could do it, same as any other kid.

Then he wanted to play football and, of all things, he got the desire to excel in a special talent. He found he could kick a football farther than anybody with whom he played. To capitalize on that ability he had a special shoe designed. With never a negative thought about that half right foot and deformed right hand, he showed up at a kicking tryout camp and was given a contract with the Chargers.

The coach, as gently as he could say it, gave him the word that he "didn't have what it takes to make it in pro football," and urged him to try something else.

Finally he applied to the New Orleans Saints and begged for a chance. The coach was doubtful, but was impressed by the boy's belief in himself, so took him on.

Two weeks later the coach was even more impressed when Tom Dempsey kicked a 55-yard field goal in an exhibition game. That got him the job of regular kicker for the Saints, and in that season he scored 99 points for his team.

Then came the big moment. The stadium was packed with 66,000 fans. The ball was on the 28-yard line, with only a few seconds left to play. The play advanced the ball to the 45-yard line. Now there was time for only one play. "Go in there and kick it, Dempsey," the coach shouted.

As Tom ran onto the field he knew his team was 55 yards from the goal line, or 63 yards from the point at which he would have to kick. The longest kick ever in a regular game had been 55 yards by Bert Rechichar of the Baltimore Colts.

The snap of the ball was perfect. Dempsey put his foot into the ball squarely. It went straight, but would it be far enough? The 66,000 spectators watched breathlessly. Then the official in the end zone raised his hands, signaling it was good. The ball had cleared the bar by inches. The team won, 19–17. The stands went wild, thrilled by the longest field goal ever kicked. And by a player with half a foot and a deformed hand!

"Unbelievable!" someone shouted. But Dempsey smiled. He remembered his parents. They had always told him what he could do, not what he couldn't do. He accomplished this tremendous feat because, as he so well put it, "They never told me I couldn't."

Never tell yourself that you can't do this or that; never assert negatively that it just isn't possible. Only tell yourself that you can. First think that you can, proceed to try and try, and then you will find that you can, indeed. Remember that chicken-eagle story? Be the eagle that you really are!

Perhaps you may feel that we go too far in emphasizing the "you can if you think you can" idea, that some things are simply not possible at all. It has been my experience that under-motivated people always tend to fall back on that excuse as if the last word in any difficult situation is the word impossible.

The principle, you can if you think you can, is valid and viable also under painful and even incredibly difficult situations. For example, on February 22, 1971, John McWethy was driving at a speed of seventy miles an hour on Interstate Route 70 near St. Louis. Dozing at the wheel, he found his car suddenly careening into the median strip, rolling over and crushing in the roof. In that tragic moment John McWethy suffered "the most severe injury a person can endure and still survive," according to Dr. Joel S. Rosen.

Mr. McWethy is paralyzed from the chest down, his hands almost nonfunctioning. He is a quadriplegic, confined to a wheelchair and unable to feel sensation in most of his body.

Dick Griffin,* who tells the graphic story, describes the abyss of depression, fear and self-pity which engulfed this formerly vigorous man. But he found within himself courage and determination to undertake the long climb from despair to victory. Mr. Griffin points out that on October 29, 1971, just thirty-five weeks and five days after the accident, John McWethy went back

_____* *Chicago Daily News* business and financial editor, writing in *The National Observer* (June 30, 1973), reprinted from the *Journal of American Insurance.*

to work as Midwest Manager of the *Wall Street Journal.*
For insurance purposes he is considered totally disabled, but he carries his own weight on his important
job.

There are always negativists eager to take exception
to such a positive philosophy as you can if you think you
can. They constantly emphasize what people cannot
do: They cannot find a chance in life; they cannot rise
out of poverty; they cannot come back from physical
disability. Unhappily, some may listen to these croakers
and settle for the "I cannot" point of view. But how
confused they must be by the John McWethys of this
world, who overcome the most frightful conditions by
knowing that you can if you think you can.

NOW HE CLIMBS SPIRITUAL MOUNTAINS

Consider another crisis, that of a friend, Ben B.
Franklin of Topeka, Kansas. I include his story here for
the purpose of illustrating the power of the concept,
you can if you think you can, especially when it is
spiritually conditioned. Ben says: *

I was 18 when the mountain turned on me.

Until then, I had been its master, for climbing
was my great love. I spent each summer climbing
and each winter dreaming of the next summer
when I would climb again.

But on April 14, 1963, I fell. With two fellow
freshmen from the University of Colorado I was
scaling a perpendicular facing when my rope
frayed on a jagged ridge. It parted and I pitched

_____* *Guideposts* (January 1972).

backward, plummeting the equivalent of seven
stories to the canyon floor.

My first sensation was floating within black wool.
Through the pain all I could think of was: What
happened to my rope? What happened to my
rope? The voices of my companions, who had fran-
tically rappelled down, filtered dimly through to
me.

By the time the rescue squad had arrived with
a stretcher, I'd become delirious. I was strapped
into it, carried down the canyon to an ambulance
which screamed the 30 miles into Denver.

Surgeons pieced together my shattered pelvis
and labored for hours on my back which was broken in four places. Many days in intensive care
followed. Then, as my pain muted and I became
more rational, the agony of my spirit began.

The sheet over my body wouldn't move. I could
wriggle my fingers and twist my wrists; but with
mounting terror I learned that my body was dead
from the waist down. Lose those legs that had lifted
me up mountains? No!

Anger charged me. Those legs were mine; they
would move at my command. Brutally I tried to
find some muscle to contract, some nerve to pierce
that deathly stillness beneath the sheets. I twisted
every emotional fiber in me to will my leg to move.
Nothing.

I struggled for hope. Days went on, and my legs
began to wither. I began to pray—pray desperately. It was in this crisis of utter hopelessness that
I surrendered myself to God. At night, alone in my
room, I spoke to Him: "You know that I want to
walk again. But I can't do it. I don't have anything
left, dear God. I've tried as hard as I know and have
only discovered that my will means nothing. If not
my will, then, Thine be done."

I drifted into a deep, relaxing sleep. For the first time since the mountain, I experienced the serenity of peaceful dreams. They were so beautiful; my feeling of helplessness was gone. In that agonizing prayer when I turned all control over to God, I had accepted my accident. In so doing I had relinquished my will to His. And I didn't have to fight anymore.

The next evening I moved a toe.

Had it really moved? Or was it only a flickering shadow?

I stared in terrible fascination at that point of the sheet, afraid to try again. Then, very cautiously, I did try.

Again the sheet moved. I exploded into ecstatic joy, laughing and shouting. An anxious-faced nurse burst into the room. I tried to kiss her; she bounced right out. I poured out a grateful prayer to God, with thanksgiving streaming down my face.

Years have passed since that night, but my happiness continues. I am still partially paralyzed. But after only a year in the wheelchair, I progressed to crutches with leg braces. I have since graduated from college and now work with my father, a lecture manager, and travel around the world on my crutches.

And I am grateful for each step I take. I am even thankful to the mountain. For it was through my accident that I discovered deeper joys than climbing. I'm happy I was only 18 when it happened.

GET RID OF "IMPOSSIBLE"!

As to the concept, "impossible," I recall the curious procedure of a well-known inspirational writer named Napoleon Hill. As a young man he had the ambition to be a writer. To accomplish this objective he knew he would need to become expert in the use of words. Words would be his stock-in-trade, but since he was a poor boy and deficient in education, "kind friends" assured him his ambition was impossible.

Young Hill saved his money and bought the finest, most complete and beautiful dictionary available. All the words he would ever need were in that dictionary, and he meant to master them. But then he did a strange thing. He turned to the word "impossible" and with fine scissors clipped it out of the dictionary and threw it away. Then he had a book of words devoid of that negative concept, impossible. Thereafter he built his whole career on the premise that nothing is impossible to the person who wants to grow and outgrow.

I am not suggesting that you cut the word "impossible" out of your dictionary. But I most certainly suggest that you cut it out of your mind. Eliminate it from your conversation, drop it from your thoughts, erase it from your attitudes. Get rid of it—get through with it. Stop rationalizing it. Cease excusing for it. Let that word and that concept go for good, and substitute for it that bright and shining word "possible," which is to say— you can if you think you can.

Remember those magnificent words: "If ye have faith as a grain of mustard seed . . . nothing shall be impossible unto you." * Write that on a card and carry it in your wallet. Better still, write it indelibly on your consciousness. Live by it. Live with it, and in the deepest sense you will get with it. You will accomplish outstanding possibles.

To get good results, develop a healthy disrespect for

_____* Matthew 17:20.

that word "impossible." Examine it ruthlessly and
scientifically. When something is considered impossible, it actually represents ignorance of the facts. It is
the passing along of an error. When careful, objective
study is made, the declaration that "it is impossible" is
shown to be lacking in substance. I recall that in my
younger years the ultimate in impossibles was expressed by a common saying, "You can no more do that
than fly to the moon."

THE "IMPOSSIBLE" BRIDGE

The building of a great bridge over the Straits of
Mackinac is a story * that deserves a place in the litera-
ture of doing what can't be done by thinking that it can,
and also by scientifically exploding the myth of the impossible.

It seems the building of the bridge had been blocked
for more than half a century because so many people
were so sure it was impossible. As early as the 1880's
forward-looking Michigan business people were saying
there should be a bridge across the Straits. The railroads
already had branch lines running east through Michigan's Upper Peninsula to St. Ignace on the north shore
of the Straits, and running north from Detroit to Mack-
inaw City on the south shore. There was also ferry service carrying passengers and goods back and forth across
the five miles of water separating the two railheads. In
winter, however, when the Straits were icebound,

_____* "The Story of the Mackinac Bridge," by Walter L. Cisler,
published by the Newcomen Society in North America.

nothing moved, and this was a hindrance to economic development in the Upper Peninsula.

Various groups kept promoting the idea of a bridge, but again and again they were met with the assertion, "It's impossible." It was impossible, said the wiseacres, because you could never build a bridge that would stand up against the high-velocity winds that go roaring through the Straits. It was impossible, some said, because the terrific winter ice pressure would crack and undermine the piers and foundations. It was impossible, others maintained, because there was evidence that the bottom under the Straits consisted of shale, too weak to support the weight of bridge foundations and extending too far down before bedrock.

For decades these objections that it couldn't be done prevented any progress toward a bridge. Then shortly after World War II Senator Prentiss M. Brown arranged for a scientific investigation of the alleged obstacles.

Research disclosed that the highest wind velocity ever recorded at the Straits was seventy-eight miles per hour during a November storm in 1940. Civil engineers affirmed there was no reason why the contemplated bridge could not be designed to withstand two and a half times that wind velocity.

Engineers also came up with specifications for piers and foundations capable of withstanding five times the greatest ice pressure ever encountered anywhere on earth!

Exhaustive tests showed that the rock beneath the Straits could support more than sixty tons of load per square foot. Calculations indicated that the foundations could be so designed as to keep the loading pressure safely under fifteen tons per square foot.

Once these findings had disposed of the ola negativisms, plans for the long-declared "impossible" bridge were adopted. But then, just as construction was about to start, a bridge at Tacoma, Washington, suddenly collapsed from the force of wind pressure in the gorge beneath pushing up against the under side of the span. What if the same kind of upward pressure should develop in the Mackinac Straits? That objection got answered very promptly. The engineers simply took the Tacoma catastrophe as a lesson in the importance of installing gratings in bridge roadways to provide an outlet for upthrust wind.

So at long last the dreamed-of bridge across the Mackinac Straits—the one that was impossible— became a reality, five miles long and rising 552 feet above the water.

The project engineer declared, "Given willpower enough and brains enough and faith enough, almost anything can be done." How right he is! As Harry Emerson Fosdick once said, "The world is moving so fast these days that the man who says it can't be done is generally interrupted by someone doing it."

If you are faced by a problem and are harassed by the impossibility concept, begin a factual, objective study of the so-called impossible factors in the situation. The verdict, "impossible," is usually derived from an emotional reaction to the problem, and it can often be overcome by substituting a cool, unemotional, intellectual examination of the elements involved, as in the case of the bridge.

It cannot be overemphasized that myths always give way to facts. "It's impossible" is a myth! "It can be done and you can do it" is a fact. So get with the facts. Bypass the myths. Reassert and reaffirm the fact that by the application of creative thinking you can eliminate the impossible.

The great fact is that by right thinking, faith and courage, the so-called impossible can be made possible. And the type of individual who accomplishes that achievement is the one who will never settle for defeat; who keeps fighting, working and, above all, who never stops believing in God, in life, and in himself.

CANCER COULDN'T STOP HIM

The newspapers told about a man who had been made a rear admiral. As a junior naval officer he was discharged from the service because he had cancer. He survived four tough bouts with that disease. At one time he was informed he had only two weeks to live. But the treatments, plus his dogged faith, worked, and his cancer condition was arrested.

This man had worked all his life to be a naval officer, but with a record of cancer, naval regulations forbade reinstatement. He was told "there wasn't a chance," but he kept on fighting. He finally learned that it would take an Act of Congress to get him back in the Navy. So he went after the Act of Congress. And President Truman signed into law a special bill that reinstated him in the Navy.

This man, Irwin W. Rosenberg, became Rear Admiral of the United States' Seventh Fleet. Admiral Rosenberg never gave up. He had a goal and refused to believe it was impossible to achieve it. All of which proves that a human being can take the big impossibles of life and make them possible. With God's help and your own attitude the impossible can become possible.

The principle of imaging results, of discounting the impossibles, is practiced not only by bridge builders and admirals but also by people like wives and mothers, as, for example, the following letter telling of a deeply human experience of positive faith:

TO HAVE A BABY—IMPOSSIBLE!

After three years of marriage and no children, I began to wonder—Why? So I went to five doctors and each one told me the same story. By this time I was desperate for I wanted a child very much. My husband would tell me it didn't matter, but to me it did. All the doctors said along with an infantile womb I also had a rare blood type (Group A) PH (D) negative, and women with this type of blood could have no children.

After the last visit I told the doctor, "There is One greater than any of you." I went home and got out a picture of a beautiful little baby girl with curly hair. This picture was an advertisement for baby products. From that moment on I would look at that picture and pray to my God that if it was His will let me become with child before a major surgery scheduled for the month of May. My last visit to the doctor was the last of February. Before long I knew God was answering my prayer.

So I waited until the last of May to go back to see him. Then I said to him and his wife who assisted him, "I'm with child." They laughed. Then I demanded they examine me to see. After he saw I was determined, the examination was made. They stared at each other in amazement. I said to them, "I've been consulting that Physician I told you about." I was then over two months and he said I could not carry the baby three months. I did. Then he said, "You cannot carry it more than seven months." That I did.

From that time on I have never had any doubt in my mind that God does answer prayers. My daughter is now married and has two boys, and neither she nor the boys have my blood type, but her father's.

Some people settle for defeat all too easily. Others do not settle easily, but trouble and failure gradually wear them down and eventually they become tired and discouraged and give up. It's the individual who has a deep faith and gut courage who comes through life's tough battles with a victory instead of a defeat.

DON'T BE AFRAID TO BE AFRAID

Some time ago the famous entertainer, Maurice Chevalier, departed this life. But he left the memory of a courageous and undefeatable human being. For many decades this amazing man delighted audiences all over the world with his jaunty straw hat, his crooning voice, and whimsical smile. He was the debonair boulevardier, America's number-one Frenchman. There was never anyone quite like him.

Why did so many people admire him? Was it his charm, his talent, his enthusiasm, his amazing stamina? Perhaps, but I admired him because he was so very human; there was nothing phony about him. And I admired his courage. He had plenty of that, and he needed it, too.

Courage can be many things, but the secret of courage is simply and honestly to admit your feelings of failure. And then with God's help go on and do your job in spite of them.

One night during his brilliant career, Maurice Chevalier suddenly felt extremely dizzy. It was just before he was to go on stage. His brain seemed on fire. Cues seemed to reach him from far away. He tried desperately to get back on the track, but his mind was a jumble. He felt hopelessly lost. His fellow actors covered up for him, but the debonair ease which was Maurice Chevalier's trademark was not there. He hesitated and stammered. For the first time in his professional life, failure had come to this great performer.

He was ordered to rest and went to the southern part of France, where he came under the care of Dr. Robert Dubois. "I'm a beaten man," he told the doctor. "I'm afraid of being a failure. There is no future for me now." He was advised to take long walks to repair his damaged nervous system. But the inner turmoil did not leave him. He was deeply afraid. He had lost all confidence.

After a time when Dr. Dubois thought the actor was ready for it, he suggested that Chevalier entertain before a small group in the village hall. "But," said Maurice, "I am terrified at the thought. What guarantee is there that my mind will not go blank again, that the dizziness will not return?"

"There is no guarantee," replied the doctor, "but you must not be afraid of failing. You are afraid to step on a stage again and so you are telling yourself that you're finished. But fear is never a reason for quitting; it is only an excuse. When a brave man encounters fear he admits it, and goes on despite it. Don't be afraid to be afraid. Go on and perform even so."

Maurice suffered untold agony of fear before his appearance in that little town before those few people, but he went on and performed very well. Joy welled up inside him. "I knew that I had not permanently conquered fear. But I had admitted it and went on despite it. The scheme worked!"

After that evening in that little village in France six decades ago, Maurice Chevalier performed before huge audiences everywhere. "There have been many moments of fear," said the entertainer. "The gentle doctor was right; there is no guarantee. But being frightened has never made me want to quit."

And Maurice added: "My own experience has taught me this. If you wait for the perfect moment when all is safe and assured it may never arrive. Mountains will not be climbed, races won or lasting happiness achieved."

And Maurice Chevalier achieved happiness. He never quit on life. He danced and sang his way into the hearts of millions who loved and respected him. And his memory will linger on, for he was a man who won over himself. He did not settle for defeat. And the reason he did not accept defeat was that he learned the great lesson inherent in all human problems—you can if you think you can.

FAITH IS UNDEFEATABLE

When Almighty God created a human being He put a touch of greatness into his nature. A man is a mixture, that's for sure. But however weak, mixed up, however defeated he can be, there is still this element: Something in him entitles him to be called a child of God.

No matter what happens to him in the way of difficulty and trouble, he still has what it takes to come out of it with dignity and power and get on top.

This fact was summed up quite well, I thought, by a taxi driver who took me into the city from Kennedy Airport one afternoon. I liked this taxi driver from the start. He flashed me a big smile. We drove along, chatting casually. Stopping for a red light, he looked around and asked, "What's your name?" When I gave it he said, "I thought so. Listen to you on radio. Thought I recognized your voice."

Then he continued, "I am glad to meet you, too. Funny, you getting into my cab at this time." The words came slowly, with effort. "You see, my wife died. The funeral was yesterday. We were married almost thirty years. You never saw a sweeter woman in your life. She was an angel. There was nothing but good in her. She loved everybody and everybody loved her. She was so good to me all those years . . . I can't imagine living without her."

As gently as I knew how, I said, "I don't believe you really will be without her. She will always be thinking of you. She will be with you in spirit. You will feel her love comforting you."

"Thanks. Thanks a lot," he said feelingly. "She was so wonderful. I wish you could have known her."

He was silent for a moment, then spoke again. "Life is full of trouble, isn't it? I've got five children. Four of them are real good, but one sure is a problem. He has taken to drugs and runs around with a bad crowd. He is full of hate and meanness. I am very worried about him. Can't seem to do a thing with him. It broke his poor mother's heart. Now I've got to be both mother and father to this kid."

I started to sympathize, but he interjected, "I know what you're going to say." And he assured me, "With the help of God I can handle it. Don't worry about me. I'm O.K."

Then he got off a tremendous statement; real truth is in it. He said, "You can be greater than anything that can happen to you." What a terrific fact!

This man was a strong personality who knew that a person with faith is undefeatable. And he was holding onto that. So even in the pain and sorrow of bereavement and his anxiety for a son seriously off the beam, he was able to say, "You can be greater than anything that can happen to you." There are some great human beings in this world and that man is one of them. Potentially we all have the quality of invincibility. You can if you think you can.

Now what have we been saying in this chapter?

1. *You can if you think you can. As you think, so shall it be. Then think that you can and you can, indeed.*

2. *Remember Thomas A. Edison's dynamic statement: "If we did all the things we are capable of, we would literally astound ourselves."*

3. *As Rudyard Kipling says, "We have forty million reasons for failure but not a single excuse."*

4. *There may not be a tiger in your tank, but there for sure is an eagle in your mind.*

5. *Be glad you were never told what you couldn't do. And if you have been, repudiate the statement.*

6. *Drop the word "impossible" from your mental processes.*

7. *"The world is moving so fast that the man who says it can't be done is interrupted by someone doing it."*
8. *You can make the impossible possible.*
9. *Never—never—settle for defeat.*
10. *You can be greater than anything that can happen to you.*

SEVEN

※

WHAT ARE YOU AFRAID OF?
FORGET IT!

There are a hundred and one secret fears. So reports a hospital "fear inventory." Fears, they tell us, range all the way from agoraphobia (fear of open spaces) to claustrophobia (fear of enclosed places) to acrophobia (fear of high places). And, believe it or not, there are ninety-eight more on the above-mentioned list. So fear seems quite a potent problem. To overcome fear is vastly important if you want to live effectively and be a happy person.

Dr. Charles Mayo, founder of the famed Mayo Clinic, said, "Worry affects the circulation, the heart, the glands, the whole nervous system, and profoundly affects the heart." Robert Frost declared, "The reason why worry kills more people than work is that more people worry than work."

This author is, of course, neither a psychiatrist nor a psychologist, but I have been trying for years, not without some success, to help people rid themselves of abnormal fear. And that is what this nontechnical chapter is all about.

It's to ask, what are you afraid of? And to suggest that you can forget it! And to do that, start the process of canceling out fear with faith. For there is no force in this world more powerful than faith when it is faith in depth, faith that is real, bona fide. The most amazing things can happen as a result of it. Faith is no palliative; it's the cure—the only sure cure—for fear.

There are two massive thought forces competing for control of the mind: fear and faith, and faith is stronger—much stronger. Hold that thought of faith's greater power until you believe it, for it can be the difference not only between success and failure, but perhaps even between life and death. Remember always—you do not need to be controlled by fear. The power of faith can drive off fear. The experience of many persons, formerly anxiety-ridden, bears out the fact that it was faith that finally eliminated fear from their minds. And you can gain victory over your fear if you learn to think that you can and apply faith strongly.

When you completely depend upon faith, the release and joy you feel will be akin to the paratrooper who said: "The first time I jumped from a plane everything in me resisted. All there was between death and me was a piece of cord and a little patch of silk, and I must admit I was afraid. But when I actually found out for myself that the patch of silk would hold me, I had the most marvelous feeling of exultation in all my life. I had the positively glorious feeling that I wasn't afraid of anything, and the release from fear filled me with incredible delight. I really did not want to come down; I was terrifically happy."

Fear haunts and defeats us because of our hesitation to trust what we regard as a fragile thing, a patch of silk called faith. But like the paratrooper, when we have faith and trust, we find that this mystic and seemingly unsubstantial factor actually holds us up. When you get that exciting realization you will be happier than you ever thought possible, for faith releases unsuspected powers.

THE ADRENALIN OF FAITH

For example, let me tell you about a young mother who had a horrible fear of the water. She had never learned to swim and avoided any body of water as much as possible. That wasn't too easy, however, for the family lived on the bank of a deep and swift-moving stream.

But let her tell her own story: *

It is sunny and my three pre-schoolers are playing in the backyard where I can watch them from the kitchen window.

Marijane, 3, comes in. "Mommie, I'm all muddy." As I change her dark brown dress for a bright orange one, I help her with one hand. Because of the accident last month, my right hand is still bandaged and useless at my side.

Marijane goes out to her swing again as my husband drops a kiss on my cheek, muttering something about "Going to the store . . . back in a few minutes." The doorbell rings. A friend is there. We visit a few minutes on the porch, then she leaves. I go to check on the children.

Benicia, 5, and Lee, 4, are in the yard alone. "Where is Marijane?" I ask.

_____* "I Fought the River for my Child," by Helen Miller. *Guideposts* (August 1961).

"She went to catch a duckie, Mommie." Benicia points to the creek.

The creek!

The creek bank is empty. In an instant I am at the edge of the stream. It is swollen almost to overflowing, the center a churning, twisting current racing to the waterfall a short distance below. I sigh with relief—she isn't here. But wait! What is that spot of bright color in the distant shadows along the bank? From that moment on, my mind is divorced from my body. It has no weight, no feeling, no sense of time or distance . . . only blind, unreasoning, suffocating fear.

That bright orange spot in the dangerous stream is my baby.

I must get help. Run. Run. The street is half a block away, but I find myself there, looking, looking, for someone to help. The street is empty.

I rush back, fighting my way through the brush, the briars. I plunge into the water. It's over my head and freezing cold. I can't touch bottom! *Why* have I never learned to swim? My heart sends up a prayer—dear Lord, help me. Help me, please! I reach up and grasp the broken roots.

The swirling current threatens, but there, between the current and the bank, is a quiet eddy of water, and in that eddy is my baby—drifting. She lies on her back, as though asleep, her arms floating by her sides. Her eyes are closed, her face purple. Dear Lord, help! Another second, and she'll be where I can reach her.

With one hand I hold onto the roots. With the other, the useless hand, I reach for her. Useless? Not now! Now there is no pain, no weakness. My hand touches Janie, lifts her just above the surface.

SHE SAVES HER CHILD

But how can I get her to safety? The bank is two feet above my head. She seems to weigh nothing as I lift and throw her upon the bank. She lands with a sodden thud, and to my horror slides slowly back again into my waiting hand. Again I throw her little body. Again, she lands with a heartbreaking thud. But now there's a gasp, a whimper, and she does not slide back. I grasp the roots and pull myself out of the water. As I pick her up, the whimper changes to a wail. It's a glorious sound.

Vaguely, the echo of screams penetrates my ear. An eternity later, I realize the screams are my own. A woman materializes and takes Janie from me.

The first-aid men are here. My husband arrives, white with fear. Could all this have happened in the time it took him to walk to the store and back? He goes with them as they take Marijane to the hospital.

I do not know how I get home, but the shadowy figure of the woman is with me. A disembodied voice speaks of "shock" . . . "hot bath" . . . A face swims slowly into focus as the woman helps to strip the sopping clothes from me.

Only now do I realize that my feet are bare. How gladly I yield to the creek its only prize—my shoes. Only now do I realize I am aflame with pain, and see the long, bloody stripes where the roots have torn my flesh—the same blessed roots that provided the life-saving hand holds.

They're back. My husband carries Janie in. Judging from her body temperature of 94 degrees, the doctor said, she must have been in that icy water for 30 minutes. But she will be all right. Tenderly, she is tucked into bed.

I kneel beside the bed and watch my baby. Why haven't I thought before how wonderful it is to watch a child breathe? Thank you, dear Lord, thank you.

In a terrible crisis when her little girl's life was at stake, this mother found that right inside herself was a power greater than her fear. So profound was that power, that enormous strength surged into her and she was able to perform an incredible feat of courage and endurance.

The reason fear defeats us, holds us back, makes us feel weak, is solely and simply due to the fact that the mind is conditioned by fear. But let some crisis arise, like that of the mother and her small child, and we experience a superpowerful upthrust of hitherto hidden and unreleased strength. As a result we can do things we wouldn't have dreamed possible because they just have to be done. Then you truly know that you can because your mind accepts the fact of an unrealized power release. And this is more than a terrific shot of adrenalin. It's a powerful shot of faith that burns out and eliminates fear completely.

If the human mental mechanism reacts in this manner under crises, why cannot it be trained to do equally incredible things without the crisis element and in the routine circumstances of everyday existence? The answer is, indeed it can—by practice; by practicing faith rather than fear until the faith reaction becomes habitual. We have only to change our thoughts and think that we can. Then, indeed, we will perform amazingly.

The basic method for developing to that level of performance is to understand that shadowy thing called fear—to know it for what it is, to stand up to it and to confront fear with faith. Actually, there is nothing that can hurt or harm you if you have enough faith.

UNDERSTANDING FEAR

In an Associated Press interview, Captain Jeremiah A. Denton, Jr., U.S.N., famed returned prisoner of war, recounts the amazing power of faith over torture, pain, and fear as experienced in a North Vietnamese prison:

> In looking back over all the challenges and trials of my experience as a POW, I believe the spiritual sustenance attained through others' prayers, and my own, was the most important factor in my survival.
>
> I believe most POWs feel the same way. Almost all of us are at peace with ourselves now. From what I observed of the performance of others, I believe the main lesson to be learned is that human nature is capable of remarkable performance when placed under duress.
>
> There was a time in October 1966, while I was at the Zoo [a POW camp] in torture, when I just turned myself over to God and I have never had a prayer answered so spectacularly in my life.
>
> A persuasive but sinister officer had put pressure on me to stop inciting the others. He finally gave up on the soft approach and had me put in a torture rig for five days. It was very painful. He wanted me to write something about the communications system between the prisoners in the camp.
>
> At the end of five days I wrote something harmless about communications which I knew wouldn't give away anything they already didn't know. I

hoped they would accept it because they would
have saved face by getting me to write just something. But they didn't buy it.

They put me back in the same rig for five more
days and that was the time at which I simply told
God He would just have to take over. I had reached
the end.

I knew that if I had to write the next time I would
write something harmful, so I just turned myself
over to Him.

I have never had a prayer answered so spectacularly in my life.

As soon as I got that prayer out, this mantle of
comfort came over me and I couldn't feel any more
pain. Even when they beat the hell out of me and
tightened up right to the maximum, I was just as
comfortable as if I were sitting in a plush auto.

Learn to live with that powerful reality called faith,
for faith is your friend, not your enemy, as the experience of Captain Denton so powerfully proves.

Determine never to be pushed around by your fears.
Stand up to them mentally and deny them the power
to dominate you, even in the less dramatic lives most
of us live.

DO THE THING YOU ARE AFRAID OF

Somewhere I read the interesting recollections of an
old man about his life in the West in the early days. A
telegraph operator in a lonely mountain railroad station, he was assigned to work from seven in the evening
until seven in the morning. The first night on the job
he was dropped off from a freight train at the isolated

station and he felt a sense of fear. There he was, all by himself in that lonely spot. After the freight train rumbled on down the valley, its whistle fading in the distance, he became aware of the encompassing silence. There was only silence—deep, lonely, ominous silence. Then came the realization that he was miles from another human being, and this filled him with nervous apprehension. Going into the office, he turned on all the lights, shut the door and securely locked it. Nervously he pulled down the shades, barricading himself inside that station for the night, afraid of the darkness and loneliness that surrounded him.

During the night he could hear all sorts of sounds from around the station. He was terrified, visualizing wild animals and maybe bandits. He could hardly wait for dawn to come and with it the bright light of morning. "I'll never last at this job," he said to himself. But he stuck to it even though with each successive night the fear seemed to get worse.

Finally one morning, when his relief man came on duty, he said, "Look, Bill, I can't take this job anymore. I've got to admit that the darkness scares the life out of me."

"I understand," said Bill, "but maybe the trouble is that you don't really know the dark. You haven't bothered to get acquainted with it. The darkness isn't your enemy. Try it one more night and this time try to get to know the darkness. Don't shut yourself in like a scared rabbit. There's nothing to be afraid of."

The next night, frightened though he was, he left the door wide open and the windows too, with the shades up. To his surprise, it was most rewarding. He got the scent and the aroma of the night. Finally he stood outside and looked up at the canopy of the heavens filled

with stars. The moon shone down in silvery radiance.
Later he stated that it was one of his greatest experiences. He had learned to face the night and stand up
to his fears. By learning to know the darkness, he had
destroyed the dread it held for him.

The problem of getting control over your fears has
top priority. Thomas Carlyle, the great English writer,
said, "The first duty for a man is still that of subduing
fear." And in accomplishing this subduing process one
thing is vital: action—positive, forthright action. Fear
must be dealt with, so deal with it—take action. Theodore Roosevelt employed this strong action method.
He could do this well, for he was a man of great mental
strength. He said, "I have often been afraid but I
wouldn't give in to it. I made myself act as though I was
not afraid, and gradually my fear disappeared."

When you are afraid of something, do not let yourself
be hung up in imaginings concerning it; rather, take
summary action; attack—hit it hard. The harder you
strike, the more quickly and surely the fear will subside.

In a Midwestern city I was met at the airport by a
sales manager, a dynamic young man, who drove me
to my hotel and then on to a hall where I spoke to a
crowd of some two thousand sales personnel.

On the way we got to talking about him and his
rather amazing rise in sales management. It seems that
a few years previously he went into sales work with a
company whose sales manager parcelled out leads to
his salesmen. These had not been previously cultivated,
being merely suggested prospects who might or might
not be interested in purchasing. This young man went
over his list the night before and planned his routing
for the next day.

However, when morning came he found many reasons for delaying his calls. He just did not feel quite ready; perhaps the route he had laid out was not quite the best way to reach his prospects; it wasn't a very good time—a holiday was approaching; and one excuse after the other. The following day his excuses continued; he wasn't feeling quite up to it; he had a headache and was in no position to make his best approach. "I even got to the point," he said, "where I lay down and moaned to my wife how badly I felt; I was coming down with a cold—maybe the flu.

"Then, in a moment of truth which I tried to avoid and indignantly repudiated, my wife came up with the observation that she 'guessed I was just afraid to make those calls.' In fact, she even went so far as to suggest that she was disappointed in me, that I was a poor fish or something, just a plain coward.

"Well, naturally this irritated me no end and I stormed and fumed, but she wasn't impressed; only asked me why I didn't get off my fanny and act like a man. Tough woman, my wife!

"I had to admit to myself that I was for a fact just plain afraid to tackle those prospects, to do what was essentially cold selling. But then I figured, why should I, a man with my education and ability, be just an ordinary peddler? I was intended for a managerial executive position, not to be chasing abjectly from prospect to prospect. Any jerk could do that. And," he continued, "believe it or not, a company did approach me about a nice, easy, inside job. Of course the pay wasn't anything great, but at least it was a recognition of my dignity, and I was about to take it.

"But when I told my wife about it she just looked at me. 'Still afraid, eh?' was all she said.

"So finally I decided to forget my fear and go out and

sell. With great effort I pulled myself up and literally drove myself to make those calls. Sure, I had turndowns, plenty of them, but then I began to make a few sales. And I began to get the thrill of successful achievement. Indeed, it got so that I actually enjoyed pitting myself against a hard-boiled buyer. I learned the hard way that when you are afraid, the only thing to do is to do the thing you're afraid of, and when you do that, pretty soon you won't be afraid of it anymore!"

How right he is. So what are you afraid of? Forget it!

It is of course a fact that much fear currently manifesting itself may be traced to one's childhood experience. To deal with it effectively, professional and expert counseling may in some cases be indicated.

SELF-KNOWLEDGE HELPS RELEASE YOU FROM FEAR

The man I met on an airplane is illustrative of many who carry a bewildering burden of fear. But this man had found an answer to his long-held fear.

Scarcely have I seen a man so immensely relieved —you might even say released. He was actually bursting with joy. "A tremendous thing has happened to me!" he exulted. "I have at last given the brush-off to fear. I am over my old fear of what might happen! And it's wonderful, believe me."

We were seatmates on an airplane and he was so caught up that his story fairly gushed out. But happy as he was, this man was no oddball. He was a personable fellow in his thirties who, it seemed, had suffered all his life from anxiety and fear. Indeed, he had been fearful out of all proportion to reason. And often for no apparent reason he would be seized with a feeling that something dreadful was about to happen. Finally he sought professional counseling about this condition. Only then did he come to understand its origin.

It seems that he had a super-loving, overprotective mother who was herself a victim of anxieties. She had a bad habit of overdramatizing fearful possibilities. Whether this was because she craved sympathy, or unconsciously wanted to dominate, or whatever the psychodynamics of it were, the strain on her son's sense of security was great, indeed.

She constantly made vague allusions about the boy's father, who apparently was an irresponsible doubledealer whose relations with women were scarcely on the up-and-up. The boy did not know this, for people avoided speaking of it in front of him, but he got an uncomfortable impression that there was something wrong with his father. The mother often remarked gloomily, "Your father will come to no good end. You just wait and see." So the boy lived in fear of something happening to his father, and that fear added to his insecurity.

Probably as a result of fear and tension, the mother developed a heart condition. This, too, she magnified and dramatized, telling her children solemnly, "You must be prepared for something to happen to me at any time. I may look healthy but I'm not, really. And perhaps some night the doctor will come and you will know that something serious has happened. Or if you are away, be prepared for the telephone call that your mother has died. I am telling you this that you may be prepared."

So years later when the boy had grown up and was a salesman on the road, he would lie in bed in his hotel room only half asleep, unconsciously waiting for that tragic telephone message that his mother had died.

This constant anxiety and insecurity eventually took its toll on the man's physical vitality. Suspecting that he might himself be developing a heart condition, he went to a doctor who advised him to get psychological and spiritual counseling. Gradually he gained insight and came to realize that his fears were basically phantoms which his mother's own acute self-pitying anxiety complex had lodged within his mind. He was helped to develop dynamic faith. Finally the old fears lifted from his mind and he felt liberated. And it was not difficult to appreciate the relief and happiness that resulted.

Chronic anxiety often stems from fears contracted in childhood through the power of suggestibility. Another big cause is a sense of guilt that develops. Counseling can bring the sufferer to see the connection between his fears and his guilt—and thereby motivate him to a moral housecleaning.

It has been said that self-knowledge is the beginning of wisdom. Often it is also the beginning of a cure. But for actual healing of fear, more is needed. Old fears must be replaced with something positive—a strong faith—else they recur or new fears take their place.

At this point spiritual therapy is important, for it strengthens faith. Where real faith is present, fear tends to weaken and lose its power. It must be emphasized again and again that while fear is strong, very strong —faith is stronger, much stronger. And faith in due course can drive out fear.

How mentally healthy we all would be were we able from birth to be free of any form of fear psychosis! We pick up fear from those around us who would not for all the world do anything to harm us. But unconsciously fears are projected upon children who thereafter must suffer and struggle with this strange malady unless, by right thinking, by professional assistance, and by acquiring a healthy-minded faith, they find deliverance and relief.

Perhaps the method for counteracting the development of fear in children used by one physician should be more widely practiced. He takes the baby from the mother's womb and as he works he talks: "Hello, little one, welcome to this world. You've come into a wonderful world where you are wanted and everyone loves you. Don't be afraid, little one. God will take care of you always. So never be afraid."

Whether this curious procedure, these wise words, reach into the infantile consciousness is of course a matter of conjecture. But if they could do so, how inexpressibly wonderful would be the buildup of faith and confidence; how great it would be never to experience the misery of abnormal fear!

BELIEVE IN YOURSELF

I can write feelingly and somewhat knowledgably about the painful effect of fear growing out of youthful experience. Always I was driven by a strong compulsive motivation but at the same time was hampered by an equally strong self-doubt. I had feelings of inadequacy and possessed perhaps the biggest inferiority complex in existence, or at least it seemed so to me.

I kept telling myself that I didn't amount to anything; no brains, no personality. I was shy, shrinking, bashful —and that old-fashioned word is potently descriptive, meaning, as it does, fearful and abashed. I discovered that people were agreeing with me about myself. And it is a fact that others are likely to appraise you at the level of your own self-image.

On the night before my graduation from college we had a farewell dinner at our fraternity house and the president of the college was the honored guest. Dr. John W. Hoffman was a man's man. He had been a football star. He had an attractive outgoing personality built into a powerful physique. He knew men through and through and his penetrating insight read their strengths and weaknesses. And beside all this, a huge heart of love beat in his chest.

As the dinner broke up Dr. Hoffman said, "Walk up to my house with me, Norman, I want to talk with you." Quickly fear assailed me. Was I going to flunk out after all? No, that couldn't be, for the commencement programs had been printed and my name was among the list of graduates. My marks were satisfactory!

As we walked along through that moonlight night he talked about life and what could be made of it by thinking right, by believing right and by doing right. When we arrived in front of his home he lingered a moment, then put his hand on my shoulder. "Norman," he said, "you know something? I believe in you. You've got some good ability if you can just learn to release it. I believe you can become a public speaker."

He looked at me for a long moment. "But," he went on, "you've got to learn to believe in yourself and stop being afraid and inferior and self-doubting. Never, never be afraid of anybody or anything or of yourself." He punched me hard in the chest. "I love you, boy, and will always believe in you. There's nothing to be afraid of. So forget it and live—really live."

I walked on air as I made my way down the street. This great man whom I idolized believed in me! Suddenly I wasn't afraid or shy anymore. From that moment I experienced a glorious release and equally glorious relief. Naturally, I had many ups and downs with my own fear problem, but I date the beginning of final victory from that night when a wonderful man made a fearful boy start believing that maybe he could do something with his life.

I loved Dr. Hoffman ever after. Many years later word came that he was dying with cancer of the throat. I went to Pasadena, California, to see him. The once golden voice that could electrify great audiences had now been stilled. But the same old wonderful smile still lighted up his face and his big hand crushed mine in the same old man-sized grip.

Since he could no longer speak, he was forced to carry on a conversation by writing. He was still a believer, a believer in "his boys." "How glad I am to see you," he wrote. "I've been following you with pride." Tears welled up in my eyes. And noticing, he turned the conversation to anecdotes of the old days. We laughed and maybe cried a bit together, each trying to hide it from the other. It was an unforgettable, in-depth experience of friendship, one of the greatest in my life.

Finally it came time to go. Taking his hand, I said, "Dr. Hoffman, do you remember that night long ago when you spoke so wonderfully to me as we stood before your house? I will never forget as long as I live what you said and how you said it. You started the process of setting me free from my fear-bound self and . . . and I just want you to know that I love you and always will."

I knew it was the last time I would ever see him on

earth, this man who meant so much to me. I put my hand on his head just to touch him affectionately. He punched me lightly in the chest, but maybe not so lightly. "And I love you, too, boy. I always will," he wrote. "And I'll believe in you to the last. Go with God's strength and never be afraid." I stopped at the door to look back. He lifted his clasped hands, and my last memory was of that old smile I knew so well.

In overcoming fear it is important to be free of all mental conflict so that you are able to approach situations with normal naturalness. Take every proper precaution. Have faith in God, in yourself, and in people. Then just go about your job normally and without fear.

OUT OF A TWENTY-SECOND-FLOOR WINDOW

One day I was sitting in my room on the twenty-second floor of a hotel in Chicago which looked out over Michigan Avenue to the lake beyond. It was a twenty-two-floor sheer drop down to the sidewalk. There came a rap at my door. I opened it, and there stood a young fellow with a pail and some cleaning cloths and a window wiper. "Would it disturb you if I washed your windows?" he asked.

"No, come in," I said. While we were talking he walked over and, looking in my direction, pulled up the window, snapped on his belt and put one leg out. "Hey!" I said, "It's twenty-two stories down to the street."

"Well, so what? I know it, but you can't wash the windows from the inside."

"I know, but there you are with one leg out the window, just like that."

"Don't let that bother you," he told me. "I know how to do this."

"Do you really like this window-washing business?" I asked.

"Sure," he replied. "I'm way above everybody else all the time."

"But how are you able to do it without being afraid?"

"Oh," he replied, "that's simple. The first thing is to fasten your belt and be sure that it is fastened. Then you have faith in your belt. You know it will hold. Then you knock on wood, say a prayer, and get busy."

Whereupon he climbed out and went to work, grinning at me through the windowpane. He whistled a gay and merry tune. In a jiffy he was back inside, then out the other window, still whistling, humming, and even singing a snatch of a song.

"You seem happy," I commented.

"Why not?" he replied. "Nothing's worrying me. I'm enjoying myself."

"And you're never afraid?"

"Of course not. What is there to be afraid of? There's nothing to it."

This fellow, who obviously had a normal mind devoid of fear, made a great impression on me as one of those many terrific people you find everywhere. He had one of the most valuable assets a human being can possess—a good, sound, unmixed-up, normal mind in which was no fear psychosis.

He made me think of a friend who was having a struggle with a disease. This man attacked his illness in the same businesslike manner in which he dealt with all his affairs. He had it—that was that—and he just proceeded to fit the treatments into his daily schedule. He went on with his business, never showed a quiver, and remained on top of the situation. Once I asked him, "At any time during this experience have you been afraid?"

"Well, let me think," he replied. "Yes, there was a minute or two when I was afraid. That was when my temperature stayed at a hundred and four degrees for two days. The thought just crossed my mind that maybe I might not make it. But that was only temporarily. I just began to apply common sense and as I did so the fever went down. All the common sense I have tells me that the doctors on this case are confident that they are doing the right thing, and I have respect for their skill."

Then he added, "If they weren't, I'd still be in good hands. God is always looking after us. Anyway, when I get into an airplane I'm not afraid. I know the equipment is good. I know the plane has been well serviced and that the pilots and engineers know their business. I don't sit there being afraid. I apply common sense to it. So with physical existence. I'm in a scientific universe. Either here or in the beyond, I will be given every good care. With all this going for me, why waste any time being afraid?"

Both this business leader and the window-washer had developed a sound philosophy out of sound minds. They would surely exclaim in surprise, "What are you afraid of? Forget it!"

In not being afraid, in avoiding abnormal fear, it will help to stress the following:

1. *Two great forces operate in the mind: fear and faith. Fear is very powerful, but faith is more powerful.*

2. *Faith power in the mind, like adrenalin in the body, can release amazing powers within you in crisis.*

3. *And remember, the same power is there within you apart from crisis and may be drawn upon always to keep fear down.*

4. *Take a long, straight look at your fear. Know it for the ghostly thing it is and stand firmly up to it. Practice the strong action technique.*

5. *When you are afraid, do the thing you are afraid of and soon you will lose your fear of it.*

6. *Self-knowledge and insight will overcome fear. This may require professional counseling. When you know the origin of your fears you are then in position to deal with them.*

7. *Develop a strong, healthy-minded faith. Fear will wither as your faith grows.*

8. *Commit the following statement to memory and say it now and then: "I sought the Lord, and He heard me, and delivered me from all my fears." **

___* Psalm 34:4.

EIGHT

※

EXPECT A MIRACLE—
MAKE MIRACLES HAPPEN

The shopkeeper was opening a package of merchandise from England. As always he admired the efficient way in which the British pack things: the sturdy twine, the meticulous care, the careful wrapping.

On top of the contents lay a card: "Expect a Miracle." That was all, nothing else. He was about to throw the card in the wastebasket, but something stopped him. "What does that mean, 'Expect a Miracle'?" he thought.

He dropped the card on the counter. But later when disposing of the wrappings he noticed it again. "How come that card was in that package?" he wondered. "Who put it there? Was it a mistake? Maybe it fell out of someone's pocket. Or is some guy trying to send me a message? But why?"

He put the card in his shirt pocket and forgot all about it until that night in emptying his pockets he found it again. "Look at this," he said to his wife. " 'Expect a Miracle.' What is that supposed to mean?"

The wife, equally puzzled, was a bit more perceptive. "Maybe that is what we need. Our problems seem so overwhelming. Wonder what would happen if we started expecting great things instead of always expecting the worst? Could miracles take place?"

146

That phrase, "Expect a Miracle," began to get into their thoughts. Like most people, they had problems, one big one and several smaller ones. Next morning the wife said, "What do you say we take that little problem which is bothering us and let's expect a miracle. We have nothing to lose by testing this 'Expect a Miracle' business."

"You mean, some magic?"

"I don't know what I mean," she continued. "Maybe we will get some new ideas. Maybe there is a solution. Anyway, what do you say? Let's expect a miracle, really expect it for a few days and see what happens."

And what did happen? Well, the two of them took the first step toward the solution of that little problem by believing it could be solved. But then they went even further and believed that it *would* be solved; indeed, that the solution was even then being worked out. And miracles, little miracles, started happening. Strange coincidences began developing. All kinds of experiences began coming one after another—all different. They themselves became different—hopeful, optimistic. As a result, when the little problems started giving way, their big problem seemed far less formidable.

"Wonder who sent us that card, 'Expect a Miracle'?" ruminated the shopkeeper one day. "We'll never know."

"I think I know," said the wife softly, "although the One I'm thinking of doesn't usually send His messages in print and in packages."

The significant fact is that when anyone starts expecting a miracle he presently becomes so conditioned in mind that he begins actually making miracles happen. He gets on the miracle wavelength. His native abilities become focused positively rather than negatively. Creative forces are released in his mind. The flow-away of values is checked and reversed. Life now flows not away from him but toward him. The negative expectations which drove away the good are replaced by positive expectations which attract the good.

One of the dictionary definitions of the word "miracle" is, "a wonderful or surpassing example of some quality." While the word has, of course, often been used to denote some supernatural happening beyond all known human or natural powers, that is not its only connotation. It also has to do with "the power to work marvelous, outstanding or unusual effects." And that depends upon "a wonderful or surpassing example of some quality," to requote the dictionary.

It is this quality with which we wish to deal, the quality of mind in which is the capacity for wonder, the ability to believe that nothing is too good to be true. It is the capacity to expect a miracle and, indeed, make miracles (wonderful things) happen.

AMERICA, LAND OF MIRACLES

For example, as I write I can see from my hotel room far across a lake the towers and turrets of Cinderella Castle reaching for the Florida sky. And there comes to mind a once-upon-a-time story; indeed, a miracle story. It's made up of the romance of America, land of dreams and miracle-making.

The story begins long ago in Kansas City. A young fellow with an urge to draw went from newspaper to newspaper trying to sell his cartoons. But each editor coldly, and perhaps a bit cruelly, informed him that he had no talent and advised him to forget it. But he couldn't forget his dream, for it had grabbed him and wouldn't let go. How can you forget a powerful motivation?

Finally a pastor employed the young man at a pittance to draw advertising pictures for church events. But the fledgling artist had to have a "studio," another way of describing a place to sleep as well as to draw. It seems the church had an old mouse-infested garage and he was told he could stay there. And what do you know? One of those mice became world-famous, as did the young artist. The mouse became known to millions as Mickey Mouse; the artist was Walt Disney.

A wise observation by Demosthenes should be remembered by anyone who wishes to accomplish big things. Demosthenes said: "Small opportunities are often the beginnings of great enterprises." This young man made miracles happen and on a vast scale, for this once-upon-a-time miracle story grew into motion pictures which eventuated in Disneyland in California and in Disney World in Florida. And all these marvels happened in America, the land where dreams can come true, where miracles are made.

Of course, back in those days when he scarcely had two nickels to rub together and everyone was giving him the brush-off, Walt Disney could have become soured on the "establishment," growling that the country was for the rich only and the system had to be destroyed. But this man didn't go emotional and become a bitter militant. He just kept on believing in himself and working and dreaming and making miracles happen and becoming, finally, the world's greatest master of childhood fantasy. He reached the heart of America, and the people of his country—indeed, the whole world—loved him.

The American miracle story isn't dead. If a few vocal and soured failures have fooled you into thinking that, just remember Walt Disney. Your faith in the United States as the land of opportunity will be restored—and how! And you will also begin to expect miracles and make miracles happen on the basis of the law of successful achievement, the kind practiced by Disney and others.

LAW OF SUCCESSFUL ACHIEVEMENT

And what is that law? First of all, it is to have a goal; not a vague, fuzzy goal, but a sharply focused objective. You must know what you want to do and where you want to go, what you want to be. And have no doubt about it. The next step—and it's a real practical one—is to pray about this goal to be sure it is a right objective; because if it isn't right, it's wrong, and nothing wrong ever turned out right.

Then hold the goal tenaciously in the conscious mind until, by a process of intellectual osmosis, it sinks into the subconscious, and when it becomes firmly fixed in the subconscious you have it, because it has you, all of you—your hopes, your thoughts, your efforts.

Then put behind your goal not negative but positive thought. The negative thinker lets loose destructive forces that can destroy him. In sending out negative thoughts, he activates the world around him negatively. There is a law of attraction. Like attracts like. Birds of a feather flock together. Thoughts of a kind have a natural affinity. The negative thinker tends to draw back to himself negative results. He attracts them.

The positive thinker, instead, in sending out optimistic and positive thoughts, activates the world around him positively. On the basis of the same law of attraction, he draws back to himself positive results. He works and keeps on working. He thinks and keeps on thinking. He believes and keeps on believing. He never lets up, never gives in. He gives the effort the full treatment of positive faith and action. Result? He can because he thinks he can. His dreams come true . . . he attains his goals . . . miracles happen.

Get the message, for this is something you cannot afford to miss: In America motivated goals and miracles can come true. And that goes for you the same as for any other person. So when you get discouraged and feel like throwing in the sponge, just remember Walt Disney and Mickey Mouse. Expect a miracle!

Of course, when such an illustration of the miracle principle is used, inevitably someone will object, "Sure, that's great; but what about me? I'm no Walt Disney. I'm no genius, just an everyday guy. You don't really think I'm going to expect miracles and make miracles happen, do you?" The answer to that is, "Yes, I do." Because, you see, you can if you think you can.

Miracles are of all sizes: big ones, medium-sized ones, and small ones. And if you start believing in little miracles, you can work up to the bigger ones. Think and believe and work and treat people right and give it all you've got, and you will find yourself doing the most amazingly constructive things in this life.

But the self-minimizer will never do wonders or work miracles. How can he? Since he is appraising himself and his opportunities on a low-level basis, it is to such a basis, pathetically, he is condemning himself. But if such a person will reverse his thought processes— about his job, his opportunities, his abilities, about people and about himself, he will get the miracle psychology and miracles will start happening.

People who think in such an upbeat, hopeful manner inevitably do the best with life. Since thoughts tend to reproduce themselves in kind, the dismal thinker is likely to come up with dismal results, whereas the person who thinks hopefully can be expected to attract constructive results.

A remarkable business woman demonstrates the amazing power of hopeful thinking. She proves that this type of thinking keeps the mind clear to function at top efficiency. At a meeting of the business organization where she is an executive along with five men, a difficult situation had developed, a really tough problem. The executives went at the matter from every angle. The five men present finally came to the gloomy conclusion that there was just no solution. "Might as well wash it up," they agreed.

But this woman said, "Look. What is a problem? Simply a set of circumstances for which there *seems* to be no solution. But actually there is always a solution. All we have to do is find it. Then there will be no more problem." The men smiled wryly at what they obviously considered a rather naive remark.

"Now," she continued, "the first step is to start thinking hopefully. Let's cut out the dismal thinking, for that is bound to produce dismal results. Let's affirm there is a solution and that we're smart enough to think of it." This positive reasoning cleared the air, and all those around that conference table did some real thinking, but now minus gloom and negativism. They reviewed the matter step by step, found the error which had been completely overlooked, and corrected it. All because one positive person was a hopeful thinker. She taught her associates that you can if you think you can.

Never write anything off as impossible or as a failure. Remember, you have the mental capacity to think your way through any problem if you draw fully upon your mind. Think hopefully, get your mental powers really working, and things can turn out better than they now appear. The hopeful thinker projects hope and faith —both miracle elements—into the darkest situation and lights it up. As long as you keep the debilitating thought of defeat out of your mind, defeat cannot defeat you.

HE WAS NOT PARALYZED IN HIS MIND

In Tokyo I met an American, an inspiring man, from Pennsylvania. Crippled from some form of paralysis, he was on an around-the-world journey in a wheelchair, getting a huge kick out of all his experiences. I commented that nothing seemed to get him down. His reply was a classic: "It's only my body that is paralyzed. The paralysis never got into my mind."

How many unhappy people suffer the mental paralysis of fear, self-doubt, inferiority and inadequacy! Dark thoughts blind them to the possible outcomes which the mind is able to produce. But optimism infuses the mind with confidence and builds up belief in oneself. Result? The revitalized mind, newly energized, comes to grips with problems. Keep the paralysis of unhealthy thoughts out of that incomparable instrument, your mind.

The dismal thinking mentioned before is evident among some contemporary young people. They've been fed the sterile idea that everything is bad, nothing is good. Indeed, a whole generation has, in considerable measure, had the miracle wonder-working concept siphoned off because of cynicism and negativism on the part of some teachers, many writers, and part of the media. This is a crime against youth, destroying as it does their natural enthusiasm and creative capacity. And to take away a young person's right to dream is an even higher crime against personality.

But lately it seems I'm getting an increase of letters from young people who are reaching for some deeper meaning in life, and finding it, too. And do they go for it! As, for example this one:

> I'm a 17-year-old girl. I would like to thank you for your writings and tell you my story. Something happened to me. I don't know what it was, but I became very depressed and cynical. I was really sunk. I read a lot, even a book about mental illness. Suddenly, everything I had read on the subject sort of closed in around me and I became convinced that I was psychotic. I really wasn't, but I was letting myself believe that I was.
>
> I had to do a term paper on "Enjoying life." Isn't that a laugh? Well, anyway, in my research I came across your works; such statements as "Those who look forward expecting great things to happen can make them happen"; "Build upon your expectations. Expect a miracle"; "Stand up and quit feeling sorry for yourself"; "Do a rehabilitation job on your thoughts." These words and more opened my eyes again. Hope flashed into my mind. Thank you for making me aware again, for helping me out of

that dark place and into the light of happiness and faith, and for saving me with new hope. And thank you for helping me get an A-plus on my term paper.

This girl was smart. She was really with it. She learned to expect a miracle, and she made a miracle happen.

Miracles are not altogether made out of dreams. Often they are put together out of plain, everyday, nonglamorous facts. Just wanting to do something with life and with yourself goes a long way toward getting a miracle going. That urge to be something and do something, to move ahead, to climb up, to get more meaning into life, is the stuff out of which miracles are made. And remember, you actually mean "miracle" when you say to someone who has come up the hard way to real accomplishment: "My, you have done something wonderful!" That word "wonderful" refers to some achievement that is full of wonders, something above and beyond the ordinary, and vastly superior to the depressing attitude, "This is all I can do, all I'm cut out for. This is it, so why bother?"

But people who are alive and vital and enthusiastic, people who go to work and think and plan and work some more—well, they perform miracles.

MIRACLE MAKERS OF ROUTE 22

For example, take my friends, Helen and Paul Dolan, daughters Pam and Pye, and Mrs. Ruth Lindstrom, Helen's mother, affectionately known as "Mamma." They run a happiness-filled snack bar on Route 22 at Patterson, New York, where I often drop in for lunch. And is the food good? Real home cooking and how! Mamma is the baker and her pies, cakes, and rice pudding are yummy, yummy, and then some.

The entire family works, and I mean *works*. But I have yet to see anyone of them dragging low or irritable. They've got a smile and a cheery welcome for everyone. Helen Dolan is a pretty woman, always charming, with a rippling, bubbling laugh and gracious manner. Everyone loves her.

One time a few years back she was a guest on the popular TV show, "What's My Line?" This alert panel, usually skillful in guessing one's work, missed on her completely, for she was, at the time, the garbage collector for the village. But when you looked at her that was the last thing you would think of. She rode the garbage truck like a queen.

She and her hard-working husband decided to move from the garbage-collecting enterprise to the restaurant business. They built a little highway place and called it "Custard Castle." Their opening ad in the newspaper was a masterpiece in describing a happy, homey, good food, fun place for everyone.

When I first visited their new quarters I commented on the beautiful fireplace that rises to the ceiling, its narrow bricks laid up with perfection. "Who made that marvelous fireplace?" I asked. "It's a beauty. Real workmanship, if you ask me."

"I did," Helen replied, "every brick of it, with my own little hands."

"What do you know!" I remarked admiringly. "A garbage collector, a manager, a cook, a bricklayer, a wife, a mother—what else?"

"Oh," she said, "Paul and I built this place, every bit

of it. We love to work, to make things, to build, to help people be happy."

All I've got to say is that there are some real Americans in this land, indeed millions of them, like the Dolans; the kind of people who made this country and keep it made by hard work and creative enthusiasm. Taken all together, they make that miracle which is the United States.

Every winter the Dolan family takes a vacation, or is it that? Anyway, they close up the restaurant and go to Florida where they are developing a place called Dolan City. They had to level a pine forest to do it. It's developing into a fine property. "How do you make all these wonderful things happen?" I asked incredulously.

"Oh, you see, we expect miracles because we believe in miracles, and we just make miracles happen," was the classic answer.

An effort is being made by some gloom artists, self-styled intellectuals, to sell Americans on the erroneous notion that since there is a disparity of wealth in this country, it should be taken from some and given to others by political action, and that thereafter everything will be just sweetness and light. Totally ignored by these social babes-in-the-woods is the fact there is another way to distribute wealth, namely, get an idea, develop enthusiasm for it, and just plain go to work to build it into reality. There's nothing in the world that can activate prosperity like that formula!

And what a method for knocking out that so-called generation gap we used to hear so much about—a family working together! The Dolans of this world have the formula: Stop griping and complaining, get a real good idea, and go to work. If this philosophy marks this writer as a square—so what? I'll gladly settle for just that! Anyway, I go for people who expect miracles and make them happen. And the whole world goes for them as well. And no wonder, for they are the dynamic people who can because they think they can.

Another miracle, ever fascinating, is the discovery of qualities in yourself that you never dreamed existed. What a thrill when those abilities and talents that have been dormant emerge to lend a whole new dimension to a personality.

HOW TO GET IDEAS AND MAKE THEM WORK

Some years ago a New York City advertising executive, Alex Osborne, outlined a practical formula for going where you want to go, for being what you want to be, and for doing what you want to do. I myself have used these principles, labeled "Applied Imagination," and have suggested them to many people who have found them effective in developing increased creativity.

Here they are:

1. Write down on paper your three greatest wishes, numbering them one, two, three. Look at this list every day.
2. Spend an hour every day analyzing and studying your job. Do this every day and in less than five years you will be an acknowledged expert on that job.
3. Spend one hour each day with a white sheet of paper in front of you and write down every idea you can think of. You will get surprising ideas that will improve your job and your own performance.

Another idea expert describes a creative process for developing idea power: *

> Suppose I were to tell you a surefire way to at least double your idea power? Tens of thousands of individuals have in fact discovered, or more accurately, rediscovered, vast storehouses of imaginative power within themselves by deliberately applying a deceptively simple, scientifically proved principle.
>
> Take a piece of paper and in three minutes' time list ways you might improve a desk calendar. How many ideas did you put down? If you had fifteen or more, that would be outstanding! Ten to fifteen would be excellent. Five to ten would be good, but possibly you had less than five. Why? Did you have an idea that you didn't put down for some reason—because you thought it impractical, might cost too much, had been "tried before," was "too obvious"? In other words, did you try to evaluate each idea as it popped into your conscious mind? You will almost certainly find that you thought up ideas that did not seem sensible or important enough to put down. Most of us for one reason or another "edit" out ideas—and this tends to inhibit the flow of ideas.
>
> The very powerful principle is: Think First, Judge Later. Put down each and every idea or notion that occurs to you—good, bad or indifferent—practical or not—obvious or way out—*all* ideas. As you jot down your ideas one idea will trigger others. Your associative processes which are the heart of your creative power will function more naturally, if given free reign.

_____* "Six Secrets to Double Your Idea Power," by M. O. Edwards, from *Success Unlimited* (April 1973), Vol. 20, No. 4.

The way to have a good idea is to have lots of ideas. Significantly more good ideas can be produced by applying the deferred judgment principle.

SWEETEST SPOT ON HIGHWAY 88

Though at the time it had not been described to me, I used that principle, "Think First, Judge Later," effectively with a charming lady, the late Mrs. Louise Williamson, lovingly called "Miss Lou" down home in Mississippi. I was on a speaking engagement in Mobile, Alabama, when Miss Lou came to talk with me at the hotel where I was staying at Point Clear.

She was a refined, petite woman, recently widowed. Her problem was a double one: financial, and what should she do with her life now that she was alone. "All right," I said, "let's take a sheet of paper and a pencil and make a list of all the things you can do. Then we'll evaluate them and select the most appropriate."

"Oh, but you see, I can't do anything," she replied "I've never done anything. My husband made all the decisions. I have no training at all."

"Now, look," I declared, "you are an intelligent and educated person and I just won't believe that you are totally devoid of skills. There is an idea lurking in your mind which we are going to find, one which will open up a terrifically exciting life for you. So let's put down every idea we can think of in a brainstorming session and see what we come up with."

This didn't work exactly as planned because I could not get her to employ the technique of thinking now and evaluating later. She insisted on evaluating as we proceeded, and her way of evaluating was simply to say, "Oh, no, I couldn't possibly do that." But we hit the jackpot, so to speak, before we finished.

"How about a job in a store?" I asked.

"Oh, no, I just couldn't do that. Unfortunately, I was raised as a 'Southern gentlewoman,' and you know they never hold jobs. I realize that sounds pretty old-fashioned and stuff, that 'gentlewoman' business, but I guess it's too ingrained for me to change now."

"Well, then, how about china painting and flower arranging? That seems to go right well with that 'Southern gentlewoman' idea."

But that, too, was out. She just had no talent along that line. "Well, then," I said, "let's consider dressmaking."

"Oh, no, I can't sew a button on, hardly. I always had a maid to do that, though there's no more maid since paying the estate taxes."

"Ever cook? I'll guess you are a terrific cook. I can almost smell that fried chicken and corn bread."

She laughed. "I can't even boil water successfully."

"Oh, come, now—let's get with it," I said. "I know there is one thing you must be able to do and do superbly."

"Well," she hesitated, "there is just one thing, I guess. I *can* make candy. Everyone says it is delicious."

I showed real enthusiasm and began at once planning how she would make this great candy and we would merchandise it all over everywhere and get her firmly fixed on a worthwhile endeavor. But she tried to puncture my enthusiasm by telling me that no "gentlewoman" could sell her own candy. She would give it away to her friends.

It was necessary to enlighten her fully on the economic facts of life by reminding her that unless she bypassed some of her objections she would end up on relief, and how would she, with her "moonlight and old lace" background, like that? "Better choose now between going on relief or practicing the free enterprise system," I warned.

"Look," I continued, "make me a box of that candy. I'm an expert and I'll tell you if it's any good and whether you can go into the candy business." A few days later came a two-pound box containing absolutely the most luscious candy that ever melted in anybody's mouth. It was simply terrific. And in the noble cause of helping someone, my waistline has never since been the same!

I persuaded her to use the front room of her house, which was right on a main road, as a shop in which to display her goods, and to put up a sign advertising it; and signs along the road as well. Ideas were by now popping up in her fertile mind. She called the shop in Edwards, Mississippi, "The Sweetest Spot on Highway 88." Before long, tourists from everywhere were writing me about Miss Lou and her candy, for she had my picture on the wall of her shop.

Now note the results. Take a look at this miracle. A few years later Miss Lou was chosen the Woman of the Year in Vicksburg, and another time the Woman of the Year in the state of Mississippi. And this was not simply because she made a good living in the candy business. She had also become a vital part of community life, discovering new and exciting possibilities within herself. She became a happy and enthusiastic person.

Then came the great honor. The Chamber of Commerce of the United States chose six people one year as outstanding citizens of the nation. They were five

famous men and one woman. And—you guessed it—
the woman was Little Miss Lou.

Well, now this charming lady has gone on to Heaven.
A poet said, "We come trailing clouds of glory from God
who is our home." I'll say that Miss Lou went back to
God trailing clouds of glory, for she learned to expect
a miracle and she made many miracles happen. She is
unforgettable. And one Sunday, speaking at the White
House in the presence of the President of the United
States and the leaders of the Senate and House of Rep-
resentatives, I told her story. She must have looked
down from above so proudly and laughed that gay and
bubbly laugh of hers, this miracle worker from Mississippi.

A final important factor in expecting a miracle and
in making miracles happen is to inject the element of
faith into the formula. There can be no sustained motivation without faith, no carry-through in the difficulties
a miracle-maker is bound to encounter. Faith plus dynamic dreams plus real working at it is a go-ahead formula that gets you where you want to go. If you have
become blasé or sophisticated or are of the couldn't-
care-less type and have no dreams, no faith, you are in
a bad way, to be sure. But you can change. Anyone can
always change. That is to say, you can if you think you
can.

AN ARMENIAN BOY BECOMES GREAT AMERICAN

In San Francisco I always enjoy dining at Omar
Khayyam's. George Mardikian, the proprietor and dear
friend of mine, came to this country years ago as an
eighteen-year-old Armenian immigrant, a refugee

from the Turks. Some of his family had been put to death. This boy wanted to make something of his life and, since the real land of freedom was America, there was where he wanted to be. Regardless of difficulty, he came with nothing but positive faith which, of course, is no small asset.

In the old country he had watched his mother cook marvelous Armenian dishes. He discovered that he had a genius for cooking and so his motivation was born. It was to cook Armenian-style food for Americans and become one of the finest chefs in the world.

Arriving in America, though he couldn't speak a word of English, George got a job in San Francisco in a fourth-class restaurant called Coffee Dan's. His job was to wash dishes twelve hours a day. Meanwhile, he tried to pick up the language. Eventually he became manager in another restaurant at fifty dollars a week. But after a while he told the boss he wanted to be a cook instead. Told that the job paid only thirty-six dollars a week, George still said he wanted to cook.

From that lowly beginning George went on a few years later to have his own beautiful restaurant in Fresno. He began to do things for people, especially young people, and everywhere he went he told Americans about the greatness of their country, for they forget that sometimes. One day he wrote a check for ten thousand dollars and gave it to his wife. She said, "George, you haven't got ten thousand dollars!"

"I know," he replied. "I want you to put that check away. It is for our second honeymoon—we are going to take a trip around the world sometime."

He went on working and believing until finally came the day when he said to her, "Honey, we are ready now to take that trip." So they went to San Francisco and he said, "Go out and shop. Buy everything you want for our trip around the world."

Meanwhile, George dropped in to visit the restaurant that had once been Coffee Dan's. There came to him an overwhelming desire to own that restaurant where he had once washed dishes. So he bought the place. Then he went back to the hotel and found his wife resting after her shopping expedition. "Honey," he said, "I have to tell you something."

She looked at him. Most wives know their husbands better than they know themselves. "I know what you want to tell me," she said. "You've spent the ten thousand dollars." And she added, "I know what you did with it, too. You bought a restaurant."

"Yes, honey," he admitted. "I know it was a terrible thing to do. That money was for you. But maybe we'd never get another chance to buy the place for a beautiful Omar Khayyam's in San Francisco!"

His wife responded lovingly, "George, I'm glad—and so very proud of you."

George told me this story at dinner one night, our table in Omar Khayyam's being on the exact spot where he had washed dishes in the former Coffee Dan's:

During the Second World War the commanding officer of a huge Army training camp in California approached George with a problem: The soldiers weren't eating the food prepared for them. The Army was procuring the finest foods, but the men didn't like the meals—so obviously the fault was in the cooking. One of the items procured in quantity was fine zucchini squash. By the time it got to the tables, it was a mess and was finding its way into the refuse.

George studied the operation of the big Army

kitchen, then reported to the general, "The trouble is that the KP's have no pride in their work. Give them white coats and aprons and chef's caps. And put an extra stripe on the mess sergeant's sleeve, to give him more importance." George showed them how to cook zucchini. He did a lot of things to it and then had them taste it—and they smacked their lips.

His helpfulness at that camp led to performing similar services for the United States Army in Europe. In appreciation of his contribution to the nation, the President of the United States invited him to dinner at the White House. As the Armenian boy sat at table in the White House having dinner with the President, he thought wonderingly, "Where else could an immigrant boy find the inspiration and the opportunity to make his dreams come true?"

George Mardikian and I received honorary degrees together from Brigham Young University. When he had accepted his degree and came back to sit beside me on the platform, I noted there were tears running down his cheeks. I put my hand over his and said, "George, you are a wonderful person."

"Ah," he said, "it was God who did it. And this blessed country."

Yes, certainly. But it was also George Mardikian who had the dreams and the faith to expect a miracle, and the motivation to make miracles happen. And he is the kind of man who can because he thinks he can.

Now what have we been saying about the exciting process of expecting a miracle and making miracles happen?

 1. First, expect a miracle and keep your sense of wonder going.

 2. Have motivation, a deep inner self-belief, and

never let anyone or anything take it from you. Remember Walt Disney.

3. *Be proud you live in a country where miracles can happen—where you can make dreams come true.*

4. *Always think upbeat—think hopefully. Never let thought paralysis get into your mind.*

5. *Miracles are made not only from dreams, but from everyday nonglamorous facts like thinking and working and keeping on keeping on.*

6. *Keep probing for the tremendous quality built into you which has not yet emerged.*

7. *Always be on the lookout for the big idea that can change your life.*

8. *Know that you are yourself a miracle. And believe you can make miracles happen—by thinking, praying, believing, working, and by helping people.*

9. *Remember that miracles are made by people who can because they think they can.*

NINE

❧

BORED? FRUSTRATED? FED UP?
WHAT TO DO ABOUT IT

There is no need to be bored or frustrated or fed up. People in the know will tell you that life can be exciting and then some. So why not get with it, have fun, be alive? Day after day, all the way, your life can be packed full of meaning.

Certainly you are going to have your tough, hard moments, your share of pain, your experience with grief. And troubles will gang up on you, bringing with them disappointments, frustrations, problems. Also there are a lot of routine things that just have to be done, and then done again. You see, that is the way life is made. That is the system by which it is put together.

But it is a fact that the ecstasy and the happiness are experienced by getting on top of your problems, by recovering from your failures, by putting meaning into the routine. That is where the excitement lies—in the realization that you have what it takes to meet and handle anything and everything. People who are really organized, who think straight, who are in control of their attitudes and have exciting motivations, are never bored. Eric Hoffer, the writer, was talking sense when he said, "When people are bored, it is primarily with their own selves that they are bored." So perhaps we'd better get ourselves restimulated, revitalized, reorganized.

Have you heard people talking about being bored, muttering that life is dull and meaningless? Dr. Donald Curtis,* in one of his inspired books, listed some of the depressing statements he hears from people. Just run your eye down this list and see if this is the way you talk:

"Life has lost its meaning for me."
"I'm fed up."
"That gripes me."
"Everything's a mess."
"I'm pooped."
"I'm bored stiff."
"Everything bugs me."
"I'm sick and tired of it all."
"Life is the same old stuff."

Well, we might throw up our hands and call it a day if we let such dreary and negative expressions seep into our consciousness control center. And that might indeed happen if you parrot the language of the bored. But, fortunately, great numbers of people sing a different song. Everywhere you can hear such upbeat expressions as:

"Life is terrific, and I mean terrific."
"Everything's great, really great."
"Boy, am I getting a charge out of living."
"This is it and I don't mean maybe."

———* *Human Problems and How to Solve Them,* by Donald Curtis (Prentice-Hall, Inc., 1962).

"I feel good, really good."
"Bored? Are you kidding?"

"OUT OF THIS WORLD" PEOPLE

Now one might ask, how do these positive thinkers get that way? How can anyone not be bored, even disgusted, with all that goes on in this world? Of course, the answer is that such people live that way in this world because they are *out* of this world. They live in another world, the fabulous world of the mind. Into that upper-level mental state the dust and confusion kicked up by the media and polluted by modern "civilization" never enter. Accordingly, these fortunate people are on top of things because they are on top of themselves. They take the tough things in stride as an exciting challenge. And so they make everything different, for the reason that their attitude toward all of it is different—fantastically different. So get with exciting people, with alive-minded people. Turn off bored commentators, don't read bored writers. Associate with excited, really with-it types. Boredom is mental death. Intelligent excitement is mental life. So be alive.

Somewhere along the line people like this went for a philosophy expressed in the dynamic words, "Rejoice with unutterable and exalted joy." * What do you mean, bored?

A newspaper writer claims that we are in the midst of a "boredom epidemic." ** He says in part:

―――*1 Peter 1:8. RSV
―――** Peter T. Chew, in *The National Observer* (May 13, 1972).

Behavorial scientists make a strong case that
chronic boredom is epidemic in our industrial society. They call ours "the land of the free and the
home of the bored."

Most psychologists agree, boredom is simply our
emotional reaction to monotony.

Monotony permeates America today. Our super-
highways are monotonous. Our supermarkets are
monotonous. Our supercities are monotonous. Our
supercorporations are dull places to work, for
white and blue collars alike. Our leisure-time activities are often boring too.

"Most of my patients come to me simply because
they are bored," says a psychiatrist.

Actor George Sanders left a note citing boredom
as a reason for his suicide.

"You get kind of numb," says Dale Sirakis, describing his assembly-line work. Every 40 seconds
or so, all day long, Sirakis' sole duty is to snap a hook
to the underside of a moving auto body.

Psychiatrists say that if you are chronically
bored, *you* are a bore.

And what are some suggested remedies for boredom
cited by the above-mentioned writer? One is to cut out
the soft living. He quotes Dr. Robert G. Heath, chairman of the Department of Psychiatry and Neurology
at Tulane University Medical School, who says:

The seeming increase in boredom can be directly traced to our easy way of living. We don't
get enough out-and-out tough physical exercise the
way our forefathers did. We've become spectator
sportsmen. I am thoroughly convinced that this
contributes to our boredom.

Another facet of soft living that contributes to boredom and needs correction is described by psychiatrist
Henry Ward, who says, "Monotony may surround us all,
but the problem is within the individual." He bluntly
informs his patients that "Life is a simple case of being
scared much of the time—or being bored. Furthermore, if life is too easy, it's no fun. We've made it too
easy for our kids."

A psychiatrist really cannot mean it when he says,
"How do I advise my patients to cope with boredom?
I tell them to go to bed and not get up until they can
think of something they *really* want to do. When
they've done it, I tell them to go back to bed. They
never take my advice, of course." Good heavens, why
should they? The kind of people we are talking about
hate to go to bed for fear they will miss something and
can hardly wait for the next exciting day to dawn so
they can get going again!

We mean to show how to get with the pulsating,
stimulating essence of life. We have viable solutions for
getting people back into touch with real life, for estab-
lishing a permanent cure for boredom, for overcoming
that fed-up, "I've had it" feeling. We believe there is
an answer to frustration and it is not all that complex as
some "learned" and perhaps bored authorities make it.

A HIPPIE ON AN AIRPLANE

For example, take the super-bored member of the
now generation whom I encountered on an airplane.
I had the window seat. In came a young fellow who took
the aisle seat beside me. He appeared to be in his early
twenties. His hair, very long and shaggy, half hid his

face. His glasses were big and gold-rimmed. A leather jacket, blue jeans, and cowboy-type boots completed his ensemble. He had all the stereotyped and traditional habiliments of the hippie.

We nodded and he settled down to peruse a newspaper while I got busy with some paper work. Presently I was startled by a series of exclamations as he crumpled the paper and threw it on the floor. "Lousy world," he declared belligerently, although he didn't say "lousy."

It so happened that the miracle of a sunset above the clouds was in progress out the plane window. The big red sun sinking in the west was turning everything to pink and gold. Observing this, I pointed out the window. "Maybe the world has a few points."

"Oh, that," he said. "Sure, maybe you've got something there. Man hasn't completely messed that up yet." With these philosophical observations we both lapsed into silence.

Presently the young man said, "Mister, could I ask you a question? What are you doing with those papers?"

"Working," I replied.

"Well, now, where does working get you?"

I replied, "I wouldn't be happy not working."

"The establishment," he grunted.

"In a small way," I said. And again silence.

In a little while he turned again. "Mister, may I ask you another question?"

"Go ahead," I replied.

"Why do you wear your hair so short?"

This rather startled me, but I shot him a straight answer. "I'm a nonconformist, an independent, you might say a revolutionary. I just wear my hair the way I like it."

"You don't like my hair, do you?"

"Now look, my friend," I remonstrated, "I said nary a word about your hair. I couldn't care less how anyone wears his hair. Could be you are projecting your own doubts on me."

In this cryptic conversation I had a feeling that there was a kind of bond developing between us. In fact, I liked him and he didn't seem to hate me. He lapsed into silence.

The interval was longer this time. Then, "Mister, can I ask you another question? You actually look happy. How come? Why aren't you bored like I am?"

"Me bored? Don't kid me. Why should anyone be bored in a fascinating world like this? No, sir, I like it. In fact I love it. I've never been bored—that is, really bored—in my whole life. Of course I've had my down moments, but very few."

"Boy, that's something—that sure is something." He looked at me as though I were a curiosity. "In college they teach us to be bored."

"You don't say! Lousy college, in my book."

"Could be," he grinned.

Now came the payoff—a most astonishing one. "You know something, mister? You look to me like you have peace of mind. Have you really?" Obviously the boy's mind was agitated and uptight, but he was looking for some kind of reality—that was clearly apparent.

"Well, you've stated an assumption and asked a fair question. I've never had it thrown at me so suddenly. But, yes, I do have peace of mind, I'm grateful to say. It took me some years to come by it, but I found the answer to a peace of mind which has never left me. Hope you'll get it, too."

"What is this answer?" The question, softly spoken, was loaded with sincerity.

"Oh, no, I can't tell you that. It's pretty personal to me, and besides, I'm not sure you would understand."

"But why wouldn't I understand? I'm not dumb. Come on, level with me."

Still I parried, "Well, you see, you're not quite the type that would be expected to receive a simple suggestion. You impress me as, shall we say, rather complex and conflicted. Besides, you are of the now generation, and I suppose from your viewpoint I'm a square, and what gave me peace of mind you might not buy at all."

I'm sure I was trying to get him really to reach for it by this holding-back technique. I didn't want to flub this chance encounter. Of course I didn't tell him I'm a minister. Didn't want to turn him off.

"I've got brains enough to be simple," he protested in a statement remarkably potent in wisdom.

WANTS SECRET OF PEACE OF MIND

"So you want my personal answer for having peace of mind? You're not putting me on?"

"I want it," he declared.

"All right, here it is, but better hold on to your seat. And don't give me an argument, either. Take it or leave it, you asked for it. It's Jesus."

A dead silence fell. Finally, "Jesus, eh?" He seemed to savor the name. Then he added, "Jesus seems to be coming back, doesn't He?"

"I never knew He went away." We both laughed, but somewhat seriously.

By this time we were landing. The plane rolled to the gate. He turned with a serious look on his face and put out his hand. The long-hair and the short-hair shook hands.

He turned up the aisle, then looked back.

"Hey, you know something? I might just buy that some day. Be seeing you."

And why did I give him that answer to peace of mind and to no boredom or frustration? Well, he wanted it straight, and what he wanted he got. And I guess I felt he was entitled to something personal.

When I was a young man and floundering a bit I read what Jesus said: "These things have I spoken unto you . . . that your joy might be full." * For some reason that appealed to me; it actually grabbed me. So I asked, "What things?" and I added them up as faith, hope, and love. I believed in that formula and tried thinking and living on that basis. It worked. Frankly and for sure, I've never really been bored or fed up or frustrated since I adopted that teaching.

This perhaps may be discounted by some as "religious" and for that reason they won't go for it. But the young hippie on the airplane bought it. At least, he appeared to consider it favorably. Had I given him some kind of argument, paternalistically preaching at him, he would have resisted and perhaps rejected. And who could blame him? But when I simply shared in a few words, with emphasis on the "few," my own personal experience, he showed respect for an honest viewpoint and for reality.

One thing is a certain scientific fact. If a formula of thought can relieve some people of boredom and frus-

_____* John 15:11.

tration, it follows logically that it can similarly prove beneficial to others who examine and experiment with it objectively. At any rate it is possible to develop mental attitudes to a conscious level where nothing can depreciate a zestful reaction to the experience of living. And if you are so bored that you doubt the possibility of becoming this way, simply start thinking that you can and you will find that you can, indeed.

LOVE LIFE AND LIFE WILL LOVE YOU BACK

I chanced to hear a wonderful thing on television. It was an interview with Artur Rubinstein, the famous musician. Some reporter was asking him the secret of his success. Was it talent, luck, or maybe good publicity? To these uninspired questions Rubinstein made a super-inspired answer: "I have found that if you love life, life will love you back." Doesn't sound like a bored or frustrated man, does he?

Well, it is a fact that if you love life, life will indeed love you back. You will get a terrific lift in the spirit, so much so that you will have perpetual excitement and a deep feeling of happiness. With acute sensitivity you will be able to maintain a constant and eager delight in the world and in people. This lift of the spirit will condition you to upper-level experience.

Every year for over twenty-five years my wife and I have spent part of our holiday in Switzerland. And we do quite a bit of hiking in the mountains. The beautiful valley of Lauterbrunnen is a favorite hiking area. This is one of the most stupendous valleys ever cut between hills "rock-ribbed, and ancient as the sun." * Through

_____* From "Thanatopsis" by William Cullen Bryant.

it flows a glacial river rushing down from the mountain-tops.

Some years ago when we were following a trail through that valley we noticed a little rope, indeed it was not much bigger than a string, dangling down from the heights around Mürren. We came near and wondered why there should be such a small rope let down over the cliff and dangling in that fashion.

Sometime later we came by the same place and saw a larger rope hanging down. Then still later the rope had been replaced by a strong cable. We were seeing the beginnings of the mighty engineering enterprise that produced the longest cable railway in the Alps, the Schilthornbahn. And on our most recent visit to Switzerland we ascended the Schilthorn by this cableway, rising from 2,700 feet to 10,000 feet in thirty minutes of noiseless floating in the air.

From the top of the Schilthorn, because of its peculiar location, you get one of the most magnificent and colossal views anywhere in the world. The panorama stretches from the Black Forest to Mont Blanc, encompassing one great peak after another. One stands awestruck in this lonely place previously visited only by men hunting the chamois. Embedded in the rock is a bronze tablet on which are inscribed the German words

Gross und wunderbar
sind deine werke
Herr allmächtiger Gott

"Great and wonderful are Thy works, Almighty God." On that peak of the Schilthorn, filled with awe and wonder, one loves the world and feels it loving him back.

The bored, the frustrated, those who have had it and are fed up, would do well to get away from cities which are increasingly dirty and frightful with noise and get reacquainted with the great natural world. Listen to the roar of the sea on some lonely beach. Trudge alongside a singing stream. Lie down in a meadow and watch the white clouds sail like ships across a blue expanse of sky. Lift up your eyes unto the hills, for it is a fact that strength does indeed come from them.

Actually, it is mental exhilaration that knocks out boredom, eliminates frustration, and kicks the fed-up feeling for good and all. And a human being must have experiences of exhilaration that really lift him to high levels of the mind, the kind he never forgets and that live with him for always.

THRILLS OVER THE MATTERHORN

Such an experience my wife Ruth, our long-time friend Arthur Gordon and I had on August 12, 1970, for one hour between 11 A.M. and 12 noon. The day and the hour are forever indelibly imprinted upon my consciousness. If ever I should begin to slip into boredom and dullness I would instantly return to the unforgettable memory of that day and hour. For that was when we flew in a small helicopter over the Alps and very close to mighty mountains, glaciers, valleys, and finally over the Matterhorn itself. For sheer visual excitement and impact this proved to be one of the topmost incidents in our lives, which have contained not a little adventure.

I've often given my own version of this experience but must admit that Ruth has related it much more graphically. So I will let her tell the story as it appears in her book: *

We were on one of our visits to Zermatt, a little town in Switzerland that nestles in a valley at the foot of the Matterhorn. This gigantic spire of jagged granite looks like a great knife thrust into the sky. The summit is more than 14,000 feet above sea level. Not far away is the Monte Rosa, highest mountain in Switzerland, but its approaches are more gradual and it's not so dramatic. The Matterhorn stands alone, brooding, somber, pockmarked even in summer with ice and snow. For years the natives believed that it was the home of devils or evil spirits who could hurl thunderbolts or fling down great boulders upon any humans who dared to come close. Someone once said that the Matterhorn isn't just a mountain; it's a "presence." It is.

During this visit to Zermatt we stayed in the chalet of an old friend, Theodore Seiler, a Swiss banker and president of the Seiler Hotels. Ted Seiler grew up in Zermatt. His grandfather owned the first hotel there, the Monte Rosa, where Ted still welcomes guests. It was to this hotel that Whymper, the first man to climb the Matterhorn, returned from his triumphant but tragic climb on which three men died. A bronze plaque near the entrance commemorates the event.

Ted Seiler told us that, next to climbing the Matterhorn, the most dramatic way to view it was to fly around it and over it in a helicopter. He added that a pair of helicopters, flown by German pilots, was kept on the alert at all times on the outskirts

_____* *The Adventure of Being a Wife,* by Mrs. Norman Vincent Peale (Prentice-Hall, Inc., 1971).

of Zermatt. There was a small one that could carry four persons, and a larger one that could take six. They had already made several highly dramatic mountain rescues. Ted Seiler said that if the weather was right, he might be able to arrange for us to make a mountain flight over the nearby peaks and glaciers. He said that if we did, we'd never forget it.

It sounded exciting, all right, but also a little scary. I had been in a helicopter only once in my life, to view some farm acreage. But Norman, on the trip he made to Viet Nam at the request of President Nixon, had made many helicopter flights.

All through the first part of our visit, the weather was uncertain. Much of the time swirling clouds shrouded the Matterhorn. When they would part momentarily, we could see that the slopes around the great peak were covered with fresh snow. But the pinnacle itself was too steep for much snow to cling to the jagged rocks.

PERFECT DAY IN THE ALPS

The night before our last day in Zermatt, the wind switched to the north—a sign of fair weather, Ted Seiler said. Sure enough, the next day dawned sparkling and bright. The sky was a deep, cobalt blue—not a cloud in it. Golden sunlight poured down on the streets of Zermatt, gay with banners and colored awnings and window boxes full of petunias and geraniums.

A telephone call was made to the heliport, a square of concrete built into a hillside just above the railroad tracks on the north side of the town. We were told that if we would come there at eleven o'clock, there was a good chance that we could make the flight. The big helicopter was undergoing repairs, but the small one was operational. Since there would be room for three passengers in addition to the pilot, Arthur Gordon, who was also in Zermatt, said he would like to go.

It was a ten-minute walk to the tall, silo-like structure that housed the elevator that lifted visitors to the heliport. We pressed a button, identified ourselves through a transmitter like the ones you see in the lobbies of apartment houses, and shortly found ourselves standing on a huge square of concrete about half the size of a football field. A painted circle with a large H in the center was evidently the target for descending pilots. Through the open doors of a hangar we could see the large red machine being worked on. We were told that the smaller helicopter was off on patrol, but would return shortly.

We sat in the brilliant sunshine, waiting. My feelings were a mixture of excitement, anticipation, and a little apprehension at the thought of soaring off the friendly earth in a plastic bubble supported by nothing but a pair of ungainly windmill blades and a single engine. As we waited, we talked about Whymper and mountain climbing and the strange and dangerous things people seem to do in their quest for happiness.

Our ears picked up the pulsing drone of the helicopter before our eyes saw it. Then suddenly there it was, hovering like a gigantic dragonfly. The pilot swung around into the wind. With a roar and buffeting gusts of the cool mountain air, the machine settled onto the concrete platform. The pilot cut the engine. The whirling blades gradually ceased revolving and grew still.

The fuel tanks were refilled. Certain mountain-rescue equipment was taken out to make room for us. Almost before we knew what was happening, Norman and I were fastening our seatbelts in the rear seat. Arthur sat forward, on the left. The young pilot, relaxed and self-assured, was on the right. "Where do you want to go?" he asked.

At this the station manager standing on the pad spoke to the pilot through his open window. It was in German and I could not understand, but a resistance on the part of the pilot and then a shrug of the shoulder by the pilot as the station manager insisted, gave me a tremor of apprehension. Was he being asked to push this helicopter beyond its limit in order to show us the glorious mountain?

The doors swung shut. The pilot adjusted his earphones. His right hand held the stick. With his left, he twisted the throttle between the two forward seats. The helicopter vibrated, stirred, began to lift. Suddenly, with a heart-stopping lurch, it seemed to me that we simply jumped off the concrete platform into thin air. There was no forward taxiing, as in a conventional aircraft. We leaned into the wind—and leaped!

Up the little valley we rushed, not more than two hundred feet off the ground. The pilot and the passenger in the front seat could see almost straight down; I was glad we couldn't. On the instrument panel I could see the air-speed indicator; the needle was hovering between forty and fifty knots. The altimeter indicated that we were about six thousand feet above sea level, and climbing.

Up the valley we flew, between towering rock walls on either side, past lacy waterfalls, over green meadows filled with mountain wild flowers. The helicopter banked steeply and started back, still climbing.

Below us, now, we could see Zermatt spread out

like a toy village, its chalets and hotels dominated by the spire of the church. We were following the contours of the ground to the east of the town. Once or twice it seemed to me that our rate of climb was too slow to enable us to clear the ridge just ahead, but we always slid over with something to spare. Far below I could see the orange cars of a funicular crawling along, like ladybugs, between pylons. Now the dark hues of the evergreens were giving way to the browns and grays of the rugged terrain above the timberline. Ahead and to the left was a cluster of buildings marking the terminus of the cog railway that climbs steeply up from Zermatt to Gornergrat, some ten thousand feet above sea level, a favorite lookout point for tourists who want to view the whole majestic panorama of glaciers and Alpine peaks.

But few tourists ever saw them as we were seeing them now. Moments later we were over the Gorner-glacier itself, a huge river of ice, blinding white, strangely scored and indented. Where it ended, a torrent of water, gray with glacial sediment, poured from under the wall of ice. To our right, a lordly peak, the Stockhorn, pierced the sky. The altimeter now read eleven thousand feet, and some dim unwelcome memory reminded me that as a rule pilots are not supposed to fly above ten thousand without oxygen. We had no oxygen.

Up the glacier we raced at sixty knots. Tortured and barren as the ridged ice was, I was glad to have it there, only a couple of hundred feet below. If our engine stopped, I told myself cheerfully, we could just sit down on that nice solid ice and wait to be rescued—perhaps by a friendly St. Bernard. But then, looking ahead, I saw that the glacier ended. And not just the glacier, but the mountain, the world, creation ended. Rushing toward us was a

fine white line, sharp as a knife blade. Then nothing. Just a kind of livid emptiness.

OUT OVER NOTHING

Over the line we went, straight out into this awful chasm. I felt my feet pressing against the floor,
as if by doing so they could somehow hold us back.
Beneath us the precipice fell sheer, straight down,
for more than a mile. We hung suspended over a
stupendous void, ringed by the great peaks, floored
by purple shadow.

My rational mind knew that we could fly just as
well over a mile of nothingness as over a glacier,
but my stomach didn't seem to know it. My stomach, in fact, seemed to have stayed back over the
glacier. I saw that Arthur had reached for the side
of our plastic bubble as if to brace himself, and I
knew he too was wondering what four infinitesi-
mally small and unimportant human beings were
doing in such a sublimely terrifying place.

Only the pilot seemed unconcerned. We swung
behind the twin peaks of the Monte Rosa, still
higher than our heads although our altimeter now
indicated twelve thousand feet. Below us a few
ants seemed to be toiling painfully across the vast
snowfields. Climbers. "That can be dangerous,"
said the pilot, pointing at them, "unless you know
what you're doing. There are snow bridges that can
break. See those holes that look like caves? If you
fall in one of those, you're finished. No one can get
you out!"

He spotted something lying on the crest of one
of the ridges, something that might have been a
man lying in the snow. "Better take a look." The
helicopter banked steeply; the rotor blades made

a flat, thudding sound as they bit into the air. I clutched Norman's hand. "Just a tent," said the pilot as we swept over the object. "Sometimes climbers will try the Monte Rosa one day and the Matterhorn the next, and spend the night down there." I tried to imagine what it would be like underneath that tiny piece of canvas with the wind moaning in the icy blackness outside. My imagination wasn't up to it. . . .

The Matterhorn is impressive at a distance. Close up, it is overpowering. And we were close, so close that it seemed to me we could see the cracks in the towering walls. But when the pilot pointed out some climbers, they looked unbelievably tiny, just dots of color clinging to the naked rock. Past a small hut we went, perched like an eagle's nest on the edge of a stupendous precipice. "Climbers spend the night there," the pilot said. "They start climbing at dawn."

We were still climbing ourselves, in a tight spiral that circled the Matterhorn three times. It seemed to me that our engine was laboring in the thin air. I was beginning to feel some shortness of breath, and I could see that Norman was too. Now the altimeter read fourteen thousand feet; we were almost on a level with the summit. I could see clearly the iron cross that marked the spot where Whymper and his companions had stood so long ago. Higher still, so that we could look down on the summit itself. There on that dizzying height, three tiny figures stood, waving at us, and I felt a sudden surge of admiration for the restless, unquenchable spirit of adventure that had made them challenge and conquer those frowning heights. Perhaps our generation was not so soft and effete after all.

Then we were dropping down through the luminous air, the great mountain receding behind us. "Swallow hard," the pilot said. "It will ease the pressure on your ears." Zermatt came into view, tranquil in the sunlight. The landing pad looked like a linen handkerchief. We made one last turn, came up into the wind, settled down exactly in the center of the painted circle. The flight was over.

But the experience wasn't over. I stepped from the helicopter walking on air. I was exhilarated as never before. The world had a glorious radiance and wonder about it. I looked at Norman and Arthur. Their faces were alight. This tremendous upsurge of spirit stayed with us for days.

FROM HELICOPTER TO AN ANCIENT COACH

Our friend Ted Seiler had arranged for the hotel van to meet us. The two splendid horses trotted back to the village, bells jingling gaily. We sat in the old coach, not saying much. The spell of the heights was still on us, and the transition from twentieth-century helicopter to nineteenth-century horse-drawn van was so abrupt and strange that it seemed unreal.

All through the rest of that day, and many times since, I have found myself reliving the exaltation of that moment when we swept over the edge of the glacier into that vast emptiness, and the thought has come to me that perhaps dying is like that; an outward rush into the unknown where there is nothing recognizable, nothing to cling to, and yet you are sustained and supported over the great void just as you were over the comfortable and familiar terrain.

Fanciful? Perhaps. But I remember that when

we said our prayers that night, thanking God for the privilege of seeing all we had seen, and also for our safe return, it didn't seem fanciful. Not at all.

The sum of the matter is that the activated, motivated, uplifted spirit of the mind is the one certain antidote to the creeping paralysis of dull boredom.

Naturally, it is not required that one get on actual mountaintops to keep from being fed up and frustrated, but it is vital to keep the mountaintop mental experiences going. It is necessary to rise up out of the everyday routine in your thoughts, which have the power to range the world over, even while you are doing the same old things. Those same old things have to be done, but when the mind becomes alive with excitement they get done easily and without frustration. Everything changes as your attitudes change.

LISTLESS LARRY BECOMES A DYNAMO

Like "Listless" Larry, whom I met when I spoke at a luncheon of about two thousand salesmen in the ballroom of the Conrad Hilton Hotel in Chicago. During the luncheon a man came up to me and said, "Dr. Peale, I've invested five hundred dollars in your speech."

"That is a big investment," I said. "How come?"

"I brought one of my salesmen to hear you," he explained, "because he is bored and dull. It will cost me about that much to get him here, feed him, house him, and send him back. But this man has intelligence, a good education, and a pleasing personality. In fact, he has everything except energy, vitality, and excitement.

What I want you to do is to activate him, get him go-ing."

Since I have had several such experiences relative to activating bored people, I asked, "And what are you going to do? You've got to help. Suppose you start visu-alizing this bored salesman of yours as becoming a changed human being, the man he ought to be."

"Very well," he agreed, "I will, because he could be a terrific producer if he could just get some enthusiasm and some real dynamic interest."

"O.K.," I responded, "practice 'seeing' him that way. Could be your image will project to him. And let's try to teach him that once we get him started thinking that he can, he really can be outstanding."

As I made my speech I glanced at that salesman a time or two, for his boss had pointed him out to me. He did for a fact look dull and apathetic. And when my talk was over he came up and said to me, "I am Listless Larry. That is what they call me. I'm the guy in whom Mr. _____ invested five hundred dollars. His aim is to get me motivated."

I asked him how he knew that. He answered, "How can I help knowing? He's been telling everybody that you are going to build a fire under me, and that it was costing him plenty. Funny, but Mr. _____ believes in me a lot more than I believe in myself."

Well, I was really on the spot. I took him up to my suite. He was tall, lanky fellow, and when I asked him to have a seat he didn't sit; he practically lay in the chair, legs stretched out, hands hanging over the sides. I said, "Larry, that is no way to sit in a chair. Sit up straight, so that your backbone touches the back of the chair all the way up. Let me see you do that, will you?"

Pulling himself up, he objected, "It seems to me this is irrelevant to the discussion."

"No," I disagreed. "You're listless. That is why they call you Listless Larry! You've got to come alive, or Mr. _____'s five hundred dollars goes down the drain."

"Dr. Peale," he said, "I think really I am a pretty good guy. I go to church. I even go to Sunday School. I belong to a men's class. I love my wife. I have lived a decent life. I'm a good man."

"Well," I said, perhaps pretty directly, "there's a difference between being good and good for nothing." He didn't mind. He grinned at that one.

"Larry," I went on, "what is it to be alive? What is life? It is to be in relations. As a Chinese sage once pointed out, we are alive in proportion to the number of points at which we touch life. Life is vitality. Life is vigor. It is energy and excitement. A listless person is only partially alive. Tell you what, let's practice getting excited."

It so happened that the hotel management had sent me up a basket of fruit, and it was one of the most imaginative ones I had ever seen. In it was an apple that was a work of art; and a beautiful orange or two; and a great big grapefruit; and a long banana. "Larry," I said, "look at that basket of fruit. Just look at it. Did you ever see such an apple? Isn't it a beauty? That apple must come from the highlands of Oregon where the cold nights firm the flesh and make the fruit juicy. Or maybe it was grown in New York State where the apples are super. And look at that orange. It's got all the sunlight of Florida or of California in it. And the banana; it has the beauty of the tropics. Isn't that basket of fruit terrific?"

"Yes, it is," he admitted. "But why get so excited about it?"

"Because that's the way to react—see things as beautiful and wonderful, see everything that way, for that is the way they are—actually miracles, each one."

"You really believe that, don't you?" Larry said.

"I sure do. Look at that marvelous Lake Michigan out there glistening in the sunlight. Boy, isn't that something! Practice that attitude about everything. And I mean really practice it. Your thinking will equate to excitement if you do this. And one other thing: Don't hang around with bored people. They may try to give you the impression that they are the "in" type, the real sophisticates. But they couldn't be further off the beam. Actually, they are out of it. Associate with those who really have enthusiasm going for them."

"O.K.," said big old Listless Larry. He put it prosaically. "You want me to get off my fanny and get steamed up. I'll try it."

Some months later I happened to go to his town to make a speech for the Chamber of Commerce. He met my plane. "Glad to see you, boy!" he greeted me. "Let's get going. Lots to see around here!"

"Look, Larry," I said, "I've been on the go and I'm tired. I want to go to the hotel and rest. I have to make a speech, you know."

"What do you mean, rest?" asked Larry. "Where's all that energy, vitality, and excitement you talk about?"

Sheepishly I agreed, "Let's skip the hotel. Where do we start seeing the town?"

He showed me everything, commenting, "That's the greatest high school," "Terrific ball park," "Last word in a hospital." He acted as if the town belonged to him personally.

Finally he pulled up in front of a nice-looking house. "Isn't that house a beauty?" he demanded. Dragging me inside, he declared, "Here she is—my wife. Isn't she a sweetheart?" So saying, he kissed her enthusiastically. And by this time I was so excited I kissed her myself.

"Dr. Peale," she said, "Larry is so different, so positively wonderful. He's—he's—" she hesitated. "He's just plain exciting."

What happened to bored, dull Listless Larry? It's very simple, yet wonderful indeed. He came alive in his mind by the process of practicing exciting thoughts. He became an excited person. No more boredom for him.

IT'S A BEAUTIFUL DAY FOR IT

Such practicing of excitement can cancel out boredom, and if continually practiced, excitement will in due course become habitual. The late four-term Governor Wilbur L. Cross of Connecticut was noted for his unusual good morning to his family. Regardless of the weather he would say, "It's a beautiful day for it."

You can supply your own meaning to this enigmatic comment, but his grandson cannot recall that the onetime Yale professor and later governor ever had any trouble with boredom or frustration. How could a man who believed any day was "a beautiful day for it" ever possibly be fed up? Boredom and frustration are produced by bored attitudes and frustrated attitudes. Change those attitudes to equate with the thinking of Governor Cross, and every day can indeed become a beautiful day for it.

But how to change attitudes is the question. And one answer is the employment of common-sense thinking instead of reacting emotionally.

I well remember a man who called me on the tele-

phone some time ago. Obviously very tense, he declared tragically, "I'm at the end of my rope and have
decided the only thing to do is blow my brains out."

"Look," I answered, "that doesn't make sense. Why
not blow your spirit up instead? How about coming to
my office and let's talk it over."

He came. Despondently he dropped his head into his
hands and moaned, "Everything is gone, hopeless, a
flop. I'm living in a deep darkness. In fact, I've lost heart
for living altogether. I'm frustrated, bored, completely
down."

"Come on, now, let's take a look at your situation,"
I suggested. So I got out a large sheet of paper, put a
line through the middle from top to bottom, and told
him we'd put down on the left side all the things he'd
lost and on the right side the things he had left.

"Humph, that's easy," he said glumly. "One thing is
sure; you won't need that column on the right side. I
have nothing left, period."

So I asked him, "When did your wife leave you?"

"What do you mean?" he exclaimed. "She hasn't left
me. My wife loves me!"

"That's great," I said. "Then that will be number one
in the right-hand column—Wife hasn't left. Now, when
were your children jailed?"

"What a silly question!" he shouted. "My children
aren't in jail!"

"Good," I said. "That's number two in the right-hand
column—Children not in jail. But I suppose with all this
trouble your appetite is off."

"You know, it's a funny thing," he admitted, "but bad
as things are, I can eat everything in sight." So I put
down in the asset column, "Can eat everything in
sight."

Well, we went on like that for a few more items and
he began to get the point.

"I get you. Funny how things change when you think
of them that way."

When we added up all the good things going for him
I said, "Look at all the assets you've got! You don't need
to blow your brains out. All you need is to blow your
spirit up. And we haven't even scratched the surface
in listing the positives you have. Come off that dramatized frustration. What are you trying to do, be bored
like everyone says you should be?"

He used his head and did come off it.

HE'D HAD IT AT TWENTY-ONE

When you get bored to the point of frustration and
are completely fed up, it will help to remember that
there is an experience so vital that it can burn boredom
out as if it had never existed at all. Let me tell you of
one person who had it, and had it real good.

A senior in a university consulted me. He said, "I am
going to give it to you straight. I've had it. Life is rotten.
I'm not only bored, I'm fed up with the whole lousy
bit."

"Sure have covered a lot of ground, I'd say. How old
are you?" I asked.

"Twenty-one," he replied.

"And you have had it at twenty-one—had it all?"

"That's right," he said. "I've been through the whole
thing. You name it and I've had it. Sex, liquor, drugs—I
have had it all. And you know what? They have had me,
too. So I am fed up with the whole d_____d business.
So what is next? Or is there anything next?"

"Oh, yes," I said, "there is something next, something that you, who have had it all, have just never gotten around to."

"What could that be?" he asked.

"God," I answered.

"What? I thought He was dead."

"Oh, no. He is only dead for those who have lost Him, but for those who find Him He is very much alive."

"Well, now," the young man informed me, "I might as well tell you, I don't go for this God stuff."

"Then why did you come to see me?" I asked him. "You know that I believe in God." Then I answered my own question. "I'll tell you why: Although your conscious mind hates God, your unconscious mind is reaching for Him. You're not honest with yourself. You came here because you want to find God."

"No," said he, "I don't go for God at all."

"Well, take it or leave it; God is your answer, my friend," I said.

"All right. Thank you very much." And he went out into the night. I didn't think I had registered with him at all.

What happened after that was one of those rare things that occur now and then. It was a cold, rain-mixed-with-snow kind of a night. Leaving my New York office he headed west on 29th Street through a rather depressing loft and warehouse district. And as he walked along he got angry. "Same old stuff, talking about God!" he muttered. "God, God—that's all they can talk about. Nothing but God, God, more God!" Then suddenly he heard himself saying, "Oh, God, if You are, help me!"

Now that was a prayer; that was real. He was asking for it and he got it. And he got it good. All of a sudden he began to feel hot in his head—a strange burning, he said. Then this heat seemed to pass all the way down through his body to his feet and he felt as though he had been healed of something deep within.

He seemed to be surrounded by "an ethereal light." Those drab buildings looked like palaces, the faces of the few people passing by were beautiful. The sidewalk seemed to undulate as though on fire. He said to himself, "What has come over me? I'm going nuts!" And he rushed back to tell me about it, exclaiming, "My God, what is happening to me?"

"You have named it," I said. "God has happened to you."

From that moment on this young man had an incredible awareness of life and an expansion of consciousness such as he had never known before. He got organized. All that dead old boredom dropped off like leaves in the autumn.

ACTIVE PEOPLE ARE NEVER BORED

It has been my observation that people who are active and deeply interested in everything that goes on in the world are not likely to become bored, frustrated, or fed up. It seems that the more you are into things, the greater the zest. The more active the mind is, the better it will perform and the longer it will keep on performing. To slow down can result in boredom, but not if one continues to exercise the mind by reading, thinking and by participation in contemporary affairs. You can avoid boredom all your life if you keep alive mentally all your life.

Keep moving, keep thinking, keep participating—this is the golden secret of perpetually fascinating existence. A friend of mine is seventy-five years old. He only laughs when asked when he is going to slow down and retire. "Why should I?" he retorts. "I feel good physically. My mind is constantly working producing new ideas. I can still handle a huge work load. I've always worked. I love to work. I'm in the work groove. In fact, I would simply fold up if I could not work, and I mean work for long hours."

This man plays very little. No golf, for example. He does swim and enjoys a long, stiff hike. But then he quickly gets back to work. He is excited and gleeful about a new idea that may open up a new project that's going to mean more work. Fortunately, this man can delegate and has built up excellent staff in his varied organizations.

This seventy-five-year-old covers the nation and foreign countries on speaking trips, and he speaks with vigorous gestures—really pours himself into a speech. He directs publishing enterprises, writes for newspapers and magazines. He is in real estate and other business activities; heads several organizations.

I asked him once, "Come on, now, really level with me. Don't you sometimes get fed up with things? Surely you must have your moments of frustration and certainly there are times when you're really bored?"

He thought a moment. "Fed up? Frustrated? Bored?" He considered the matter. "I can only think of one time. That was when I was talked into taking a week off to do absolutely nothing. Worst experience I ever had." He shuddered. "I was bored stiff. Outside of that," he concluded, hitting me a strong blow on the back, "I've never been bored or frustrated in my life, and you won't be, either, if you keep thinking, keep moving, keep participating."

So now what is the score on this matter of being bored, frustrated, and fed up?

1. *Get this basic fact firmly in mind—you do not need to be bored, frustrated, or fed up.*

2. *Concentrate on exciting motivation. Boredom can't live with it.*

3. *Get with the philosophy which teaches us to "Rejoice with unutterable and exalted joy."*

4. *Don't shy off real spiritual faith. It's packed with excitement that burns out boredom.*

5. *Remember: If you love life, life will love you back.*

6. *Get away from dirty and noisy cities. Get with streams, meadows, mountains, if at all possible. Nature siphons off boredom.*

7. *Like once-listless Larry, practice excitement. Practice excited thinking until you become excited. And always know for a fact that you can if you think you can.*

8. *Level with yourself. Things are better than they seem.*

9. *Associate with excited people. Let their excitement rub off on you.*

10. *Keep thinking, keep moving, keep participating.*

TEN

❧

NEVER THINK OF FAILING!
YOU DON'T NEED TO

It was blustery and cold that winter night in Cleveland. Snow driven by a high wind whipped across Euclid Avenue, slanting under the streetlights.

When my taxi stopped for a red light I noticed a gasoline service station on the corner displaying a large streamer buffeted by the wind. The banner proclaimed the virtue of a certain brand of motor oil and featured in large letters the striking legend, "A Clean Engine Always Delivers Power."

Right away that statement became part of the speech I was about to make to some three thousand sales personnel who packed a theatre auditorium. In the speech my thesis was that personal achievement power is often siphoned off by the mass of wrong thoughts that clutter up the mind. "A clean mind," I declared, "always delivers power."

I suggested that if power was not being delivered, it might be that some of those present did not have a clean mental engine. Maybe it would be well to use some intellectual detergent to flush out of the mind those old, tired, listless, debilitating thoughts of inferiority, resentment, and negativism. This process might get the mental engine clean so that it could produce maximum power.

Backstage after the meeting a man came bursting up to me. He appeared to be in his thirties and seemed terrifically excited. "Something has happened to me," he declared. "Now I see why I have been failing both in business and as a person. It's because I haven't had a clean mental engine. While you were talking, do you know what I did? I just asked the Lord to clean out my mind. And He did," he concluded triumphantly. "It seems hard to believe, but I feel like a new person; I have a new power, I sure have." This was a sudden transformation but that he was correct in this appraisal of his newfound self I had no doubt. No longer would he think of failing, for with his fresh, new insights such thoughts were out.

"O.K.," I answered, "now you can if you think you can. Keep it going."

Out of a slight acquaintance the late Lord Beaverbrook, British publisher and one-time Cabinet Minister, sent me one of his books * in which he discussed philosophically and practically the problem of achieving success. He maintains that the three keys to success are judgment, industry, and health.

"A man may have two of these attributes and go far. But unless he has all three, he will not go all the way. Are there exceptions to prove the rule? I can think of only one," declared Lord Beaverbrook, "Franklin Delano Roosevelt. Roosevelt lacked good health and Roosevelt was a great man. He might have been supreme, if he had not suffered from his grave affliction.

"Sir Winston Churchill, on the other hand, was sup-

―――* *The Three Keys to Success,* by Lord Beaverbrook (Hawthorn Books, Inc., 1954).

ported in his prodigious career by all three of the keys
to success; sound judgement, immense industry and
excellent health. He was the greatest exemplar of these
basic attributes."

The three outstanding qualities, then, that make for
success are—judgment, industry, health. "And the
greatest of these is judgement." So says one of the most
successful men in Britain's recent history. In Chapter
12 we will discuss the value of health in the creative
living process and throughout this book the importance
of industry is stressed. At this point we are concerned
with the vital factor of mind in personal effectiveness.

Judgment is a process of mind; the ability to think in
a cool, logical, orderly manner and make sound decisions. Good judgment reduces the error factor in decision-making, and in the long run success depends upon
the percentage of right decisions made. Any factor
which interferes with effective judgment must be
eliminated, or at least reduced, if we expect to have
good success in any enterprise. Hence the importance
of controlled mental operation.

One quality which often impedes the exercise of
judgment and, indeed, may actually set it aside, is uncontrolled emotional reaction to people and situations.
This was the evident cause of failure of a man who, with
his wife, asked to meet with me at a national industry
convention where they had heard my talk on "Why
Positive Thinkers Get Positive Results."

"Why," this man asked, "do I consistently fail to get
positive results? As it stands now, I'm a complete failure!"

"Oh, no, Bill," protested his wife, "you're just having
a bad time of it at present but that is only temporary.
Never think of failing! You don't need to." She then

went on to explain that her husband had a good educational background, was well-trained and experienced in his line; indeed, he had "plenty of brains." But the negative factor was that he also had a temper, a quick boiling point. And he was apt to be resentful, volatile, rather unsocial. "In fact," she concluded, "the poor guy has a pretty bad time with himself."

Through hard work and intense application to his job, and by sheer ability Bill had advanced in the company, finally becoming Executive Vice-President. But he worked primarily on his nerves; a tense, irascible man who often "blew his top," especially when any of his actions were questioned. On his way up in the company he made not a few enemies and he wasn't too well liked by others.

The chief criticism of Bill, however, seemed to be his lack of objectivity in the decision-making process. Too often decisions affecting an associate were made on an emotional basis or on a personal reaction to people with whom he did business. "He got away with his job for a long time," so his wife said, quoting his associates, "because of his brilliant ability to explain away the results of his decisions or to correct them by some astute tactic."

HE HIT THE CEILING AND SUFFERED PERSONAL DAMAGE

But finally the matter came to a head when the company president retired. "Bill, who fully expected to succeed him, was bypassed by the Board and a man was brought in from the outside to head the organization. Bill really hit the ceiling," his wife said sadly. "He told everybody off. He went completely out of control. Instead of trying to calm himself, think the new situation out and intelligently adjust to it, all the inner frustration that had been building up for years spilled out."

Result? He was let out. "We really hated to let him go," the wife was told, "because Bill has tremendous ability if only he wasn't so emotional."

"What about it, Bill?" I asked. He respónded in a tone as cold as ice, "Yes, that's what they did to me. And don't think I'm not as smart as those characters. I'm going to get every one of them, so help me; and when I do I'm going to stick the knife in deep and twist it and watch their faces while I twist." Actually I was observing an acute case of hate.

I found myself wondering if this man could really think. Did he have judgment ability or was he simply a sick person emotionally? So when his tirade had subsided I asked, "Have you made a new connection?" To which he replied that he did not think he was ready; was still too upset. "Good diagnosis," I agreed. "And you won't be ready until you become a thinking, objective, judgmental man. Before you can recover yourself, which you surely can, you will have to put the lid on that volatile, emotional characteristic of yours. So what do you say, let's stop erupting and start really thinking cool, like an executive should. And no matter what your past emotional record shows, you can change if you think you can.

"Here you are," I continued, "only forty-five years of age, a real smart man acting like a child. Ever stop to think you may have developed into a grown man in your body and brain but are still infantile in your emotions?"

For some reason that remark struck him hard. He sat

quietly, then said, "Do you know, I never thought of that. Just when you made that statement I saw myself in a kind of flash. That's my trouble, for sure. I see it. I'm a man and yet I'm a baby. I've never grown up emotionally. But what can I do about it? I'm ruined."

"Oh, no, you are not ruined. Let's start some real thinking. Tell me, as a judgmental businessman, is your present attitude and approach paying off or isn't it?"

He smiled for the first time. "Of course not. It's a flop."

"O.K., then, let's ask what we do now. Mind you, no reacting—only thinking; only objective judgment. I believe you can come up with a sound decision."

Bill sat in deep thought. And he showed his ability to think. No emotionalizing now. Without hesitation, crisply decisive, he said, "I see the answer. It's the only thing to do. Embarrassing as it is, I will go to the new president of the company, tell him I am now aware of my emotional instability and at last have learned its cause. I will also tell him that I feel sure I can handle it hereafter. I'll say that if he will give me my old job back . . ." he gulped, "or any job, I will assure him of competent service."

Such change does not ordinarily come so quickly or easily, but I had the feeling that maybe, just maybe, this man's in-depth experience of self-revelation had effected a cure. Accordingly, I refrained from warning him or injecting any negative thoughts into his mind. Instead, I congratulated him on becoming, indeed, a changed person.

That he was a different man was demonstrated by the objective manner in which he dealt with his old company. He was honest, humble, and forthright. The new president, whether out of a need for Bill's ability or compassion or both, brought him into the organization on a temporary consulting basis. In the end he made the grade. He became a person motivated not by personalities but by principles; not by emotional reaction but by judgment.

WHEN YOU FIND YOURSELF

What actually happened in the foregoing case was that this man finally found himself, and at age forty-five. Some find themselves while young; others later in years. But to become competent in judgment, in the ability to think and move ahead, one must for a fact find himself sometime. He must know who he is, what he is, and what he can do best. In a word, he must become a fulfilled person able to make sound judgments and objective decisions.

Fortunate, indeed, is the individual who has the basic experience of finding and knowing himself early in life. Like offbeat teen-ager Mike, for example.

This boy, a high-school student, was bitter, sullen, and morose. He appeared to be full of unresolved conflicts and hostilities. He had gotten himself into some sort of jam and was summoned to the office of the school administrator. He sat, glum and defiant, waiting, as he later said, to be "chewed out by this guy, this stupid jerk."

But the school administrator was a relaxed man. He sat back in his chair with a kindly but thoughtful expression, studying the mixed-up boy. Finally he said, "Mike, show me your hands." Surprised, Mike held out his hands.

The principal looked searchingly at the hands, then

mused out loud, "Strong, sensitive hands—the hands of a surgeon." Then he said, "Do you know something, Mike? Maybe you were born to be a surgeon. Perhaps there is a great surgeon inside of you. Be seeing you, Mike. Goodbye."

Mike was astonished. It was incredible to him that he should be thus treated. Bewildered, he walked out and down the steps. He stopped and regarded his hands. Then he had one of those incomparable, tremendous experiences that sometimes comes to a human being. He had an experience of awareness. In that moment he determined that he could be a surgeon and that he would be. He had a deep inner intuition of personal qualities never before considered.

What a school principal! How subtle, how understanding. His job was to make men of defeated kids, to help boys know their potential. That is real teaching, real administration.

POWER OF MENTAL CONTROL

Mental control is the secret of mature and creative judgment. Your mind is an instrument designed to serve you, not to destroy you. When uncontrolled, your mind can be very damaging to you, but when controlled it can develop unlimited power. Everywhere men and women are failing simply because they have not mastered their minds. At the same time others do amazing things through the exercise of mental control.

Flying into a certain city, I was met by a stewardess or ground attendant who put me on another flight. I was impressed by this young woman's personality and her power of thought. I asked, "How did you get this way?"

"Because of my husband," she replied, which was a very unusual remark; nowadays husbands are being played down, it seems. She said, "You really ought to meet my husband."

"Well," I replied, "I surely would like to meet him. But what is it about your husband?"

"He has absolute power over his mind," she explained. "He practices mental control. For example, he had an accident, and for a long time he was in pain, but do you know what he did? He dismissed his pain mentally. By mental control he overcame his pain. And he overcomes discouragement and difficulty in the same way. My husband practices mind control and that has made him a very successful person."

"And you do the same?"

She nodded. "Mental control gives power over things that otherwise would defeat you. My husband and I never think of defeat."

Another case of mental control is evidenced in a letter I received from a man who gave his whole life history on one page, cryptically and succinctly. Here it is:

This is a note of report and thanks.

Some years ago I failed miserably. Here's where I stood. Life savings lost. $25,000 in debt. No job—couldn't find one. No income for food or clothing for my family. Had an old car. Lost my home. Moved in with my in-laws. And I had frequent visits by the sheriff taking me to court because of suits by my creditors.

Then I got a few days' job with a public accountant who loaned me your book, *The Power of Positive Thinking*. He said that's what I needed. I read it. It convinced me that I was all wrong mentally and spiritually. My negative, defeatist attitudes were bringing defeat. I turned my life over to God. I went all-out in spiritual revamping. I got a new view of myself. I learned to control my mind.

Now, ten years later—we live in a nice house on a peninsula surrounded by water. I've got an $18,-000 mortgage which I'm paying off. I'm earning a good salary. I have two modestly priced cars. I'm building a savings account. But best of all, I've found myself. And I get a huge kick out of helping people find out who and what they are and who and what they can be. Again, thanks. Sincerely yours.

This man discovered the basic principles of successful achievement; mentally turn away from your failures. Know yourself. Control your mind. Think. Make right decisions. Never accept defeat. Believe in yourself. Mentally accept your great future. Never think of failing. Believe that you can if you think you can.

One effective way of doing a successful thing is to equate with six powerful words. An article which discussed the most important words in the English language suggested such expressions as "Do it," "I am," "Act now," * and others, including the ten so-called greatest words, "To be or not to be, that is the question." But for me the six potent words that can determine the success of any enterprise or, for that matter, any person, are, "Find a need and fill it." Do something that really fills a need and you will find your needs fulfilled.

——— *"Hamlet," by William Shakespeare.

HAMBURGERS ON LONDON'S PARK LANE

Take this fascinating story right out of the now generation as an example.

Would you believe it? Giant hamburgers, mouth-
watering ice cream, and honest-to-goodness American-
style apple pie have taken the youth of London by
storm. Every noon and night they throng the Hard
Rock Cafe on stylish Park Lane in the heart of Mayfair,
at least that is the location as of this writing.

But there's little style to the cafe, simply an eating
establishment set up in a former automobile show-
room—Rolls Royce, no less! No carpets, no hangings,
just tables and chairs; but man, it's real good eating.

And there's something else; spirit—terrific spirit. The
place is packed full of happiness along with plenty of
go-go. If you like hard rock music, here's the place, and
believe me, it's plenty loud. As for me, I sure do go for
the food, but about that rock—well, a little goes a long
way.

Isaac Tigrett, of Jackson, Tennessee, is the young
man responsible for developing this unique enterprise.
When we last saw Issac he was wearing his hair long
and his face was encircled by a full beard. A collection
of chains and medals adorned his chest. He was dressed
in traditional hippie attire.

But he has the touch of a businessman and this goes
for his associates, too. In less than a year, their operation
was deep into the black. But money is not what they
are fundamentally after. Their goal is to find meaning
in life and to do something real for a lot of people.

Isaac's advertisement for waitresses was characteris-
tically untraditional. "No one under 40 need apply.

Must be good old-fashioned, motherly type. Experience doesn't matter." One buxom lady appeared in response to the ad. "You boys looking for a good old Down South gal? I'm her," she grinned. She was hired on the spot. These waitresses love the kids, and vice versa, judging from the spritely banter.

Unable to find ice cream in Britain to meet his exacting Tennessee standards, Isaac experimented and came up with his own brand; and it's out of this world! His grandmother contributed her recipe for apple pie and his mother her salad dressing recipes. Tennessee on Park Lane became the "in" thing in London town.

American soft drinks abound, and scrumptious tall milkshakes get the call from most of the youthful customers.

A few signs around the otherwise barren walls loudly proclaim the merits of Tennessee. But the biggest sign reads: "Marijuana—Assassin of Youth."

The Hard Rock Cafe is a generation gap eliminator. Adults and squares like myself really go for this place. Every kind of dress under the sun shows up. Being somewhat old-fashioned, I had on a sport jacket and tie, but who cared? I wasn't out of it at all. I was accepted even in the uniform of the establishment.

Isaac, and indeed many others of his generation, are pretty deep and thoughtful people. They are thinking through the problems of today, and when anyone really thinks, he is sure to come out O.K. All this is to voice the opinion that, like Isaac Tigrett, long hair or short, we've got some "with-it" young people! They have what it takes to constructively condition their lives. Isaac found a need and filled it. You can, too, if you think you can.

GET YOURSELF ORGANIZED

I have noted in my contacts with all sorts of people that the ones who make the grade creatively, who come up with the greatest accomplishments, are those who might be described as organized individuals. The reference is to inner organization, in which mind, spirit, and purpose operate in harmonious unity. It's the shattered people who fail, since, being unable to focus themselves, everything seems to elude them. Their grasp is weak, their direction vague, their impact uncertain.

To get "pulled together," so that an individual functions with every element of personality operating harmoniously in unified manner, is to ensure successful outcomes. Get a person pulled together and watch with astonishment the metamorphosis.

Take the dispirited salesman I met on an airplane. He was really low. His enthusiasm had entirely run out and no wonder, for he was in a state of miserable conflict, feeling that he was, as he put it, "getting absolutely nowhere, and fast." He poured out quite a depressing accumulation of woes in which self-doubt seemed to be predominant in his thinking. He just didn't believe that he had what it takes, and besides, as he put it, "Isn't salesmanship a low-grade kind of occupation, anyway? What is there to it, just being a peddler?"

"In what type of salesmanship are you engaged?" I asked.

"Oh," he replied, "my employers send me out to make inspirational speeches at sales meetings."

I chuckled. "Boy, some inspiration, judging from the way you've been talking. Your employers certainly must be stupid, sending you out on that assignment."

He really bridled at that. "They're not stupid. They're the smartest men in the business."

"Well, in that case they must see something in you that you do not see, namely, that you have the ability to inspire, to be a motivator, a real leader."

"Now," I continued, "about your estimate of salesmanship. You are away off the beam on that. Without salesmanship our great economy could not have been developed nor could it remain strong. I suggest that every day you stand in front of a mirror and pull yourself up to your full height. Then say aloud: 'I am proud to be a salesman. I'm a trustee of the free enterprise system. I'm vital to the whole process of communication and distribution. I'm a member of one of the greatest, most respected, most important professions in the entire field of business. Without me, a salesman, all scientific progress, all manufacturing of the products needed by people, would cease because distribution depends on me, a salesman, to make goods available to the consumer.' "

After this little speech the discouraged man sat silent for long minutes, it seemed. Then, to my amazement, he asked, "How about saying a prayer for me?"

"Glad to," I said. "I will remember you in my prayers tonight."

"Oh, no, not tonight; right here and now."

So I prayed aloud in a low voice something like this: "Lord, this man is supposed to inspire people, so inspire him. He is low and depressed in spirit. Give him an infusion of enthusiasm. And pull him together; organize and focus his personality. Amen."

"Thanks," he said quietly.

It seemed to register, for some time later I ran into

him at a meeting. With a confident smile he said, "You know something? God and you pulled me together on that airplane."

Well, I was indeed honored to be coupled with the Divine. But anyway, the man got focused. He did not need to fail and he didn't.

Getting what you want from life needs directed motivation. If you want to get somewhere you have to know where you want to go and how to get there. Also, it is vital to know what you want to do and what you can do best. This is part of being focused and organized. And to all this must be added deep desire, a driving force, and the willingness to work, to work, to work— and never, never, never to give up; never to quit. Always remember, "The quitter never wins and the winner never quits." That sort of thing is primary to the person who never thinks of failing and who doesn't intend to.

WHERE DO YOU WANT TO GO?

A few years ago a young man stopped me on the street. "I want to go places and get somewhere," he declared. "How do I do it?"

"Where do you want to go? Name it," I replied.

"Well . . ." he hesitated, ". . . I just don't know exactly where."

"Have you any general idea if you can't make it specific?" I asked.

Still he couldn't define his objective. It was all vague and inconclusive.

So I tried a different tack. "What can you do best? What are your special skills?"

Again, the reply was uncertain. He didn't know exactly what he could do; I gathered he didn't believe he was very competent at anything.

"Well, let's go at it this way," I said. "What do you like to do? If you could have the kind of job you really want, something you could really go for, what would it be?"

Again he shook his head. "Don't believe I've ever given that any thought. I just don't know for sure what I want."

So there we were with a young man who "wanted to go somewhere and get places" but didn't really know where he wanted to go. Moreover, he did not know what he could do or even what he wanted to do. Naturally, I advised him that his first step was to be specific in his goal, to decide what he could do, and to settle upon an objective toward which he could work and then work with dogged perseverance.

But there was no such reaction in the case of a young couple who had a definite goal and reached that goal over great odds. But let the wife tell the story in the following letter which she wrote me:

> When I was in the ninth grade my high school band went to New York City on a trip and on Sunday we heard you speak. That was about fourteen years ago, but that morning was the turning point in my life. I learned there was something in me bigger than I ever thought.
>
> A person's mind is like a river that runs wild if it is not controlled. I learned that a person has to decide what he will stand for and not back down. I became a positive-thinking person.
>
> When I married my husband I knew that he was a wonderful young man with great possibilities!

[How's that for positive thinking?] I just wanted to help him finish college and help him go to law school, and I told him that is what we had to do. [What a wife!]

We had no money, but we had the important thing: God was by our side. We had the desire and believed we could do it. I worked in a clothing factory and sewed for four years. If you have never worked on a quota you wouldn't understand how you have to get your body turned up to a fast rhythm to be able to sew 79 dozen fronts of jeans a day. I won't go into all the hurdles we had to cross to get my husband through law school, but I will say that two years ago we were sleeping on box crates, and we were not hippies, either!

We lived on $200 per month and there were three of us. We have a son who is seven years old. We went through six years of this, but now my husband has passed two bar exams in two different states and has started practicing law on his own. I am his secretary and we are just getting started, but his number one goal is justice and how can we not succeed with God as a partner?

What a girl! She believed in herself and she believed in her husband. They knew they had something in them that they could bring to a realization if they just kept working at it. There was never a thought of defeat. They just kept going.

It is important to realize the need for that kind of fortitude. Keep your courage high. Hang on; keep at it. Don't think of giving up. It may be tough going, but like that young woman and her husband, you can come through if you just remember there's something big to work for. Keep focused on it.

Remember that Lord Beaverbrook's three keys to

success included industry in addition to judgment and health. The driving energy, the vitality that keeps you moving, struggling, everlastingly working toward your goal is so important.

POSITIVE AND DYNAMIC THINKING

A conclusive factor in overcoming any form of failure is dynamic and positive thinking. As we have said elsewhere, the negative thinker, in sending out negative thoughts, activates the world around him negatively and thereby draws back to himself negative results. The positive thinker, on the contrary, sending out positive thoughts, activates his world positively and draws back to himself positive results. As birds of a feather flock together, so do thoughts of a kind have a natural affinity, reproducing according to type. Negative thoughts = negative results; positive thoughts = positive results.

I once heard a psychologist say something to the effect that there is a deep tendency in human nature to become precisely like that which we habitually imagine ourselves to be. The word "imagination" actually implies imaging. As pointed out in an earlier chapter, we become what we picture or image ourselves as being. The self-image, as Dr. Maxwell Maltz * has so well described it, is determinative of what we become.

If that self-image is one of inferiority, inadequacy, and failure, it can be changed, and when it is changed then you will change. The failure concept will give way to the "can do" image of yourself. And as William

_____* *Psycho-Cybernetics*, by Maxwell Maltz (Prentice-Hall, Inc., 1960).

James, famous American thinker, reminded us, the greatest of all discoveries is that human beings can alter their lives by altering their attitudes of mind.

The application of these creative principles to a potential failure situation, thereby reversing it into a spectacularly successful outcome, is illustrated by the development of the widely read inspirational, interfaith magazine, *Guideposts.* This magazine came into being in 1945 following a meeting in which Lowell Thomas, Governor Thomas E. Dewey, Captain Eddie Rickenbacker, Branch Rickey (former owner of the old Brooklyn Dodgers baseball team), and others participated. These men became enthusiastic about the idea of a magazine that would feature the upbeat potentials in human beings. They suggested that I be the editor and get it going. My old friend, Raymond Thornburg, was co-founder.

I responded by acknowledging the honor of being made head of a nonexistent magazine but reminded those present that such a venture required capital and they should be the first to contribute. I was amazed by the alacrity with which it was discovered that the hour was late and everyone had to get home! They all did participate later, very generously, of time and support. But that day I was left as editor of a nonexistent magazine with no money, no subscribers, no equipment, no publishing know-how; which might reasonably be regarded as an unpropitious situation. And I was about to chuck the whole thing.

But the idea of such a publication got hold of me and I was loath to abandon it. Where could I secure some financing? I rummaged through my mind for the name of someone who was wealthy and who at the same time had a generous disposition.

Sadly I discovered that these two factors were rarely found in the same person! However, I did think of a good friend, the newspaper publisher, Frank Gannett, who met the above specifications and gave him a sales talk, as a result of which he made a contribution of seven hundred dollars. With this amount I purchased the "good givers" list and sent out a mailing describing the proposed magazine. The return was good, seven thousand dollars. And with this small amount we started the magazine called *Guideposts*.

It had no advertising then (nor does it have now) so everything depended on volume sales, which grew very slowly indeed. When our subscription list reached twenty thousand our loaned office building, a dwelling house, was destroyed by fire. We had to begin again. Finally the subscription list reached forty thousand, but costs were mounting more rapidly than income and a crisis was reached. We were facing the fact that we might be forced to fold.

At this juncture a meeting of the Board of Directors was called. You may have been in gloomy meetings, but certainly nothing to compare with the abysmal gloom of this one. The directors' thought processes seemed frozen; no ideas were forthcoming. We had invited a woman to this meeting who was not a member of the Board but we included her for the very practical reason that on one previous occasion she had contributed twenty-five hundred dollars to our magazine and we figured, hopefully, that lightning might strike twice in the same place.

But, fully aware of our intent, and being of a sagacious and forthright mind, she said, "I must put you people out of your misery. I am not going to give you another nickel." Well, instead of putting us out of our misery, this remark only plunged us more deeply into it.

AN INSPIRED IDEA BETTER THAN MONEY

"But," she quickly added, "while I will not give you any more cash I will give you something of far greater value than money." At the moment, faced with a stack of bills, we could not imagine anything more important than money. "I will give you a creative and dynamic idea," she said, "and with this idea you can secure all the resources needed to carry on."

She began then to examine the situation, asking how many subscribers were needed to establish the magazine on a sound basis. I did not know for sure, but picked the figure of a hundred thousand out of the air. Since we had forty thousand we needed that extra sixty thousand people for our circulation list if we were to succeed.

"All right," said our amazing friend, "let's face the situation. We are in a condition of lack. We lack everything: money, subscribers, equipment, imagination, ideas. Now just why do we lack?" she demanded. And she supplied the answer to her own question. "We lack for the reason that we have constantly been thinking in terms of lack, so therefore we have created a condition of lack." Astonishing as this appraisal was, we could scarcely argue with it for obviously we did lack, nor could we deny that we had been thinking lack.

"O.K., what can we do about it?" I asked.

"Do about it?" she snorted, "Do about it? Why, stand up to those defeating lack thoughts like men! And tell them to get out of your minds."

"Now, look," I objected, "you can't do that. If you mount a frontal attack on an unhealthy thought pattern instead of exorcising those thoughts, you only tend to drive them more deeply into consciousness. Besides," I ended lamely, "we don't control our thoughts; our thoughts control us."

Was I to learn something! In fact, what then happened revolutionized my own thought attitudes.

I shall never forget the disgust with which the lady regarded me. "I'm amazed," she declared, "at such a weak, willy-nilly reaction. Don't you remember what the great Plato said?"

Well, frankly I hadn't the slightest idea what the great Plato said. But not wanting to reveal my ignorance, I asked brightly, "To which of the many familiar quotations of Plato do you refer?"

"I refer," she shot back, "to the one you never heard." I shall never forget hearing this astonishing woman quote what she said Plato said: "Take charge of your thoughts. You can do what you will with them."

And that is true for a fact, as I began to see. We are not meant to be worms crawling defeated in the presence of a difficult situation. We are men, women, children of God with minds for thinking. We can indeed take charge of our thoughts and do what we will with them. And that is what happened in this instance.

"How do we go about it?" I inquired.

"Spend fifteen minutes right now," she admonished, "flushing out those lack thoughts." Presently she declared, "All right, your minds are empty, which I must admit didn't take very long. But the mind will not perpetually remain empty. And those lack thoughts are hanging around waiting for the chance to creep back into your minds where for so long they have been hospitably entertained. So we must keep them displaced by filling the mind with dynamic prosperity thoughts.

"I want you to look out there in your creative imagination and see or image a hundred thousand people reading our magazine and," she added, business-wise, "who have paid for their subscriptions."

I responded, appearing to look out into the distance, "Frankly, they look mighty dim to me."

SEE AND IMAGE AND HAVE

Then I happened to look into the woman's eyes—big, black, snapping eyes—and as I did so a phrase crossed my mind: "The exalted look of the believer." And in her eyes I "saw" mirrored those hundred thousand subscribers. Becoming excited, I leaped to my feet. "I see them, I see them," I shouted.

"Ah, isn't that great," she exclaimed. "Now that we see them we have them."

Startled, I asked, "What's that?"

"Oh, yes,"she said firmly, "now that we can image them we, in effect, have them."

Then, surprisingly, she demanded, "Now let us thank God that He has given us a hundred thousand subscribers." In her prayer she did not ask God for anything; she thanked Him for everything. She also repeated a Bible statement: "Whatsoever ye shall ask in prayer, believing, ye shall receive." * Well, I became so stimulated that I could hardly wait for her to stop praying, and then I leaped to my feet and looked down at where that stack of bills had been—and there they still were.

_____* Matthew 21:22.

I guess in my exuberance I thought the Lord would come down in some sweet chariot and take all those bills away. But that isn't the way He works. When He wants to change a situation it is not done in some magical way. He changes people, and changed people change situations. And that is precisely what happened.

Our directors became unfrozen, terrifically motivated, and they began to throw ideas rapidly onto the table. Of course, ninety percent of them were no good, but ten percent were, and with those the magazine began to move. Today, *Guideposts* subscribers number well over two and a quarter million. And the magazine is taken by nearly three thousand firms for employees. It has become perhaps the greatest inspirational, nonprofit, interfaith publication in the United States, read by some six million persons monthly.

I do not recite this story to advertise *Guideposts,** although I do willingly welcome the incidental by-product of any illustration I may happen to use. This thrilling narrative is given here because it so well illustrates a basic law of successful achievement. My reader will recognize that the principles outlined here have also been stressed in other chapters. But basic are the following points:

    1. Formulate a goal; not a fuzzy, vague goal, but one that is sharp, clearly defined and specific—very specific.

    2. Pray about that goal to be sure it is right, for if it isn't right, it's wrong, and nothing wrong ever turns out right.

    3. Put that goal into your conscious mind, holding the image there tenaciously until it sinks

_____* *Guideposts,* published at Carmel, New York 10512

*into the unconscious. And when it does you
will have it, because it has you—all there is of
you.*

4. *Then give it all you've got of thought, effort,
   imagination, and innovation.*
5. *Work, and then work, and then work.*
6. *Never, never, never give up—keep it going, going, going—know that you can if you think
   you can.*
7. *Tell yourself every day of your life until you
   believe it away down deep that you shall never
   think of failing. You don't need to.*

ELEVEN

❧

ALL THE RESOURCES YOU NEED
ARE IN YOUR MIND

All the resources you need are in your mind. They are established in consciousness waiting to be summoned.

I will never forget the time I discovered that fact. It was worth a tough crisis experience to emerge with that truth which has served me well ever since. As a very young man, not long out of college, I found myself one day in a predicament requiring some fast thinking.

It was some years after the end of World War I. As the American Legion's chaplain for Kings County, New York, I was asked to give an invocation at a Memorial Day meeting on a May Sunday afternoon in Brooklyn's Prospect Park.

A big crowd was expected, but I figured I could handle the few sentences of an invocation even though I was very young and inexperienced. I did not reckon, however, on the huge crowd that gathered for that occasion or the situation that I was to face. Approaching the designated area of Prospect Park, I asked a police officer how many people were there. "Oh," he said, "about fifty thousand."

I proceeded to the platform and introduced myself to the chief speaker of the day, former President Theodore Roosevelt's son, Colonel Theodore Roosevelt, Jr.,

who later served in World War II with the rank of
general and died on the beaches of Normandy. I informed him casually that I was scheduled to give the
invocation.

Then I sat down, picked up the program and examined it. To my consternation I saw that I wasn't listed
for an invocation at all. Instead, believe it or not, I was
down for a speech just preceding Colonel Roosevelt's
talk. The program read, "Address by Norman Vincent
Peale, Chaplain of the Americar Legion of Kings
County." I gulped. Indeed, I froze. I had no speech
prepared. What was I to do?

I rushed over to the master of ceremonies and chattered, "There's been a big mistake. I was asked only to
give an invocation, but look at this program; you have
me down for a speech."

"Well," he said, matter-of-factly, "if you are down for
a speech I guess you will just have to give one."

"But," I protested, "I just can't do that. To make a
speech you have to be prepared, and I'm not. It's just
not possible. Besides, look at that big crowd. Somebody
else will have to speak in my place."

COLONEL ROOSEVELT TAKES ME IN HAND

Colonel Roosevelt, who overheard this conversation,
looked me over appraisingly. "What's the matter, son?"
he asked. "Are you afraid?"

"Afraid? That's not the half of it!" I frankly acknowledged. "A huge crowd like this is enough to scare the
life out of me! And anyway, how can I think up a speech
in the next few minutes? It just isn't in the cards."

"Oh, yes, it is," he answered, "and I'll tell you how.

For one thing, stop telling yourself that you're scared and start thinking courage. Practice affirming confidence. And another thing, I'd suggest that you stop thinking of yourself. Come over here with me a minute."

He led the way to the front of the platform and drew my attention to a big section of reserved seats all occupied by women. "Do you know who those women are?" he asked.

"They are Gold Star Mothers. That means that every one of them lost a son in the war.

"They are sitting here on this Memorial Day afternoon thinking of beloved sons who aren't with them anymore. Maybe they are remembering the days when those sons were little boys who had to be held by the hand, sometimes had to be coaxed to sleep at night. They miss their boys. They have their sorrow. They are lonely and sad.

"Isn't there anything you can say to these Gold Star Mothers? You certainly can love them. Forget yourself and start feeling compassion for those wonderful mothers. Then get up and give a talk just for them. Forget everyone else in this crowd if you want to. What you say to those mothers will reach everyone here.

"You can do it," he asserted. Then came that powerful statement that has remained with me ever since, one of the greatest of all truths. Colonel Roosevelt said, "Look, Norman, all the resources you need are in your mind. Sure, you can do it by just drawing on them. That speech is right there in that mind of yours. Relax, start thinking, and it will come to you."

And he threw me two final words: "Think courage." He hit me sort of affectionately on the back.

I drew a deep breath and said, "All right, Colonel, I'll try. But it's going to be a very short speech."

"The shorter it is," he grinned, "the better it will be. But put your whole self into it. Send out love to those people and you will shake off that fear of yours."

So I made my little speech. When I finished and sat down Colonel Roosevelt leaned over and clapped me on the knee. "Boy, that was great! You rang the bell!" I am sure it wasn't very great and the bell didn't ring very loudly, but of course I have remembered that great man with affection ever since.

He was right about one thing. When you rely on your mind it will deliver, provided you've put something into it. And that is doubly true when you forget yourself and sincerely try to do something to make life happier for other people.

Forget yourself! Think courage. Believe that all the resources you need are in your mind. That is a formula that works, really works.

When we say that all the resources you need are in your mind we are not suggesting that the dependence is solely upon mechanical mentality. The Divine force is in the mind, and it is only in mind that a human being can have contact with God. A drawing upon spiritual power takes place through the intellect, through the ability to think and believe. Therefore the greatest of all resources, that of God power, is available through a spiritually controlled operation of the thought processes.

When the Bible says, "The kingdom of God is within you," * it is asserting that in essence all of God's power and truth are built into you. And just where in you? Where else but in your mind! Obviously, then, the principle that all the resources you need are in your mind profoundly takes account of spiritual resources.

___* Luke 17:21.

When anyone can be persuaded to think spiritually, to have faith and to believe, then the mind, being motivated to a higher level, opens to maximum strength and the amazing powers it possesses go to work on situations to bring about good results.

HE KICKS DRUGS

In a magazine article entitled "Back from Happy Town," * Daniel Negris substantiates these resource principles. Negris was a genius at the piano from childhood. He started working with dance bands at fifteen, and in his late teens and early twenties he played with Coleman Hawkins, Henry Jerome, Ben Webster, Red Norvo, Dizzy Gillespie, and Billie Holliday, reputed to be among the best-known jazz musicians in the United States. Well, one night this youngster Negris was with a saxophonist, an older man, who reached into his shirt pocket and pulled out a long, slender cigarette and gave it to Daniel, saying, "C'mon, man, get with it."

The boy knew at once that it was marijuana. He did not want to show how inexperienced he was, so he took a long drag on it. Nothing happened at first. Then he began to feel numb from his toes up through his legs and into the upper part of his body. And it seems that once you begin, you feel you've got to smoke this weed. He got so he smoked between jobs, smoked in the morning, smoked at night, smoked at all hours.

Then he tried heroin, which, he says, has a different effect from "pot" smoking. He got so he could not control himself and he did not care. The junkies assured

_____* *Guideposts* (January 1968).

him that is how it works—so he should "keep cool." He would arrive late for work and be very "high" much too often. The bandleader, disgusted, fired him. He lost job after job. While he had not used heroin enough to become a true addict, he had sampled too much, he says, to break completely free. He realized he needed help, but didn't know where to turn.

Each time Daniel went on a tour his mother put a Bible among his clothes in his suitcase. He never read the Bible—he just let it remain in his bag out of deference to her. Then one night in his hotel room he felt so low that he almost wanted to die. At twenty-three he felt he was through, washed up, finished. And as he sat staring at the blank walls of that cheap hotel room he thought of the Bible. He took it out of the suitcase and flipped through the pages until finally he saw and read the words of Matthew 11:28: "Come unto me, all ye that labor and are heavy laden, and I will give you rest."

Suddenly, in compulsive terror of what he had fallen into, he jumped up, took his supply of drugs and washed them down the drain. Trembling, he fell to his knees, wept, and then prayed. Immediately, he says, he was filled with Christ's Spirit, felt cleansed and overwhelmed by God's love. And he writes: "I have never touched drugs since that night; amazingly enough, my flight from 'happy town' has been total."

This amazing ability to kick the drug habit in one minute of time dramatically underscores the powers inherently resident in the mind. When activated by a desperate need, an overwhelming desire and a powerful surge of faith and belief, they come forth to produce dramatic results. Always waiting in the mind and ready to help you, whatever your need, are those resources which are releasable by the astonishing combination of faith and thought.

NEVER BUILD A CASE AGAINST YOURSELF

What gives a person inner strength in crisis? It is, of course, belief, coupled with thought-releasing mind resources. Referring again to William James, famed philosopher and psychologist, he taught that belief creates the actual fact! It is therefore most important to keep the mind free of disbelief and eliminate negative thoughts.

Years ago an old friend, Robert Rowbottom, gave me one of the most powerful truths I have ever received. It was this: Never build a case against yourself. It is only natural sometimes to feel overwhelmed by problems and difficulties. In fact, they may be so tough that we contemplate giving up. At that moment always remember the encouraging fact that all the resources you need are in your mind; that you have within you the capacity to handle anything that comes at you. Again, remember: Never build a case against yourself. Stop minimizing yourself. Realize you are greater than you've ever considered yourself to be. And don't wait to be faced with a crisis before you realize and use the power that is in you. Use your mental resources every day in every situation. Then you will be ready to use them in a crisis. Like Frank, for instance.

Frank really knew how to handle a rough situation. He demonstrated that mental outlook can be determinative of one's future when a crisis develops.

He telephoned one day. "How are things?" I asked.

"O.K.," he replied, then added casually, "I've lost my job."

I was amazed at his matter-of-fact reaction. He had occupied a top-level position in his company and I knew that his superiors appreciated his work performance. Indeed, everything seemed to assure him a promising future. But, as sometimes happens, intra-company political maneuvering developed and he was, with another young executive, suddenly let out. "Just like that," he said, "out, on the street, both of us."

Expressing regret and concern, I suggested we talk over his problem. But he said that he only wanted me to know about his situation and "to do some positive thinking" about him. "I'll do all right," he asserted confidently.

"I sure do admire your spirit," I told him, "but what are you going to do?"

"I don't know exactly, yet. When I've had a chance to do some constructive thinking I'll let you know. Right now I'm looking for new ideas. Believe me, I'm drawing on all the resources my head contains."

This conversation took place several years ago. And the different ways in which things worked out for the two ousted young executives provide an interesting example of how mental outlook can determine a person's future career.

Our man Frank reasoned on a positive basis: "I'm going to take the attitude that this misfortune can turn into good fortune. I'm going to believe that every disadvantage can be turned into an advantage." Beyond that he practiced being objective and unresentful. He got busy doing some solid thinking. He discovered new qualities within himself. As a consequence he moved away from the past toward the better future in which he had conditioned himself confidently to believe.

His thinking gave him an idea. Ideas are bound to come if you really think. Anyone can think himself out of any difficulty, even the hardest problems. The idea he put into operation was to write a letter to a hundred executives of local companies. It was a brief, business-like letter that went somewhat as follows: "Since every business organization brings in new personnel from time to time, perhaps your company could use a man like me. The summary enclosed will give you an idea of my background, my experience, my training and my abilities. I have some weak points, too, which I have frankly enumerated. But I honestly think my strengths outweigh the weaknesses. So if by chance you need someone with my particular qualifications and experience, perhaps you may want to follow it up with an interview . . ." and he added optimistically, "before someone buys my services."

Believe it or not, this forthright letter appealed to some of the employers and it resulted in several job offers. The one he accepted landed him in a better position than his previous post. And the creativity he brought to the job led to steady advancement. By a positive mental attitude he found the advantage that is always present in a disadvantage.

What about the other fellow who lost his job at the same time? Well, at first he did not fare so well. Angered and bitter, he went on a sulking jag, spending his time hating and worrying and drinking heavily. Result? He worked himself into an incipient nervous break-down. But he came out of it finally and shook off the negativisms and resentments. He, too, started cultivating a positive mental attitude. He took a job far below his basic qualifications, but is beginning to move ahead in direct relation to his changed attitude. But think of the time and possible opportunities he lost.

WHAT ABOUT SETBACKS?

Charles F. Kettering, the great inventive genius, once remarked, "I am not interested in the past. I am interested only in the future, for that is where I expect to spend the rest of my life." And remember, that future where you are to spend the rest of your life is determined by your outlook. You'll find all the resources for it in your mind.

Naturally, setbacks come to everyone. And sure, you can have a rough time of it. Who doesn't? But as you develop and hold the thought that any adversity can actually be turned to your advantage, you then have an immense mental asset going for you. Concentrate on the fact that your future is not determined by circumstances over which you have no control, but by proper mental outlook over which you do have control. Thus, you truly can shape your own future.

The question is: How do you get that right mental outlook? The answer is to start developing what is called rightness in thinking. Start siphoning off the error in your mind. For error results in wrong thinking, which in turn results in wrong action, which produces wrong outcomes. The only remedy for error is rightness. And this requires a quality of study and thought that will in time develop keener insight and perceptiveness. Then that better outlook will create the conditions of a better future.

Since the mind is a vast reservoir of needed resources, it follows that any kind of foreign matter that may block off the orderly flow of those resources will need to be eliminated. No doubt the explanation of much frustration and failure may be attributed to those blocks to the free passage of creative thought which have been permitted to lodge in the mind. Thus, the tremendous resources needed to accomplish the job well or even to live well are dammed up and cannot get through.

"EVERYTHING GOES WRONG BECAUSE I'M WRONG"

In this connection I often think of an old friend; Louis is his name. He had a great many ups and downs, mostly downs, I must say. But finally the ups began to take over and he became an "up" type of individual. But during the earlier stages he used to be on my doorstep quite often, and always he was complaining about the tough breaks that seemed to plague him. "Why?" he asked. "Just why does everything always go wrong for me? Am I that dumb that I can't seem to get right results? What's wrong with me, that everything keeps on going wrong? And besides," he added, concluding his tale of woe, "I've got some pain."

"Pain?" I echoed, surprised. "That's strange, for you look healthy enough."

"Oh, I don't mean physical pain. What I'm talking about is a kind of what you might call mental pain. I'm hurting in my thoughts." It was a curiously apt psychological diagnosis, and it amazed me, for I really didn't think Louis was capable of that grade of insight and the ability to describe such a phenomenon.

He was always coming around for what the professionals call "counseling," but since I'm not in that business I shunted him off to those better able to deal with such problems and who, unlike myself, had time available for long personal interviews. It seemed to me that Louis was constantly playing the same old "frustrated failure" record.

However, that "pain in the mind" was a matter for concern. It occurred to me to tell him about a curious series of events which Lowell Thomas had related to me. It was about a man in New England who went to a dentist about twenty-five years ago. In the treatment the tip of a drill broke. The dentist fished for it carefully and thought all pieces were recovered. However, without any supposition that there was any connection with the dental experience, this man months later began to feel some slight pain in his neck. Much later the pain transferred to the shoulder. Years later the pain appeared in the arm, which finally was X-rayed and a small object removed which proved to be a fragment of the drill. Now I have no way of checking the medical facts of that case, but I used it to point out to Louis that perhaps he had dropped something into his mind that had created some "infection" in his thoughts.

"It could be some off-color deal," I observed.

"Well, I've done plenty," he honestly admitted. I told him about Dr. Sara Jordan of the Lahey Clinic, who said, "Every day give yourself a mental shampoo."

"O.K., Louis, better get it cleaned up, whatever it is," I advised. He knew what it was, all right. He did clean it up. The "mental pain" passed. While he felt better, still he continued to perform ineffectively. And he also continued to contact me with the old plaint, "What is the matter with me? Why do so many things go wrong?"

It so happened that one afternoon I left my office to drive about a hundred miles to a speaking engagement in Pennsylvania. I intended driving alone to have opportunity to think over my speech on the way. But just as I was about to enter my car, who should appear but Louis! I explained that it was impossible to talk, as there was just enough time to make my engagement. "I'll go along, if you don't mind," he volunteered, meanwhile climbing into the car.

"O.K.," I agreed, a bit reluctantly, "you drive so I can work on my talk."

But I couldn't shut him up. He talked about himself all during the one-hundred-mile journey. After my speaking engagement we started back and he continued talking. And it was the same old tune: "Why does everything go wrong for me?"

Along about midnight I suggested we stop at an attractive diner for a cup of coffee and a hamburger sandwich. We perched on stools, started eating our sandwiches, and then it happened. Suddenly banging his fist down on the counter, making the silver and dishes rattle, he shouted, "I see it, I see it! Why have I been so dumb? Now I know why everything goes wrong with me; it's because I'm wrong myself!"

People turned to stare, but that didn't faze Louis at all. He was really excited by what must have been an extraordinary and flashing self-revelation. All the way home he was riding on air, literally—so much so that I had to slow down his driving speed a couple of times. I told him I never realized there was that much power in a hamburger to effect so overwhelming a change in a person.

But he was now perceptive. "The power was not in the hamburger," he said. "The power came through my mind. It was like a curtain drawn aside and for one second I saw into myself. But believe me, that one second was enough for me to see that there is more in that brain of mine than I knew. Now you just watch me get going." And get going he did. Oh, he made many mistakes and flubbed a few things, but his direction had changed because he had changed.

Gradually he began to do much better. In fact, I was often amazed by the capacity he revealed. He now had a grip on himself. His attitudes were positive; his thinking sharp and creative. He had discovered that all the resources he needed were in his mind.

Louis died young, but the last dozen years of his short life left a memory of a man who really found himself. His experience proved that an insight into the great resources of the mind, whether instantaneous or gradual or through the guidance of some wise person, is a powerful supportive experience in dealing with problems.

THE TWO SADDEST WORDS IN ANY LANGUAGE

Arthur Gordon,* one of America's outstanding writers, outlines an extremely valid process through which he found deepened insight into the vast resources inherent in the mind:

> Nothing in life is more exciting and rewarding than the sudden flash of insight that leaves you a changed person—not only changed, but changed for the better. Such moments are rare, certainly, but they come to all of us.
> That wintry afternoon in Manhattan, waiting in

_____* "Two Words to Avoid, Two to Remember" (Reader's Digest, January 1968).

the little French restaurant, I was feeling frustrated and depressed. Because of several miscalculations on my part, a project of considerable importance in my life had fallen through. Even the prospect of seeing a dear friend (the Old Man, as I privately and affectionately thought of him) failed to cheer me as it usually did. I sat there frowning at the checkered tablecloth, chewing the bitter cud of hindsight.

He came across the street, finally, muffled in his ancient overcoat, shapeless felt hat pulled down over his bald head, looking more like an energetic gnome than an eminent psychiatrist. His offices were nearby; I knew he had just left his last patient of the day. He was close to 80, but he still carried a full case load, still acted as director of a large foundation, still loved to escape to the golf course whenever he could.

"Well, young man," he said without preliminary, "what's troubling you?"

I had long since ceased to be surprised at his perceptiveness. So I proceeded to tell him, at some length, just what was bothering me. With a kind of melancholy pride, I tried to be very honest. I blamed no one else for my disappointment, only myself. I analyzed the whole thing, all the bad judgments, the false moves. I went on for perhaps 15 minutes. When I finished, he said, "Come on, let's go back to my office. I want your reaction to something."

The Old Man took a tape from a flat cardboard box and fitted it onto the machine. "On this tape," he said, "are three short recordings made by three persons who came to me for help. They are not identified, of course. I want you to listen to the recordings and see if you can pick out the two-word phrase that is the common denominator in all three cases." He smiled. "Don't look so puzzled. I have my reasons."

What the owners of the voices on the tape had in common, it seemed to me, was unhappiness. The man who spoke first evidently had suffered some kind of business loss or failure; he berated himself for not having worked harder, for not having looked ahead. The woman who spoke next had never married because of a sense of obligation to her widowed mother; she recalled bitterly all the marital chances she had let go by. The third voice belonged to a mother whose teen-age son was in trouble with the police; she blamed herself endlessly.

The Old Man switched off the machine and leaned back in his chair. "Six times in those recordings a phrase is used that's full of subtle poison. Did you spot it? No? Well, perhaps that's because you used it three times yourself down in the restaurant a little while ago." He picked up the box that had held the tape and tossed it over to me. "There they are, right on the label. The two saddest words in any language."

I looked down. Printed neatly in red ink were the words: *If only.*

"You'd be amazed," said the Old Man, "if you knew how many thousands of times I've sat in this chair and listened to woeful sentences beginning with those two words. 'If only,' they say to me, 'I had done it differently—or not done it at all. If only I hadn't lost my temper, said that cruel thing, made that dishonest move, told that foolish lie. If only I had been wiser, or more unselfish, or more self-controlled.' They go on and on until I stop them. Sometimes I make them listen to the recordings you just heard. 'If only,' I say to them, 'you'd stop saying *if only*, we might begin to get somewhere!' "

The Old Man stretched out his legs. "The trouble with 'if only,' " he said, "is that it doesn't change anything. It keeps the person facing the wrong way—backward instead of forward. It wastes time. In the end, if you let it become a habit, it can become a real roadblock, an excuse for not trying anymore.

"Now take your own case: Your plans didn't work out. Why? Because you made certain mistakes. Well, that's all right: Everyone makes mistakes. Mistakes are what we learn from. But when you were telling me about them, lamenting this, regretting that, you weren't really learning from them."

"How do you know?" I said, a bit defensively.

"Because," said the Old Man, "you never got out of the past tense. Not once did you mention the future. And in a way—be honest, now!—you were enjoying it. There's a perverse streak in all of us that makes us like to hash over old mistakes. After all, when you relate the story of some disaster or disappointment that has happened to you, you're still the chief character, still in the center of the stage."

I shook my head ruefully. "Well, what's the remedy?"

"Shift the focus," said the Old Man promptly. "Change the key words and substitute a phrase that supplies lift instead of creating drag."

"Do you have such a phrase to recommend?"

"Certainly. Strike out the words 'if only'; substitute the phrase 'next time.' "

"Next time?"

"That's right. I've seen it work minor miracles right here in this room. As long as a patient keeps saying 'if only' to me, he's in trouble. But when he looks me in the eye and says 'next time,' I know he's on his way to overcoming his problem. It means he has decided to apply the lessons he has learned from his experience, however grim or painful it may have been. It means he's going to push aside the roadblock of regret, move forward, take action, resume living. Try it yourself. You'll see."

My old friend stopped speaking. Outside, I could hear the rain whispering against the windowpane. I tried sliding one phrase out of my mind and replacing it with the other. It was fanciful, of course, but I could hear the new words lock into place with an audible click.

More than a year has passed since that rainy afternoon in Manhattan. But to this day, whenever I find myself thinking "if only," I change it to "next time." Then I wait for that almost-perceptible mental click. And when I hear it, I think of the Old Man.

The "if only" attitude leads to a dull and uninspired reaction to things. But "next time" signifies a positive and courageous attack on problems. Drop the "if only" concept, pick up the "next time" idea, and you will have the ability to do your best and move ahead unhampered by whatever happens.

Live a day at a time and do a job at a time. Then go on to the next time. That makes sense. But, unhappily, lots of people don't do that. Instead, they live in the past, present, and future all at the same time. And that doesn't make sense. What an error to waste mental energy brooding over past events or worrying about problems that might develop at some future time and then again might not. The successful person learns to live in the present only, but always headed toward next time.

SKIP THE POST-MORTEMS

The futility of post-mortems was forcefully impressed upon me when I first began making speeches. I would make a careful outline, know my material, and then speak without notes, standing out free and clear of a speaker's stand, as I have continued doing. This gives a direct, two-way communication and closer relationship to the audience. But as a young man, after every speech I would start agonizing inwardly over stupid things I had said or clever things I might have said but didn't.

"Why did I ever say that?" I would exclaim, getting hot all over. Or, "If only I had said . . . ." Sometimes hours later I would still be harping on all the slips, faults, and flubs, mentally kicking myself for being so inept.

One day an older man, a well-known speaker to whom I mentioned the misery of these experiences, gave me some sound advice: "When you speak, do your best while you are at it, but when you have finished your speech, walk off the platform and forget it. Your audience probably will—so why not make it unanimous?"

It was good advice. Never get hung-up on "if only." Forget it and get ready for the next time.

If you carry around in your mind from one day to the

next a load of dejection because things haven't gone as well as you had hoped, you will run completely out of energy.

"Finish every day and be done with it," wrote Emerson. "You have done what you could. Some blunders and absurdities no doubt crept in; forget them as soon as you can. Tomorrow is a new day; begin it well and serenely and with too high a spirit to be cumbered with your old nonsense. This day is all that is good and fair. It is too dear, with its hopes and invitations, to waste a moment on yesterdays." That is advice worth heeding.

These thoughts remind me of a painful occasion when I spoke to a big industrial convention one night in New Jersey. It was on a February 12, back when they had the antiquated habit of celebrating Lincoln's birthday on the anniversary of the day he was born, instead of a device to get a longer weekend! I was asked to speak on Lincoln.

I went out on a suburban train and was going over my speech when a man sitting alongside and observing my notes asked if I was in the speaking business, adding that he was also. In fact, he said, "I'm the main speaker tonight at a convention," naming the same organization to which I was scheduled to speak.

"That's odd," I said. "I thought I was the main speaker at that affair." We both laughed and decided we were a double-header.

He pulled a folder from his pocket which advertised him as the "World's greatest humorist—the funniest man alive." "Boy, you must be good," I commented. "I sure don't want to follow you, so I hope I go on first."

Arriving at the ballroom, we found twelve hundred people at dinner. The program listed my newfound

friend as the first speaker; then I was to come along
with my Lincoln talk. The master of ceremonies went
all-out in his introduction, telling how funny this humorist was. "Hang onto your seats, folks, or you'll roll
in the aisles. This man will rock you. You've never
laughed like you're going to laugh tonight. I present for
your hilarious entertainment the world's greatest
humorist—the funniest man alive!"

I felt that he was building our friend up a bit too
much. There is a fine line to be drawn in such introduc-
tions. Build a speaker up to a reasonable point and the
audience is impressed and tends to like him. But going
beyond that point and overplaying him may turn off the
audience's favorable attitude and into a sort of "Oh,
yeah?" reaction. And that is what happened in this instance.

The humorist opened with what I was sure was one
of his best jokes and got a fair laugh but short of a
full-bodied one. With each succeeding joke the laughter was less, dropping at times to mere titters. I laughed
as loudly as I could, trying to get it going. With perspira-
tion streaming down his face, the humorist said to me
out of the corner of his mouth, "Sure is a tough crowd.
Boy, this is terrible."

There is a curious psychology between an audience
and a speaker. One night your speech will go over with
power; there is a marvelous rapport between the
speaker and the audience, and enthusiasm fills the air.
Then the next time—same type of audience—same
speaker—same jokes—same speech; yet the same feeling isn't there. As long as I have been speaking to audiences everywhere, I've never been able to figure this
subtle chemistry.

Well, the humorist finally ground to a stop and re-

ceived hardly more than a polite hand. On the basis of
the reaction to his jokes, I decided to use none at all,
although I have a few sure-fire, time-tested stories. Instead I decided to be dead serious. But, alas, my experience, though in reverse, was no better—the audience
laughed at my serious remarks.

Perspiring and chastened, the humorist and I took
the train back to the city. But he was a wise man. "No
post-mortems," he said. "This engagement is past. Only
thing is to forget it. No 'if only's.' Have you a speaking
date tomorrow night?" When I told him Yes, he said
he did also. "And that's good, real good," he added
sturdily. "Never stick around mentally with a defeat.
It's the next time that counts."

Well, this delightful man has gone on now, but I
never forgot him, nor his philosophy of bypassing "if
only" and going for "next time." He was really a great
person and one of the best humorists I ever heard, for
I spoke with him later on several occasions. He had a
line open to the resources in the mind, and they served
him well.

PEOPLE DO AMAZING THINGS

If we develop greater appreciation of the immense
resources built into the mind, we can do amazing things
—even greater than we dare to imagine. What a person
can be and what he can do is largely determined by the
degree of self-limitation which he mentally imposes on
himself. If he images himself on a restrictive level, the
flow of resources from the mind will be reduced and
maintained at a trickle of the full potential. If, on the
contrary, his image of himself and his possibilities is

comprehensive and exact, the volume of resource power from the mind will be correspondingly larger. A certain degree of boldness is required of the individual who wishes to make more of himself. Boldness is an activator of power from the mind. As an author once said, "Go at it boldly, and you'll find unexpected forces closing round you and coming to your aid." * The mind, ever the willing servant, will respond to boldness, for boldness, in effect, is a command to deliver mental resources. Boldly expect, and the power will come through.

If you don't think you can draw upon power resources, read this story.

At a Chinese dinner in Taipei, Taiwan, I met an old friend, Gladys Aylward, a lady diminutive in stature but powerful in mind. I noticed that, while seated, her feet did not touch the floor. She was dressed in Chinese costume, even though British, quite British. Born in the Cockney section of London of a poor family, she worked as a maid in the home of a wealthy man.

One day in London, she came upon a Salvation Army street meeting. Attracted by the music, she stopped and listened to the message of the speaker. For some reason she decided right then and there to become a missionary. But how could a poor, uneducated girl accomplish that objective?

Her employer, who had a splendid library on China, found her reading and reproached her. "I hired you to dust and clean, not to read my books," he said.

"But, sir," she explained, "I am so interested in China. Please let me read your books."

_____* *The Conquest of Fear,* by Basil King (New York: Doubleday and Company, Inc., 1948).

"Very well, but not until after you get the housework done," he replied.

She continued to read until she became a sort of living encyclopedia on China. And then she felt the compulsion to become a missionary to that country. She applied to the Mission Board, whose officials were highly intellectual ecclesiastics. They gave this sincere girl an educational test which she could not pass. "You do not measure up to our standards; sorry, you can't go," they told her.

But did that faze her? Not at all. She saved her money shilling by shilling, and finally went out to China on her own. She began to speak in the streets of Nanking and Peking. So remarkable was the career of Gladys Aylward that, years later, a motion picture was made of it called, "Inn of the Sixth Happiness." And it was a hit picture.

This little Gladys Aylward, a personality filled with concentrated power, told me about how she spoke in the streets, telling the people that no power on earth could overcome the believer, that God was always with him.

This type of speaking went on week after week in many Chinese cities. And it finally put her to the most dramatic test of her life.

SHE TAKES THE CRIMINAL'S BLOODY KNIFE

One day the governor of the province sent for her and said, "We have a terrible situation. There is a riot in the prison. Murderers and vicious men have overcome the guards and are running amuck. We can't go in; they will kill any guard who tries to enter. And one of the worst criminals in the prison has gone completely berserk. He is wielding a huge meat cleaver and has already killed two men and terrified everyone. I know you, for I have heard you speak. You have a God who gives all power. Please go in and disarm that man."

"You must be out of your mind, sir," she said, aghast.

"But I have listened to you in the street telling that your God is always with you."

"But, Excellency, you misunderstand."

"Oh, then you have not been telling the truth. I only know what I heard you say, and I believed you."

She realized then that if she ever hoped to influence the Chinese people she would have to go into that prison and demonstrate her belief.

Gladys Aylward walked through the tunnel, was admitted to the prison yard, and the gate quickly locked behind her. She saw the madman, wielding the meat cleaver dripping with blood, wildly running about, everyone desperately trying to get out of his way. Suddenly he was in front of her. He stopped short, amazed. They stood facing one another—the little woman and the incensed giant.

She looked into his wild and feverish eyes, held out her small hand and calmly said, "Give me that weapon." He hesitated, bewildered—then meekly handed the meat cleaver to her. She told the prisoners she would plead for clemency if they would surrender. And, strangely enough, they did as she asked. Later she helped arrange with the governor a just settlement of their grievances. What a spiritual power demonstration of the principle, you can if you think you can!

Your problem of course may never be even a fraction as dramatic as that which Gladys Aylward had to handle. But never forget that there is a power in you that can be summoned in any situation. Maltbie D. Babcock said: "The tests of life are to make, not break us." And nothing can break you when you have going for you the powerful resources of your mind.

Finally, let's sum up some of the principles stated in this chapter:

1. *Believe that you have inherent in your mind all the resources you will ever need.*

2. *Build up your resources inventory by faith and know-how.*

3. *Remember that spiritual power activates your forces of mind and spirit.*

4. *Never minimize your ability to think your way through any situation.*

5. *If power isn't coming through, find the block and remove it.*

6. *Keep alert for those flashes of insight which come when you're really thinking.*

7. *Skip "if only"; concentrate on "next time."*

8. *Never bog down in a defeat psychology. Always, in the midst of defeat, keep looking for victory.*

9. *Be bold, and mighty powers will come to your aid.*

10. *The tests of life are not to break you but to make you.*

TWELVE

WAYS TO FOSTER HEALTH, VITALITY, ALIVENESS

A woman in her thirties, sickly and frail, went from physician to physician haunting their offices. Despite the efforts of competent doctors she continued in slow decline. Whether she had something really wrong with her, or was ill of a sick psychosis which drove her obsessively from doctor to doctor always looking for an illusive assurance of health, the fact remained that she got worse rather than better.

Then she encountered another form of treatment. She heard a speaker discuss the power of the mind in the healing process. For the first time this woman became aware that spiritual healing is a scientific use of thinking, not only in psychological problems but also in actual physical conditions.

It was pointed out that the "life force" can be either stimulated or depressed by attitudes of mind, including faith. The talk was given not by a "faith healer" but by a scientifically conditioned teacher who had made a study of the effect of thought upon mental and physical states. This was in the early days of a science that has become highly sophisticated and generally respected under the term, psychosomatic medicine, pertaining to the interrelationships of mind and body.

The lady was profoundly impressed by this concept, which was new to her. And its therapeutic value was demonstrated by the phenomenon which occurred following the meeting. Walking along the street with her husband, she suddenly stopped in a quiet place under some trees. Aloud she made an affirmation: "I affirm that I was created by God, and that He who creates can also re-create. I affirm that the life force is now surging through my physical body. I have been impeding it by my sick thoughts. I affirm that from this moment I will think health, believe health, act health. Vitality and aliveness are now operating in my entire being. My whole physical organism is released to function as the Creator intended. I affirm and reaffirm dynamic life force."

While she did not experience change overnight, or even quickly, she did begin to show a new and healthier attitude. Her thought pattern was overhauled. She consulted doctors in a normal way for check-ups. Her medicine phobia was reduced to a sensible use of prescribed medication. The change must have had validity, for it is reported that the lady lived an active, healthy life, dying at ninety of a normal malady called old age.

HEALTH OF MIND AND HEALTH OF BODY

The foregoing case history suggests that when real health of mind is attained one has gone far toward enjoying health of body also. As Dr. Paul Tournier, well-known Swiss doctor, points out, physical health depends to a large extent on mental attitudes and the spiritual condition of the personality.

If this is true, and we have no reason to doubt the thesis, it follows that anything which contributes helpfully to mental, emotional, and spiritual well-being of the individual can be an important factor in health of mind and body.

Frequently someone will say, "I am sick with worry." This is more than a mere routine expression designating intense anxiety. A person definitely can become sick from worry. One doctor has stated that fifty percent of his patients have definite worry symptoms, and Dr. Smiley Blanton said, as I quoted earlier and I repeat because of its importance, "Anxiety is the great modern plague."

Resentment, hate, and ill will also have their demonstrated place in the bad health picture. A physician said of a certain man who held a long-term hate that he actually died of "grudgitis." Perhaps the doctor could not enter this officially as cause of death, but he described how the patient's color sickened, his eyes lost luster, his organs functioned with increasing sluggishness, and his breath became extremely foul. "His whole being deteriorated and he became lacking in resistance and easy prey to disease," said the doctor. "Yes," he insisted, "the man died of a virulent long-held hate."

Obviously this is an extreme case, but thousands of dull, listless, and lethargic individuals with aches and pains drag through life low in energy and vitality primarily because of a diseased emotional and spiritual condition. Such a condition undermines the body tone, leaving it open to the encroachment of disease. This is not to say, of course, that all sickness is emotionally induced. But it is well to remember that a distinguished Canadian physician advanced the theory that stress is an active agent in all disease.

SHE ITCHED IN CHURCH

In my experience I have noted not a few personal situations in which unhealthy mental and spiritual attitudes gave rise to emotional conditions that in turn had pronounced physical manifestations. For example, after I had given a talk in a church a woman spoke to me with the blunt announcement, "I itch terribly. Whatever shall I do about this itching?"

"Well, madam," I replied, "I've had all kinds of reactions to my talks, but this is the first time I can remember stimulating itching."

"I've had it off and on for about three years, but for some strange reason it's particularly bad when I am in church. Look at my arm, see how it itches." The exposed arm showed nothing except maybe a slight redness. I was curious as to why the itching was particularly noticeable when she came to church. In talking with her, the only inkling that emerged from our conversation, and it came out strong, was hatred of her sister. I mean hatred, vehement and virulent.

She claimed that her older sister, as executor of their father's estate, had defrauded her of a considerable portion of her "rightful" inheritance. I reasoned that since she was a long-time church member, the hatred was compounded with a sense of guilt when she came to church, and concluded that the itching might well be a concomitant of the guilt-hate complex.

Becoming curious about the case, I received permission to discuss it with her physician. He was obviously interested when I told him of her hate confession. "She never opened up on that with me," he said. "This woman may have what might be called an internal eczema. She has been scratching herself on the inside and producing an outward pseudo-itching. I have a hunch that if she could be persuaded to drop the hatred she might get over it. At least it's worth trying."

The doctor talked with the patient along this line and sent her back to me with the stern warning, "You'll itch yourself into a breakdown if you don't straighten up your sick thought pattern."

She responded to the suggested therapy, but not without considerable resistance, for the hate was deeply imbedded. She forgave her sister, which was the first step in giving up the hate. As the guilt feeling lessened, the itching was reduced and finally ceased altogether. Apparently her changed attitude also had a salutary effect on the grasping sister-executor, for she straightened out the financial situation to mutual satisfaction.

Of course, it must be stressed that changing a thought pattern is no easy process. Sick thoughts, negative thoughts, thoughts of resentment, of hate, of inferiority, wear a "groove" into the consciousness that isn't quickly overcome. One might wish for some magic pill to heal these maladies, but perhaps that would not be best even if it were possible. It could be that health of personality is better served by struggle and discipline and the curative practice of thought reversal.

TO GET BODY TONE, GET IN TUNE

I recall a man who, if not actually ill, at least had desultory and low-grade physical health. His doctor said the whole "body tone" was down, and prescribed a curious remedy, advising his patient: "To improve that tone, get in tune." The doctor did not explain this enigmatic prescription. The man asked me what I thought. I guessed that perhaps the physician might have in mind the decidedly unhealthy thought pattern of the patient and was suggesting that he tune up his thinking.

"To foster health, vitality, and aliveness," I suggested, "why not attempt for just one day to think on a healthier basis? For one day do not think or voice a negative thought, express no resentment. Instead, affirm that you are a well and happy human being. Try that procedure for one day and note whether it has any effect in toning you up to feel more alive." I took a pad and figured that if this man lived to be eighty years old, he would live 701,280 hours, including leap years. I suggested that it made sense to experiment with twenty-four of those hours to test whether a reversal of thought would help to achieve a healthier mind and body.

His unenthusiastic response to that suggestion was: "Maybe I'll do that sometime."

"No," I admonished. " 'Sometime' only means no time; if you are ever going to try this therapy, get with it. Tomorrow is the day." Thus prodded, he agreed to have a go at it the next day.

The patient kept his promise. He used the method of the Monkey of Nikko: He really attempted all day long to think no evil, hear no evil, speak no evil. "You have no idea what disciplinary attention it required," he told me. "It was uncanny how automatically I started to come out with those same old depressing, negative thoughts to which I've been so long accustomed. I really tried. I watched myself every minute and went around all day thinking and talking positively. I complimented everyone about anything I could think of." He carried out the experiment and admitted at the end of the day that he felt "strangely content, with a sense of relief I had never felt before. And did I feel good! I just felt good all over. It was amazing."

Indeed, the result was so good that he became excited about the project and eagerly went at it for another day and then still another. But this strong and unaccustomed thinking was hard going. "I was just all worn out trying to be all that good," as he described it. And he slumped back into the old thought pattern, but not all the way back, for he had gotten a taste of living on an upgraded thought level. So he worked his way up and down in the project of change. After this kind of struggle he finally arrived at a permanent level of better thinking. And while he confessed to stumbling a bit at times, he began to feel so much better physically and mentally that he vowed there was no chance ever again of his returning to a mentally unhealthy state. "Why should I?" he demanded. "When you're on the way to health, vitality, and aliveness it's so exciting that you don't want to have it any other way."

EFFECT OF THINKING ON HEALTH

Let me repeat again, to be healthy, vital, and alive it is very important how you think. To a degree you can "think" yourself sick or you can "think" yourself well. In a very deep sense you are what you think. "The soul," says Marcus Aurelius, "becomes dyed with the color of its thoughts." Think unhealthy thoughts and you will tend to become unhealthy in fact. And similarly, healthy thoughts can make you well.

Dr. Joseph Krimsky, distinguished medical doctor

and author of the book, *The Wonder of Man,* says: "The strongest bulwarks against invading disease germs are the inner defenses, the *vis medicatrix naturae:* the normal, natural forces within us that stand guard against the infiltrating and attacking hordes of the enemy germs and viruses. The modern term for this complex of forces is 'psychosomatic' [a combined word of *psyche,* which means mind, and *soma,* which means body]—the concept of an integrated and interrelated body and mind.

"It has been demonstrated scientifically," continues Dr. Krimsky, "that emotional tensions, emotional stresses and strains, may produce chronic depression and fatigue with the lowering of bodily resistance to infection and disease. Prolonged anxiety and worry, uncontrolled passion and temper, the high pressure and tempo of present-day life will bring on degenerative changes in the heart, kidneys, liver and other vital organs, together with hypertension and arteriosclerosis. Hate and fear can poison the body as much as any toxic chemicals."

Healthy thinking can be a vitality-producing process. Such thoughts help to keep the body in balance and functioning in a normal manner. Think defeat and you will tend to create the circumstances that lead to defeat. Think inadequacy and you may ultimately fail to perform in an adequate manner. But if you think victory and success—really think it, really believe it—then you will tend to perform in a manner that leads to such an outcome. Similarly, in the matter of well-being, positive results come from visualizing yourself as whole. See your mind and body as strong and vital and they will tend to become as you image them.

I encountered a vibrant young black man who practiced this principle. One very cold morning my wife and I were at a motel in Chicago. As a matter of fact, the doorman told me it was zero degrees! He also informed me that the weatherman reported a wind-chill factor that made the temperature feel like minus thirty!

"It sure must be cold outside!" I said to my wife.

"Well," she replied, "no doubt it is, but we're bundled up. Besides, we're healthy, aren't we?"

The motel's courtesy car rolled up and the young black driver got out. "Good morning," he said cheerfully. "Isn't this a terrific morning!"

As the wind whipped my face, I muttered, "It's a bit cold."

"I know," he replied, "but it's a beautiful cold. I hope you enjoyed our motel last night," he continued, as he handled our bags.

"Yes," I answered, "we certainly did."

"How are you feeling this morning?" he asked, as he jumped into the driver's seat.

"I'm pretty good," I chattered.

"*Pretty* good?" he exclaimed. "*Pretty* good isn't enough."

"Well," I asked, "how are you?"

"I am just great. I'm terrific! I think well and I am well." He really went all-out.

As we drove I said, "You know, my friend, I'm glad to meet you because I'm going to give a talk tomorrow, Sunday, on the topic, 'How to be Healthy, Vital, and Alive.'"

"Where are you speaking?" he asked. "You're talking my language. I'm off Sundays. I'll be there!"

"Well, it happens to be in New York, and that's quite a way from here!"

He turned around and smiled. "Thought I recognized you. You're Dr. Peale, aren't you? And you often tell people that the way to feel healthy is to think healthy. You're so right. I made up my mind to practice being vital and alive, and now that's just the way I feel every day."

There is always somebody ready to argue with the idea that practicing healthy thoughts can foster well feelings. They will say glumly, "But I've got something really wrong with me." Of course people may have "something really wrong." We do not minimize organic disease at all. But even if there is something wrong, the forces of vitality and health can either be stimulated or reduced by the manner of thought which is applied. And thought-faith power can help bring about good results even in serious sickness.

Like the woman I called on at Memorial Hospital in New York. Her husband left the room and in his absence she said, "I have a cancer condition which I know is going to be cured. But my husband is the real problem. He is in a negative gloominess all the time; always thinking the worst. Will you work on him and help him to think creative health thoughts? I want him to see me in his mind as a well person, not as a victim of cancer or a wife he's going to lose. Because he isn't going to lose me, I don't intend to die!"

One could have regarded this as whistling in the dark, talking big. But her powerful faith, her strong thinking conveyed optimism.

"Believe me," she said, "I'm all right. But please pray for my husband. Help him to get well in his thoughts."

Several weeks later a dynamic, vital woman came to me. "Do you remember me?" she asked.

"How could I ever forget you?" I said. "Your faith and healthy-mindedness made a profound impression on me." And I added, "You look very well."

"Why," she exclaimed joyfully, "of course I'm well! I made up my mind that with God's help I would be well." On several subsequent occasions I saw her; she was still well. This was a case in which faith and right thinking aided in a healing.

Healthy thinking is increasingly recognized as an important factor in well-being. Years ago a doctor might depend upon medicine only. But because man is a unity—body, mind, and spirit; and the psyche and the soma are closely related—scientific thought treatment is generally considered entirely relevant to the healing process.

I CURE MY COLD TENDENCY

Consider my own personal experience, though it is not to be compared to the case of the young woman mentioned above. Every winter, it seemed, I had one major cold, and always it would run a course which finally affected my vocal chords so that I could scarcely speak. This often proved embarrassing, inasmuch as I carry a heavy schedule of speaking engagements which have usually been dated months or even a year in advance. It does not set well with a local committee to have your secretary telephone at the last minute and say that you have lost your voice! And I have a sense of responsibility about keeping a date.

Once, I recall, a local committee of a national convention insisted I come anyway, since I was under contract. But when I arrived in that city I was speaking only in a whisper and was faced with the problem of making myself heard at a dinner for which seventeen hundred tickets had been sold. I sucked, or at least it seemed that way, every lozenge in the drugstore, filled myself with vitamin C, gulped vast quantities of liquid, did everything that I had ever heard would help cure a cold: a real crash program.

In the afternoon I inquired about a throat doctor and went to his office. He was an older man, a relaxed, easy-going type of person. "Doctor, please fix me up," I croaked, "so I can get through this talk tonight. I am on the program for a forty-minute speech. In fact, I'm the only thing on the program."

"What do you want me to do?" he asked, to my surprise.

"Do? Why, how should I know? You're the doctor— spray and swab my throat, I guess. The usual."

"Think that will make you feel better?" he asked. "O.K., we'll give you the treatment." He did everything I thought he should do. "Now," he said, peering over the top of his glasses which seemed to perch halfway down his nose, "you are on the way to recovery, but I've got a prescription for you. It's this: Start now saying to yourself, 'I'm going to have enough voice for that talk and my positive thoughts are now helping me to improve systemically.'

"And beyond that," he added, "spend the afternoon getting rid of that tension. You're all wound up. Forget about this evening and whether or not you will be able to talk. Those vocal cords show that you are uptight. Go back to the hotel, take off your clothes and get into bed. Leave a call for seven P.M. Go to sleep. You won't be speaking until eight-thirty. Order some tea and toast from room service. Visualize those vocal cords as relax-

ing. If you do, and mean it, they will. Then," he concluded, "say a prayer of thanks and affirmation. Go to
the high school gym just at eight-thirty P.M. and give
them a bang-up talk."

Well, whatever it was—the relaxed attitude of the
doctor, the bed rest, the new attitude of nonchalance,
the faith and the prayer, or a combination of all these
factors—I got through the speech with sufficient vocal
power. And, grinning at me from down in the audience, I spotted the face of the doctor. He held up his
hand in the O.K. gesture.

From then on I began wondering if perhaps I was
getting this devastating cold along about February every year because I was mentally expecting it. I really
did not believe you could attract a cold by the thought
and expectation process. But that I was regularly taken
down by a heavy cold was a fact, and that I was expecting it was also a fact; so perhaps—just perhaps—there
could be an interrelation between the two facts.

Therefore I decided to reject the possibility that in
February of the next year the usual throat-crippling
cold would get me. I sought medical advice for sound
and sensible precautions. I made it a habit, when at all
possible, to get to bed earlier. I practiced relaxation.
When the newspapers, purveyors always of bad news,
began to shout terrifyingly of a new strain of flu—Hong
Kong or London or what have you—I mentally rejected
the negativism. Well, perhaps I'd better knock on
wood, but outside of a few little sniffles, I have not had
a real cold for several years. And never one that really
affected my vocal cords. I've just kept on talking and
talking, speaking everywhere. The old doctor taught
me one of the best lessons I've ever had about how to
be healthy, vital, and alive.

One thing is very sure, and ought to be more widely understood and practiced. It is simply this: The teachings of Jesus Christ are designed, among other things, to make people come alive, not only spiritually, but also mentally and physically. Running all through like a golden thread is the message that you can be healthy, vital, and alive.

An old friend and classmate, Laurence H. Blackburn, a leader in the spiritual healing ministry, points out in his book * that one out of every seven verses in the Gospels relates to healing. Bernard Martin calls attention to the fact that there are recorded in the Gospels forty-eight instances where Jesus healed people individually and eighteen instances where He healed en masse. This indicates that His teaching deals not only with philosophy, theology, morality, and sociology, but also with the "good news" about healing.

Spiritual thinking will not, of course, guarantee that you will be without sickness, but it definitely can improve your health average.

Three principles may be employed:

1. *Think* health for vitality and aliveness.
2. *Practice* health for vitality and aliveness.
3. *Pray* health for vitality and aliveness.

In writing about health, vitality, and aliveness, I would be completely remiss, and as a matter of fact irresponsible, if I failed to remind my readers of the enormous and incredible healing power resident in spiritual faith and attitudes. So if you are not feeling well, if you are sick or ill in any way, go to your doctor,

_____* *God Wants You to Be Well* (Morehouse-Barlow Co., 1970).

but also develop an open mind to the immense possibilities of healing through those mental and spiritual processes which have been experienced by so many sane, logical, and responsible people.

A REMARKABLE RECOVERY FROM ILLNESS

I recall one man, for example, who was then president of a national business association. He and I got to talking as we sat at the head table during a national convention luncheon. We were looking out over a great crowd of industry operators and executives and, to my astonishment, I found myself listening to a most interesting healing story. He had no zephyr-like voice, either; in fact, everyone within twenty-five feet could hear what he was saying.

You would not expect anything like this to happen at an industry convention—but why not? Those who run our great business organizations are human, same as the rest of us. This man was a burly, diamond-in-the-rough sort of fellow. And the first thing he did was to ask, "Do you believe that Jesus Christ can heal people?" —just like that. In those surroundings it was an unexpected and startling question.

"Of course I do," I replied.

"You haven't any doubt?" he asked.

"No doubt at all," I answered.

"I'm glad to hear that," he continued, "for I have talked with some ministers who come up with nothing but weasel words in reply to that question. I am glad you come out unequivocally in your belief."

"Right! I do."

"Well," he said, "so do I."

Naturally, I prodded him for his story. But he needed no prodding. It flowed out enthusiastically. He told me he had been very ill; at death's door. In fact he got the feeling he had been given up, that there was nothing to be done for him except to make him as comfortable as possible. As he lay in bed at home, very depressed, all of a sudden he got an idea. He called to his wife and asked, "Have we got a Bible around this house any place? I don't remember ever having seen one."

"Oh," she said, "yes, I've got my mother's Bible. It is in a bureau drawer upstairs."

"Will you bring it to me?" he requested.

"What on earth do you want with a Bible?" she asked. "You have never read it in your life."

"I don't know," he answered, "but I feel like I want to read it now, that's all. Go get it for me, will you, please?" So she brought him the Bible.

"I hadn't the faintest notion where to begin," he continued. "But I opened it and started reading. Some of it seemed very uninteresting, but I finally got around to Matthew, Mark, Luke, and John and it began to grab me. I could see that this book, the Bible, really had something special—very special. It fascinated me. There was a strange, compelling interest in it. I read on and on and on. I read about all the people Jesus healed. And they were pretty tough cases. Some of them had been given up by the doctor. So I got to thinking.

" 'Jesus is a square shooter,' I said to myself. 'He wouldn't put you on. He would give it to you straight. He wouldn't fail you; He wouldn't let you down. And if He says He can heal people, then I believe Him. If the Bible says these people were healed, I believe that.'

"And then," he continued, "I came on a statement

which said that Jesus Christ is the same yesterday and today and forever. So I thought to myself, if He could heal those people then, He can heal me now. And so I prayed and said, 'Dear Lord, the doctors around here have given me up. I put myself in Your hands. I believe that You can heal me.' I just had no doubt about it from then on."

"Well," I asked, "how are you?"

"Take a look at me," he answered. "How do I look?"

"You certainly look healthy."

"I am healthy, but there's more to it than that. I realized I had to go deeper into what I was reading and go beyond healing. So I kept on reading. I came to a place where it said that whoever tried to save his own life would lose it, but whoever gave his life would find it. So that is what I have been trying to do. I'd never given anything. I didn't give to the church. I gave as little as possible to the community chest. I was a big money-grabber but short on giving. And I saw what was happening; I was losing my life because I wasn't giving —of money or of time or of myself.

"After I got well I went to the minister of the local church and told him I was on his team from then on if he could use me. I have been giving time and thought and energy and money to the church and to the town. I've gotten into activities. That's why I am president of this business association. My life has been given back to me and I intend to keep it strong and healthy by giving myself."

Quite a philosophy, I'd say.

"Anyway," he concluded, "the spiritual health and life principle is going for me."

There is a vast and wistful interest in this matter of physical well-being, energy, and healthiness. And why shouldn't there be? For when you lose your health, when energy and vitality go down, then the whole life process suffers. Enthusiasm and dynamic essence go out of living. Perhaps it is for this reason that everywhere in the world healing services are crowded, not only with the sick who want to get well, but also with the healthy who want to stay well.

HEALING MEETING IN AUSTRALIA

This interest is worldwide and was deeply impressed upon me when I was asked by Dr. A. W. Morton, Dean of St. Andrew's Cathedral in Sydney, Australia, to speak at a healing service during my visit in that country. To my surprise, the vast structure was packed to capacity and the atmosphere was impressively charged with faith. I could feel it actually taking hold of everyone, including myself.

As I looked out over the great audience I sensed an intensity of desire for some valid ideas on the subject of well-being. So I want to include here some of my remarks on that occasion, for they pertain to being healthy, vital, and alive.

And that is exactly what we are intended to be. When God created us He breathed into us the breath of life, and this vitality was for life. It is said that, "In him we live, and move, and have our being." * And a reason that we are not vital or truly alive may be because we have let the life force be interfered with; we erode it, even destroy it. It is my opinion that whoever will believe and live on the healing words of Scripture will be

____* Acts 17:28.

on the way to health, vitality, and aliveness: "But they that wait upon the Lord shall renew their strength; they shall mount up with wings as eagles." *

Did you ever see an eagle rise up? I rose up the other day on a 747, but it wasn't anything like the dramatic way an eagle rises. Once I saw one take off from a rocky crag in the Yosemite. He reached for the sky, of which he was the master. "They that wait upon the Lord . . . shall mount up with wings as eagles," but that isn't the end of it: "they shall run, and not be weary;" nor is that the end of it: "and they shall walk, and not faint." * The Creator built energy into you and me when we were babies. He implanted in us the life force, and true faith can keep this life force alive.

A friend of mine went to a physician one day to get a report on tests, and the doctor said to him, "My scientific findings point to serious trouble ahead for you. In fact, I am obliged to tell you that your life expectancy is limited."

"Well," said his shocked patient, "how long?"

"I cannot give you a specific time, but in all honesty it could be a matter of months."

The man asked, "Is there no hope for me?"

Now this was a wonderful doctor. "Yes," he said, "there is hope if you will practice hope. Now, remember, my friend, I am only a person who works with God. We treat the patient; God heals him. Perhaps if you establish a close relationship with God, you might prove my diagnosis to be in error."

This man was very thoughtful as he walked up Park Avenue on that spring day. It was April and the flowers were starting to bloom; leaves were beginning to come out on the trees. The thought occurred to him, "Isn't

——* Isaiah 40:31.

this strange, that these trees and these perennial flowers seem to know when it's spring and they emerge to new life?" He reasoned that the operation of recurring new life in the natural world was also applicable to him. So, standing there on that avenue, he did a curious thing, a very curious thing, and I have done the same myself since he told me about it. He made the same affirmation as was made by the woman referred to earlier in this chapter. He said, "I now affirm the emergence of the life force, and what is happening in nature is now happening in my physical body." He maintained this affirmation for days. On subsequent trips to the doctor's office the physician nodded his head with a smile, and finally after many months said, "The conditions that I found some months ago no longer exist. You are, from my point of view, on the way to being a healthy man." And when the man told the doctor what he had done, the physician said, "Apparently you are thinking and praying and affirming your way back to health."

Among the many actions to be taken if one expects to be healthy, vital, and alive is to wash out of the mind all old, tired, dead, listless, unhappy thoughts. Again quoting Dr. Sara Jordan of Boston's Lahey Clinic, "Every day give yourself a mental shampoo. And if this is done," she said, "there will be fewer people in our clinics." Many cases indicate that unhealthy thoughts siphon off healthiness.

A TAXICAB HEALING STORY

I was in a taxicab in New York with three other men. It was a beautiful day, and as I got into the cab I said to the driver, "Nice day, isn't it?"

But he grunted, "So what? It's all right now, but it'll rain before night, maybe snow," and various other negativisms. As we rode along these other men were calling me "doctor" from time to time. Finally the driver turned around and looked at me, apparently thinking he had a medico in the cab and that maybe he could get a little free treatment. "Doc," he said, "I have pains in my back all the time. What about it?"

"Why," I said, "you shouldn't have pains in your back, a young fellow like you. How old are you?"

"I'm thirty-seven," he replied, "and I just ache all over. I can't eat very well because I also have pains in my stomach, and I just don't feel good. What do you think may be wrong with me?"

I said, "Look, my friend," maintaining the medical doctor manner, "I'm sure it's not the thing to practice medicine in taxicabs. But you seem to be a nice fellow, and I think I can diagnose your problem. What I really think you have is psychosclerosis." This shocked him so that he nearly ran up on the sidewalk.

"Psychosclerosis?" he exclaimed, "What in the world is that?"

Well, I wasn't too sure myself, but I said, "You know about arteriosclerosis, don't you?"

"No," he said, "I don't know what that is."

"Well, that means hardening of the arteries, and that's a bad thing to get. But psychosclerosis is infinitely worse. That means hardening of the thoughts, and ever since I've been in this taxicab you've been exhibiting the symptoms of psychosclerosis. If you don't get over psychosclerosis, the next thing you know you may have arteriosclerosis."

"Well," he asked nervously, "what am I going to do?"

"I'll tell you," I replied. "You come to my office and we'll give you a treatment."

He didn't know me at all. I handed him my card and he said, "Why, you're not a doctor of medicine; you're a religious doctor."

"Maybe that's the kind of doctor you need," I said. "Perhaps you don't need a medical doctor nearly as much as you need a doctor of the mind; perhaps even a doctor of the soul." He came to my office and we gave him the treatment comprised of the principles in this book. And after a while he was cured of his psychosclerosis, and it didn't cost him anything, either, except the struggle of cleaning out diseased thoughts.

Thousands of people are making themselves ill and encouraging other maladies and diseases by unhealthy thinking. So the solution is to affirm the life force; drop uptightness; cast out all hate; emphasize love. The most curative thought in the world is the thought of love. Go around loving people; thinking good thoughts about everyone. Cast out all negative thoughts and fill the mind with positive thoughts. Eliminate all inferiority thoughts. Fill the mind with victorious thoughts. Healthy-mindedness makes people healthy, vital, and alive.

Like the man mentioned earlier, try living one day without any unhealthy thoughts. You'll have the time of your life. It may be very difficult, and the second day you may not want to try it again because it will have made you tired; but try another day, until it becomes habitual, and life will move in the direction of becoming healthy, vital, and alive.

SOME PEOPLE'S HEARTS KEEP GOING STRONG

But suppose we turn finally to a scientific source for confirmation of the health, vitality, and aliveness principles described in this chapter, the acceptance and

practice of which can increase your joy in living and
your effectiveness as a person.

Mary McSherry, in an article called, "Why Some Men
Live Longer," * says:

> What some doctors are calling the biggest news
> about the heart in twenty years was recently
> released by a nineteen-man team from the Depart-
> ment of Nutrition, Harvard's School of Public
> Health, and the School of Medicine at Trinity Col-
> lege, Dublin. The news concerns discoveries made
> by a two-country medical group headed by Har-
> vard's prominent nutritionist Dr. Fredrick J. Stare
> during a unique, nine-year study of 575 pairs of
> brothers born in Ireland. The study turned up as-
> tonishing differences in health between Irish and
> American hearts.

These brothers were all raised in Ireland and therefore had a similar physical and psychological heritage:
They were raised in the same house, ate the same food,
were brought up in the same manner, enjoyed the
same degree of comfort (or discomfort) and affection.
Then, at about age twenty, 575 of them emigrated to
the United States and for the most part settled around
Boston. The other 575 stayed in Ireland.

It had long been felt that people have healthier
hearts in Ireland than in the United States. So therefore
it was thought an investigation of this phenomenon
would be worthwhile. The assumption was that diet
was involved. Heart disease is supposed to be a disease
of prosperity. If you have enough money to eat well,
you eat lots of saturated fats and often create a choles-
terol condition. This forms a deposit, it narrows the

———* *Woman's Day* (October 1971).

arteries in the heart, and can lead to a heart attack. For this reason many people in this country are concerned about eating eggs and meat and the like.

Examination of the diet situation in Ireland revealed that the Irish diet consists of few vegetables or salads, and little fruit. It consists of meat, potatoes, milk and cream, and huge slabs of whole wheat bread covered thickly with butter. And the condition of the heart of the Irish runs younger than their American brothers. It was found that the Irishman walks; he uses his legs; whereas the Boston brother pushes, pushes, pushes, but he pushes an accelerator. He doesn't use his legs; he doesn't walk. And he is very short on time. But the Irishman says, "If we don't get it done today, we'll get it done tomorrow."

The Boston brother worries; the Irish brother has faith. The Boston brother is inclined to be irascible; the Irish brother has a sunny disposition. The Boston brother feels that everything depends on him. The Irish brother feels that if you put your trust in God, things will turn out all right Hence the Irish brother lives longer than the Boston brother.

Mary McSherry's article points up the important intangible difference in these two sets of Irish brothers. She says:

Finally Dr. Stare thinks Americans might learn one more thing from the Irish. "It's nothing you can weigh or graph, but whether you can measure it or not, it's there. I mean the Irish attitude. When you survey a great many people, you can't help noticing that there's a hopefulness, a courage they get from trust in God. I believe this is a factor in their health. I can't prove, of course, that the uncomplaining, looking-on-the-bright-side attitude of the Irish stems from their faith, but it's there. I think it may have a bearing on their hearts, and I think Americans could add this lesson to the others our study offers."

So the thesis is—and it is being demonstrated by thousands of people—that health, vitality, and aliveness can be a way of life. And what a way it is—fantastically full of zest, enthusiasm, and joy! And it's there for you. Why not go for it—really go for it?

Finally, here are a few guideposts to foster health, vitality, and aliveness:

1. *Realize that you can of yourself do much to make yourself a healthy, vital, and alive individual.*

2. *Affirm and keep on affirming that the powerful life force is flowing through your mind, your spirit, your body.*

3. *Rid yourself of all sick thoughts—hate, resentment, inferiority, and the like.*

4. *Every day practice emptying your mind of all unhealthy attitudes.*

5. *Keep your mind tuned up to keep your body in tone.*

6. *Hold the thought of all elements of the body working together in perfect rhythm.*

7. *Help the doctor by thinking healthy thoughts. Remember that while the doctor treats you, God heals you.*

8. *Think health, practice health, pray health.*

9. *See yourself as a whole person.*

10. *Visualize God, who created you, as constantly re-creating you in every element of being.*

THIRTEEN

EASE UP! HAVE A SENSE OF HUMOR

At our farm on Quaker Hill in Dutchess County, New York, hard by the Connecticut border, we have a venerable apple tree. My good friend and farm superintendent, John Imre, says the tree is eighty or ninety years old if it's a day.

It must have been a big, strong apple tree in days gone by, with wide-spreading branches. But now it is old and gnarled, and its once huge trunk is only a rounded shell on one side, not more than three inches thick. And even this has several large holes in it.

But the tree means a lot to me, and I've learned much from it. For you see, that apple tree has been acting positively all these years. It does not seem to know that it is old and only a remnant of what it once was. Because every springtime it puts forth a great array of beautiful blossoms, then leafs out fully. And then it just goes on about its business of producing apples. As far as I know, it has never been sprayed. But it produces apples. Of course they are not big and round and shiny like those you see in supermarkets. They are out of shape and a bit crabbed and have some dark spots; sometimes even worms; but do you know, those apples are really sweet.

Nature is a subtle teacher of human beings, and when

275

I start driving myself and taking myself and things too seriously and get the notion that maybe I am not delivering as well as formerly, I simply go and commune with the apple tree. And then, encouraged, start putting out some new blossoms myself. I remind myself that even if the apples on that ancient tree are warped and wormy, as long as they are sweet and in part edible, the tree is still in business; is still doing the job it was designed to perform. So it would seem that our old apple tree teaches, among other things, to ease up, have a sense of humor, and keep on doing the job you were intended to do.

As my old friend, Dr. Smiley Blanton, used to say, "Practice easing your way along. Don't get het up or in a dither. Do your best; take it as it comes. You can handle anything if you just think you can. Just keep your cool, and keep your sense of humor going."

Emerson urged the practice of serenity and what he called "self-possession." That latter word seems packed with meaning; obviously, self-possession means to possess yourself. In other words, never let your controlled self get out of control. Practice serenity and urbanity, old-fashioned words scarcely ever used in this get-with-it age, this jittery, tense, hot-TV-news era.

WE GOT ALONG WITHOUT TV, RADIO, OR NEWSPAPERS

Some time ago my wife Ruth and I were on a safari (cameras, not guns) in East Africa, particularly in Kenya and Tanzania. For two weeks we were far out in the bush country—no newspapers, no radio, no TV; sleepy-headed every night by 8 P.M., then up early and over the majestic Serengeti plains. We could feel the up-and-with-it tension subsiding.

It was startling to return to blaring radios, to the tense immediacy of news broadcasts on TV, and to loud-shouting newspaper headlines. And one asked himself, "So what? Strange, but it really doesn't seem to matter a whole lot! With slight variations, we're hearing the same old stuff we listened to or read before we took off for the African bush." One who makes such an escape from so-called civilization becomes gratefully aware of this thing called serenity. He finds himself easing up and beginning to look at the news-conscious and frantic world with a kind of urbane sense of humor. He is reminded that there isn't anything really new, apart from the more sophisticated buildup. It's all happened before, and before that, and repeatedly before that. There is, we are rightly told, nothing new under the sun.

Of course, we who happen to live in New York, probably not one of the best governed or safest cities in the world, would gladly settle for anything that could increase our serenity.

We were at the home of friends, Mr. And Mrs. Vadja Vadin Kolombatovic, in Madrid. Mr. Kolombatovic is legal attaché at the American Embassy. They live in a quiet and pleasant section of the Spanish capital. On leaving their home about eleven o'clock at night, as we stood in the street, Vadja clapped his hands loudly and a man instantly came running. Our host told him he was taking his car out to carry us to our hotel.

Mr. Kolombatovic explained that this man is a *sereno,* or private guard, employed by residents on the block to keep an eye open all night long to protect all the houses, apartments, and people. This particular man had been the *sereno* on that block for twenty-five years, succeeding his father who had served in that same capacity for some forty years. "How wonderful," we insecure New Yorkers exclaimed, "to have a *sereno* (a name derived from the same root as serenity) watching over you and your neighbors all night long!"

And a second word so desperately needed is one that the famous physician, Sir William Osler, considered vital to health. That word is "equanimity." What a picture it conjures up of a person who, no matter what, remains poised, in perfect balance, inwardly controlled; indeed, one who is able to ease up and maintain a sense of humor. This philosophy may be simply stated. So what? Even this will pass away. Don't take any event, any turmoil, or even yourself, too seriously.

Years ago in Vienna Dr. Paul Dubois is said to have practiced what he called "word therapy." The treatment was by the use of a word that was opposite to the particular destructive emotion of the patient. For example, if the patient felt a pervading sense of defeat, he was to say aloud and regularly the word "invulnerability." If he was uptight, his healing word might be "serenity," or perhaps another word that is not unlike liquid music, the word "tranquillity." If all around the patient was confusion, the conflicting chatter or strident shouting of many voices, if everyone was in a tizzy about this or that, the healing word was "equanimity."

KEEP YOUR TRANQUILLITY AND EQUANIMITY GOING

Keep your emotions in balance, keep them level; keep your sense of humor about those who think all civilization began this morning and that everything has to be settled right away, now, before tonight. When everyone exclaims, "Isn't it awful!" "Oh, what are we going to do now?" "Why doesn't somebody do something, and fast, or civilization will collapse?"—that is when good old "equanimity" comes in handy. You, for one, can just ease up and practice your sense of humor. For, as they say, everything finally "comes out in the wash." At least, it comes out. Plato may have been going a bit far when he said, "No human thing is of serious importance," but even so, it's a point to consider.

The wisdom of equanimity is actually based on a sense-of-humor reaction about all human activity. And the person who masters this quality is bound to enjoy life far better than the excitable and super-concerned, eager-beaver type so common nowadays.

To become adept in equanimity it is helpful to read one of the world's greatest thinkers, Marcus Aurelius. Among other wise remarks, as mentioned earlier, he advises: "Vex not thy spirit at the course of things. They heed not thy vexation." And again: "How ludicrous and outlandish is astonishment at anything that happens in life." In Hong Kong I saw a proverb by an ancient Chinese sage whose name is unknown. But what he says marks him as an urbane master of equanimity. It is this: "Take an emergency leisurely." Two other sense-of-humor type of words that can really ease you up are "urbanity" and "imperturbability." In colloquial speech these words might identify with the old phrase, "Never let anything get your goat," or, more modernly, "Don't let it throw you." Just employ your sense of humor, take it easy and wait it out, for nothing lasts forever. Can you remember, for example, what every TV news broadcaster was upset about, say, five years ago? This, too, will fade into the past. And incidentally, the past is a great invention; it mercifully swallows up all those tensed-up, so-called immediacy matters.

I once made a speech to some five thousand school teachers at a State Education Association convention and talked along the lines of this chapter, emphasizing word therapy. Apparently one teacher was terribly impressed by that word "imperturbability"; so much so, in fact, that when her pupils presented her with a dog, she promptly named it "Imperturbability." This was the most astonishing result I ever had from a public speech! Well, anyway, no wonder she was liked by her students; she had a sense of humor.

A sense of humor is so very helpful in turning potentially sensitive situations into assets. A friend of mine has a daughter who, as a child, simply could not properly pronounce the word "spaghetti." She was a rather sensitive child and this could have been a source of embarrassment to her. But instead she laughed at herself when she tried to say it and others found it a source of good fun as did she. In fact, she seemed a bit disappointed when she finally learned to say it correctly, for it had become one of her ways to entertain people.

Another case where a sense of humor creatively improved what could have been an unhappy psychological situation concerned Uncle John. He was in a serious accident and his leg was amputated. "Poor John," the neighbors said, for a leg amputation and resulting wooden leg can be a serious problem. The tendency is for the victim to shy away from other people and keep to himself.

Not so with Uncle John. Children came to see his wooden leg, children he had never known before, and they became great friends. He always signed his letters, "Uncle John with the wooden leg." He got more mileage out of the wooden leg than he ever did out of his natural one.

Then there is my friend, Amos Parrish, one of the greatest merchandising experts in the country. A. P. has stuttered for years, but instead of letting it embarrass or inhibit him, he turns it into a kind of trademark, an asset. People wait until he overcomes the stutter, for they know full well when the words come he will really say something. I heard him speak to a huge crowd of national department store executives in the grand ballroom of the Waldorf Astoria. He went along for quite a while, then became hung up on the word "Cadillac." The great audience strained with him to get that word out and finally he said, "C -a -a -a -dillac. I c -a -an't even say it, let alone b -u -uy one." The audience roared, as did Amos Parrish also. They loved it and him.

One of the most beloved personalities of modern times was the late Pope John XXIII. Reasons for his immense popularity are not difficult to compile; he was dedicated, compassionate, catholic in spirit, ecumenical, and very human as well as saintly. Perhaps above all else he was a humble man who, despite his vast distinction, did not take himself too seriously. And he had a delightful sense of humor.

One story concerning this great pope appeals to me and I believe it is true. It's about the time his family came up from the country to visit him following his elevation to the papacy. These sturdy, religious peasant people were awed by the pomp and ceremony surrounding their famous relative. But he put them at their ease. Laughingly and tenderly the pontiff said, "Don't be so nervous—it's only me."

PRESIDENT EISENHOWER AND HIS SENSE OF HUMOR

One thing people liked about President Dwight D. Eisenhower was his slow, easy grin and the fact that even though he was one of the most famous men of his time he wasn't all that impressed with himself; he didn't take himself too seriously. Despite the fact that he was the successful supreme commander of the allied forces in World War II, the world's idol and President of the United States, as far as he was concerned he was still Ike, the boy from Abilene. He could handle himself on a great historic stage, but his book, *At Ease*, was well named. He was an urbane, imperturbable, lovable human being with a well-developed sense of humor. Since he was the complete antithesis of a stuffed shirt, totally lacking in pomposity, the people took him to their hearts as one of them.

I had the privilege of knowing him personally, and vividly recall one amazing private conversation I had with him. I had been asked by J. Edgar Hoover to give a talk at a meeting of police chiefs held under the auspices of the F.B.I. in Washington. They represented several hundred of the leading law enforcement officials of the nation.

Seated on the platform, I noticed that the chair next to me had on it a "Reserved" sign. Soon, to my astonishment, President Eisenhower entered and took the seat. Immediately I said, "Mr. President, you must give the speech today. I wouldn't think of talking, with you present."

Ike grinned. "Why leave me out?" he said. "I need some positive thinking, believe me. No, you can't get out of it. You do the talking and I'll do the listening. And come up with something really good; I need it." Then he added, "All I'm going to do here today is receive a Special Agent's badge of the F.B.I." Then, with a kind of boyish pride, "You know, I always wanted to belong to the F.B.I."

Well, I gave my little speech and when I sat down he graciously told me it was "great." He said, "I like to see a speaker tear into it and wave his arms." Despite the aura of the presidency, he was one of the easiest men to be with that I ever knew. You soon forgot he was the President and felt only you were in the company of a delightful and very engaging man. After my speech and the presentation to the President of the Special Agent's badge, Mr. Hoover went into the business of presenting diplomas or certificates to each of the several hundred police chiefs who were graduating from an intensive eight-week course in law enforcement. I felt sure the President would leave, but he didn't seem to be in any hurry; in fact, he told me it would be a discourtesy to all those police officials were he to leave.

But all during the long time it took to present the diplomas, he talked to me just like an old friend. I have on my office wall a newspaper picture showing him during that personal chat. He has one leg pulled up, his hands informally clasping his knee, and the pant-leg caught up, showing a garter and a wide expanse of bare leg.

The President seemed to want to talk and he spoke fascinatingly about many things, indeed he seemed to be entirely uninhibited. One remark I recall was that anyone who wanted his job of being president "should have his head examined."

I said, "Mr. President, I would like to tell you that I pray for you every day."

"Oh, thanks—thanks a lot. Keep those prayers going, for I sure need 'em. Tell you something; I always pray, and God really hears my prayers and helps me. I just couldn't live with this job if He didn't," he declared, meaning it as much as any man I ever heard testify to the reality of prayer.

"Do you ever get nervous, Mr. President?" I asked.

"Oh, sure, but when it starts getting to me I just say to myself, 'Forget it, Ike; who do think you are, Caesar Augustus? Remember, you're just Ike Eisenhower, that's all. So do the best you can, and angels can do no better.' " He warmed to the subject and it was evident this matter of prayer meant much to him. "No, sir, when I go to bed at night I thank the Lord for helping me during the day. I ask Him to overlook any mistakes I made. Then I ask Him to forgive any sins I may have committed. I commit my dear ones to His loving care. Then I say, 'Lord, I'm going to sleep. You just take care of the country during the night.' Then, knowing everything is in far better hands than mine, I go off to sleep."

I never spoke or wrote of this unforgettable personal conversation during General Eisenhower's lifetime, but report it faithfully here and am sure he would not mind. This never-to-be-forgotten visit with one of the few greatest men of history is clearly etched on my mind. And I shall always think of him as a self-possessed, completely genuine and sincere man who had a sense of humor, not overly impressed with his own importance but simply trying to do the great job destiny had given him, and doing it superbly.

During the conversation, for some reason it occurred to me to ask, "Mr. President, in your wide acquaintance with the great of this earth, who would you consider the greatest man you ever met?"

At our left sat a dozen of the leading men of the time. Impishly, he gestured in their direction. "Well, I hate to say it, but it's none of those fellows over there! But," he added, "aren't they wonderful, those young men I've brought into government?"

THE PRESIDENT NAMES THE GREATEST PERSON

"The greatest man I ever met was not a man, but a woman—my mother," he said. "She was not well-educated from the standpoint of formal schooling, but she had insight, understanding and wisdom, deep wisdom. In fact," he continued a bit wistfully, "often since I've been in this job I've wished I could ask her advice, for she was a straight thinker and knew human nature through and through. One of the wisest principles I ever learned was given to me years ago by Mother. One night in our farm home up in Pennsylvania my mother, my brothers, and I were playing cards. Now get this straight," he injected, "we were not using regular playing cards, for my mother was very straitlaced. I think we were playing an old-fashioned game called 'Flinch,' or something.

"Anyway, Mother was the dealer and she dealt me the worst possible hand. I knew I hadn't the slightest chance of winning with a hand like that, and since I always did like to win, I began complaining and griping. Well, sir," continued the President, "Mother said, 'All right, boys, put your cards face down on the table. I want to tell you all something, especially you, Ike.'

"She said, 'This is only a game, but it's like life itself. You're going to have many a bad hand dealt to you. What you've got to do is to take each hand, good or bad, and don't whine and complain, but just take that hand and play it out. If you're men enough to do that—to play out the hand—God will help you and you'll come out all right in the end.' How many times I've had occasion to discover the truth of my mother's wise teaching!"

And then as the meeting broke up, what do you suppose the President of the United States said? "Thanks for letting me talk about some things that mean a lot to me. Thanks for listening. God bless you." *He* was actually thanking *me!* With that, he was gone, and I stood deeply moved by a man great enough to ease it up, with a sense of humor, and a disarming humility—a great, natural, lovable human being.

Many people fail to do creative jobs in the world, not because they are not capable enough, but because they push it too hard; they overpress. The secret of efficiency is to think and plan and give the project all that one has of constructive effort and then rest it; don't overpress; relax; ease up.

MY BROTHER, DOCTOR BOB

One of the most successful men I've ever known was my brother, Robert Clifford Peale, M.D. Bob practiced medicine until the great Doctor called him, turning the key in his office door forever.

Over his threshold for years had come the poor and the rich, the black and white, the young and old, all seeking healing of their ills. He took them in turn, no one being more important than another. But each one was important to him. He loved them all like his own children.

When now and then he lost one to the grim reaper,

his big heart was anguished. But always he had done his best. "I treat the patient as best I know. And if sometimes God takes him, His will be done." All his life he fought disease and death, until finally, like all mortal men, he succumbed to the old enemy. He died peacefully and with faith.

Then the people started coming to pay their respects; oh, no, much more than that—their love. "I remember the night he saved my wife." "And our little boy; we were afraid he would never walk again." So went the heartfelt tributes. "He took care of me for twenty years. Whatever will I do without him?" Never before did I realize the deep love in which a doctor is held.

Bob was by choice a small-town physician. Before arthritis afflicted his fingers, he was a gifted surgeon. One of the greatest doctors in the Midwest wanted him as a protegé to succeed him in a lucrative practice. But Doctor Bob wanted neither fame nor money. He was a natural-born doctor for the small town, for there he could know and enter into the lives of the plain people. He achieved success, the success of helping people and being loved by them.

My brother often told me of the ill effects of brooding over past failures. Sometimes people became sick because they had mistreated their bodies and minds by such unhealthy thoughts as "Why did I do that?" or "Why didn't I do this?" As a result, anxiety and fear took hold of them. Finally they ended up in the office of this kindly and understanding doctor. And he told how stress and overpressing created hypertension and heart problems. "Ease up. Have a sense of humor. Don't take things so seriously, yourself included, " I heard him say time and time again, not only to his patients but also to our brother, Leonard, and to me.

He administered proper treatment and medication,

but he also gave a deeper therapy. "Forget the past. There is only sickness for you if you don't. Forget it, and look to the future. There is healing for you in the future. Get healthy in your thoughts. Trust God, forget the mistakes of the past, and don't get tense or uptight. God loves you." Again and again I've seen patients come from his office, faces shining. "I feel so much better every time I see Doctor Bob," they said. "He is a doctor you can talk to."

In his empty office I sat in his old chair. His blood-pressure-measuring instrument rested in its accustomed place on his desk. His list of patients for that last day of his practice was there. I picked up his stethoscope, then put it in my ears. With it he had listened to the heartbeat of humans for forty-five years. "Stop worrying, ease up your tension. Look at the sky, love flowers. Lift up your eyes unto the hills. Take it easy. Don't strain. Get God's peace into that heart of yours, and you'll be all right." So he told them.

I got the message, and walked out of the old office not in sadness, but with gratitude that Doctor Bob, a great and successful physician, had been my brother. "Don't dwell in the past. Look forward. Ease it up, don't push so hard. And keep your heart at peace," he seemed to say. It was his final prescription.

In my personal experience I've often found it advisable to practice easing up and falling back on a sense of humor. That attitude toward situations does indeed pay off. It so happens that much of my activity is that of speaking to large national business conventions, sales and marketing meetings, indeed all sorts of gatherings, only a very few of which are under religious auspices. And strangely enough, even after carrying out this routine for over forty years in all parts of America, I will still hear some fellow ask in surprise, "How come they got a minister to speak at this business convention?"

TELL A JOKE ON YOURSELF

I've been meeting this situation, in which a minister seems to have two strikes against him (which somehow reflects on the reputation of ministers as communicators to general audiences) by easing it up and practicing a sense of humor. And this is accomplished by anticipating the criticism. One way to do this is to deflate yourself humorously. For example, in opening my speech to a business or sales convention I begin by saying something like this: "When I heard myself, a minister, being introduced, I am sad to report that I saw no evidence of burning enthusiasm. It is entirely possible, even in this friendly audience, that there may be some fellow who asks, 'Why in the world did the program committee get a preacher to speak to this insurance (or office equipment, or whatever) convention?'

"Well, if there is such a person present, I hope these circumstances will not cause him to feel so badly as did a certain gentleman whom I met not so long ago. I was the speaker at the annual dinner of a national bankers' association and arrived at the hotel where this dinner was scheduled to be held about an hour late, unavoidably. I went to my room and changed into a tuxedo or dinner jacket.

"Thus attired, I descended in the elevator to find that all the bankers had gone into the dining room save one stray banker whom I encountered in the elevator. This banker, I am sad to relate, had obviously been communing with a form of spirits which were certainly not religious. He was swaying rather uncertainly on his feet. He fixed a thin, watery eye on me and looked me over speculatively.

"Obviously he did not know me and, dressed as I was, he did not take me for a minister, for in an intimate sort of way he said, "Hello there, buddy." This was not the form of address to which I was usually accustomed. But I answered in kind and for a couple of minutes there ensued a conversation which might roughly be described as—jocular.

"Becoming a little more confidential and rocking unsteadily, he asked, 'Where you going tonight, buddy?'

" 'Well,' I replied, 'I'm going into the dinner of the bankers' association. Where you going?'

" 'Oh,' he said disgustedly, 'I guess I'll have to go in there, too, but I don't want to, for it won't be any good.'

" 'Why,' I asked, 'won't it be any good?'

" 'Oh, believe it or not, they've got some preacher from New York to speak in there tonight.'

" 'You don't mean it!' I exclaimed.

" 'Yessir,' he declared, 'it's a positive fact.'

" 'But why in the world did they get a preacher to speak to the bankers' association?'

" 'You've got me, buddy; unless it must be they are running out of money.'

" 'Well,' I said, 'I guess I'll go on in there, anyway. There's nothing else to do around here.' He said he guessed he would, too, but he reiterated, 'I'm telling you, buddy; it won't be any good.'

"I said, 'Brother, you don't know the half of it. I *know* it won't be any good.' Having agreed that the speaker wouldn't be any good and having settled this matter to our mutual satisfaction, he went his way and I went mine.

"I went to the speaker's table and took my seat along-side the master of ceremonies and forgot all about my friend of the elevator. Until, when I rose up to speak, the first eye I caught away back in the audience was this character. To say that he was surprised is to put it mildly. He threw up his hands in a gesture of dismay and sank down out of sight. But presently he came up for air and listened to my speech. When it was over I was shaking hands with such persons as came forward to greet me when I saw him coming off from the left.

"He was now completely sobered up. I could see that he hated coming up to speak to me, but I liked him, for he proved to be a dead-game sport. Getting up in front of me, he put out his hand and said, 'Put 'er there, buddy. We were both right, weren't we?' "

This sort of easing into a situation and this sense-of-humor approach seems to serve well in the establishment of a rapport with an audience, and it opens a line of communication. Granted, the humor is the home-spun type, but the fact that it is turned on oneself seems to develop an atmosphere of good will, thus creating a friendly reaction.

The principle of easing it and cultivating a sense of humor is valid in any line of activity. Do not take yourself too seriously, but believe in yourself completely. Work diligently. Think creatively. Do all possible to insure a successful outcome. Apply intelligent thought in depth. Do your homework. Never overpress. Ease up. You have done all that you can. Let it work out. It will, and much better than if you keep fussing with it.

I well recall a taxi driver I rode with one morning in New York City. The traffic was absolutely incredible. This driver was about as super-uptight as you could imagine. And irascible, too. All the other drivers seemed to irritate him no end. And he would lean out the window and in a loud voice instruct them on how to drive. In the process he used some pretty rough and forthright language.

I noticed that he had a printed card scotch-taped to his instrument panel. It read, "If you can keep your head in all this confusion you don't understand the situation." I studied this tense man as we inched along, then I printed another card and handed it to him when I paid him off. It read: "Thou wilt keep him in perfect peace, whose mind is stayed on thee." *

"What's this?" he asked. Then he read it aloud slowly, and looking up said, "Hey, you know something, that's pretty good. Where did you get it?"

"Oh," I replied, "out of a book that can help you ease it and have a sense of humor."

Last I saw of him, he was sitting there reading that while drivers were honking at him.

NEVER LET ANYTHING AGITATE YOU

Imperturbable, serene, urbane, never letting anything rile you, letting nothing disturb you, taking things as they come, with equanimity—this is the package that is vital to successful living. And only the person who performs in this manner is able to achieve the philosophical cast of mind that can surmount current tension and stress. Then, no matter how much may be thrown at him, his inner quality of equanimity and imperturbability can ride it out. Like the man I met in St. Louis.

That morning it was really winter. The temperature was down toward zero and it was snowing hard. I called

_____* Isaiah 26:3.

the airport because I had to go to Kansas City, and was told no planes were flying. So I resorted to the railroad. When I checked out of the hotel the clerk said, "Sure is a bad day. Look outside there. Look at that snow!"

The doorman said, as he got me a taxi, "What terrible weather!"

The taxi driver looked glum, and I gave him a cheery "Good morning!"

He countered, "So what? It's a bad day." The heavy snow kept obscuring his windshield, and he complained about it all the way to the station.

The porter who picked up my bags said, "It's a bad day!" We walked toward the train. On all sides, people were coming up with the profound observation that it was a bad day. When we got to the train platform there were holes in the station roof and the wind was pushing huge gobs of snow down my neck. And I heard another fellow moan, "It's a bad day!"

A GLORIOUS BAD DAY

As I was about to follow the porter into my car I heard my name called. I turned around and here came a stocky man. He wore a light raincoat and he didn't even have it buttoned. He was striding along, obviously full of good humor. "Good morning!" he said. "It's a glorious bad day, isn't it?"

We proceeded into the train. "That's some phrase you got off," I said, " 'glorious bad day.' How come?"

He looked at me with a twinkle in his eyes. "You'd really like to know, wouldn't you? Well, I'll tell you. For forty years I was the worst sour-puss west of the Allegheny Mountains. I took a pessimistic attitude toward events and people and conditions. I was always negative. I had a gloomy outlook on everything and was always creating bad days for myself. And besides, I was as uptight as they come. Then I did a housecleaning job on myself. As a result I eased up. 'Easy does it' became my technique. I saw that I could do better if I didn't push it so stressfully. I got with it and acquired a sense of humor."

"You have that, for sure," I said admiringly. " 'Glorious bad day,' eh? Guess only you could have thought of that one."

Now let us add up a few points on this principle of easing up and having a sense of humor:

1. *Don't get stirred up and in a dither. Take it easy-like.*

2. *Take all the fuming and fretting of the media with a grain of salt. Much of today's news isn't really new. Most of it has happened before and before that.*

3. *Practice word therapy—serenity, urbanity, imperturbability, equanimity. Say those powerful, mind-healing words over to yourself every day. Let them sink into consciousness, reconditioning your stressful attitudes.*

4. *Like General Eisenhower, take the hands which life deals you and play them out without griping. You will come out O.K.*

5. *Get in harmony; easy does it; don't over-press.*

6. *Don't take yourself too seriously.*

7. *Never let the excitable immediacy of our time throw you. Keep your sense of humor. It's not all that bad.*

8. *You can live with all the confusion of today's world if you think you can. So practice thinking that you can.*

FOURTEEN

❧

GET ON TOP OF THINGS
AND STAY THERE

People who think they can are always getting on top of things. And what is equally important, they stay there.

Everyone encounters defeating factors in life, but those who think they can do not give in. By drawing upon their inner powers of mind and spirit they simply refuse to be defeated. They are aware that even the most difficult situations can be overcome, so they proceed to overcome them.

Those who practice the dynamic victory principle of you can if you think you can are truly wonderful individuals. And they range all the way from young people, to men and women of all ages, to business executives, even to lords of the realm. You can find such great people everywhere, even within yourself, for you are one, too. Let's start with the experience of a frightened and defeated small boy who with great effort and determination got on top of things and is staying there very successfully indeed. The story is related in the moving letter which follows:

> After 13 years, today is *Victory Day* at our house! Our son graduates tonight from high school! Why

is that so marvelous? Because about 10 years ago we were told, "You have a slow child; he will probably never learn to read much and will end up with an emotional problem!"

Well, those words of "wisdom" just about *"did me in."* I wrote to you for your sermons, booklets, started reading all your books. I couldn't seem to get the help I needed until I started studying your material. Then I realized that *I* had a problem, namely, I didn't really believe what I thought I believed. Well, once I got over the shock of seeing myself for the first time, I began to make progress.

I immediately said to my son who was 9 years old then, "You have a problem. Now I know you can overcome this problem, but more important, you must believe you can overcome it."

He said to me, and I will never forget what he said, "Mama, I'm afraid to try, I've failed so much trying to learn to read, I'm afraid to fail."

So I said to him, "Things are different now, you have me to help you, and you and I together have Jesus. Everything we do we will ask Jesus to help us, every time we study together, every test you have, we will first ask Jesus to help us. He will be our partner and when He's really your partner there's no way you can fail."

And I also said to him, "You say to me and I will say to you from time to time, 'One day a name will be called, and it will be your name, and you will walk across a stage and receive your high school diploma.' " This we have done for 10 years, and we have struggled and sometimes it seemed there was no end, but then I would stop, pray, read the Bible, read your sermons and books over and over and we would remind each other that *"one day,"* and we would bounce right back.

Our son is intelligent, happy, excels in math and is average in all other subjects. I predict that one day he will stand out as a great man in some field. At 19, he knows more about struggle than I did at 36. I write this to you for it is because of you and your guidance that today is *Victory Day* for this house!

So in this final chapter we remind you again that you can if you think you can provided you believe and persevere and hope. And hope is very important. "In all things," said Goethe, "it is better to hope than despair." And to keep hope going for you it is important to get on top of things mentally; to know that you can if you think you can in whatever situation confronts you. If you get on top of your problems so that you are looking down rather than up at them, you have a tactical advantage over difficulty.

And to keep hope going is important for another reason. It stimulates comeback power and we must all have comeback power to live in this world. When you become mentally convinced that you can make a comeback from any adversity, then all of your creative forces will come to your aid.

In a business office some years ago I remember seeing an old-fashioned lithograph on the wall. I do not recall where this experience occurred, but the facts connected with it remain vividly in mind. The picture was not particularly attractive; in fact, quite plain. But apparently it was held in high regard by its owner, for it occupied a prominent place in his office. And it had a message, one that has stayed with me.

The picture was of a big, sluggish-looking old scow. Oars were resting on the sand and the battered boat gave evidence of hard usage. The tide was out, leaving the scow stranded high on the beach. A glimpse of low water showed. The picture gave the impression that hardly anything could be more hopeless-looking, more inert, than a high-beached boat at low tide.

THE TIDE ALWAYS COMES BACK

The caption below the lithograph read: "The tide always comes back." One knew that when the tide did come back that inert thing would come alive, lifted on the mighty shoulders of the sea.

Curious, I asked, "Why do you have that picture on your office wall?"

"Well," explained the owner, "when I started as a young salesman I was having a very hard time. Everything seemed against me in business, and I had personal troubles as well. One morning when calling on a prospective customer I saw that picture in his anteroom. I sat studying it and thinking about that statement, 'The tide always comes back.' It said something to me. I was only in my twenties, but I started thinking that the tide was going to come back for me. It inspired me so that when my customer received me I sold him a good order. And then I asked him about the picture.

"He said he had gotten it some years before from a man with whom he did business. It was a time when he himself was discouraged. And it had helped him. So half in jest I said, 'When you pass on, how about leaving that picture to me? I get its message.' And believe it or not, he remembered, and at his death it came to me. So that is why it's on my office wall."

Never think that you've had it, or that you are through. Instead say affirmatively, "The tide always comes back." No matter the failures or defeats. They can be reversed. You can if you think you can.

A newspaper story tells of a man eighty-seven years of age who was killed by a truck. He had been quite active until the day of his accidental death. After the autopsy, the surgeon said to the widow, "Your husband must have been a very remarkable man. He had enough wrong with him to have caused his death years ago. It's amazing how a man with so many things wrong with him could have lived as long as he did."

"Well," she replied, "I can only tell you that my husband always had an optimistic point of view. He never went to bed any night of his life that he didn't say, 'I'm going to feel better tomorrow.' And," she added, "he was always saying, 'I have hopes.' "

Obviously this man had discovered the dynamic fact that the tide always comes back for the determined and positive person, for the one in whom hope never dies. Accordingly, he was able to get on top of things and to stay there for a long and useful life.

Some may object that, while the tide always comes back in the world of nature, it does not always do so in personal human affairs. Such objection, while containing elements of truth, may, however, within itself hold the reason why, in personal instances, the tide seems not to return. The attitude of expecting the return of good days after a difficult experience serves to motivate comeback. Positive belief that the tide always comes back helps even those who have experienced the worst in adversity to get once again on top of things.

Such belief was the motivation that changed the life of Audrey Braga. Let me tell you her story.

A TWELVE-YEAR-OLD AT FIFTY-FIVE

The middle-aged woman sitting in my office said she was twelve years old! "I have been on earth for fifty-five years," she hastened to explain. "That's by the calendar. But my real age is twelve." Mystified, I asked what she meant. Then Paul, her husband, related this remarkable personal history.

Paul and Audrey Braga lived in Hong Kong, where Mrs. Braga developed a pituitary gland disease and was treated by X-ray. In this treatment there was damage to the brain tissue, which resulted in slowed mental activity and inability to communicate. A neurosurgeon operated and corrected the condition to the extent that she regained the ability to talk and read. However, Audrey's mental capacity, while improved, was appraised as that of about a twelve-year-old. Her manner as she talked was childlike, in a sweet, engaging way, but she revealed a certain mature perceptiveness.

"I have something to show you," she said, unrolling some scrolls. To my amazement, she displayed several exquisite paintings in Chinese style done on long strips of paper-backed silk as is the ancient custom of China and Japan.

"How beautiful!" I exclaimed. "Who did them?"

"My wife," Mr. Braga answered proudly.

For four years after her operation Mrs. Braga had been painfully aware of mental limitation and a sense of uselessness. Then she had chanced to see in a French magazine some reproductions of ancient Chinese paintings. The article stated that "the art of the Western world seeks to stimulate the senses, while the art of China seeks to stimulate the mind." Here was just what she needed, something to help develop her mind.

So she started to paint in the Chinese manner. Her

first effort required five months to complete. She took some lessons and then began creating designs of her own. The amazing thing was that with no previous experience she showed signs of real talent.

An exhibition of a hundred of her paintings was held in Hong Kong's city hall. Outstanding artists were astonished by her evident genius. Her own explanation was simply: "I asked God to give me a new mind, and He gave me the soul and ability of a painter."

Everybody at one time or another finds himself in an unhappy situation. Perhaps you may be in one now as you read; if so, take heart, for you can change it. In every difficult situation is potential value. Believe this, then begin looking for it. You will find that values which might otherwise escape you are yours if you think they are. Perhaps you are reading this in the wistful hope of finding something that can help you change a tough situation. Well, re-examine the situation objectively and optimistically. Look for unsuspected values—they are there for sure. And remember that you, too, can get on top of things and stay there.

Therefore, wanting the tide to come back in your own affairs, hoping once again to get on top of your problems, remember that how you now think and act will determine ultimate outcomes. Aristotle says it well: "Men acquire a particular quality by constantly acting in a particular way."

The case of Jane Withers substantiates the validity of the principle, you can if you think you can—with God's help. Millions of TV viewers would be amazed to know that Jane Withers was at one time all but paralyzed by rheumatoid arthritis. Jane is the happy, positive-thinking "Josephine," the lady plumber of the TV commercial.

Jane Withers was one of the great child stars of motion pictures. At two years of age she was on stage singing and dancing. At age three she starred in her own radio program! At five, Jane and her mother went to Hollywood where she filled a role opposite Shirley Temple. And she was signed to a seven-year contract.

After forty-seven starring roles, Jane entered the University of California. Then came World War II and she was off to lift the morale of the troops. With enthusiasm and vitality she did over a hundred shows for the armed forces. She also continued with her film career and was, as a matter of fact, the only child star to work through the so-called "awkward age."

Jane did not stop working until ten days before her marriage. She was twenty-one at the time and gave up her career for a home and family. Her children "were beautiful individuals, as God created them, and they still are," says Jane.

Then this vigorous, creative, dynamic woman suffered a severe attack of rheumatoid arthritis. Paralyzed, she asked the doctor when she would walk again.

"Maybe in a year or two you'll be able to get around," he replied, "if things go well." But would that tide ever come back? Could she ever again get on top of things?

Jane expressed faith in her doctors, "But," she said, "I also told them that God was my partner and all my life I had put myself in His hands. And I really believed I would walk!"

SHE IMAGED HERSELF STRONG

Daily Jane reaffirmed that she would walk. She held constantly in mind an image of herself, not as incapacitated, but as strong and vigorous. She pictured herself as when she was a child, whole in joints and muscles. She held that picture resolutely in her conscious mind. Says Jane, "With this deep faith in God as the Source of my strength, I was walking and assuming all of the responsibilities for my children within nine months, and there has not been any recurrence."

A miracle? Well, just what is a miracle? Isn't it perhaps a phenomenon not presently explainable by scientific formula, but which is validated by the spiritual formula of positive faith? At any rate, it put Jane Withers back on top of things to stay there.

Regardless of how much trouble you are having, how hard going it all seems to be, keep your thoughts on a high and positive level. Do that no matter how difficult, even unreasonable, a situation may appear to be. Do not let yourself ever believe, with Samuel Butler, that life is "one long process of getting tired," or with Sigmund Freud that "the chief duty of a human being is to endure life." These great men notwithstanding, life is something to take hold of and master by getting on top of it. Always remember, there is more strength in you than you have ever realized or even imagined. Certainly, nothing can keep you down if you are determined to get on top of things and stay there. Draw upon your fantastic inner power for it is there, and fantastic is the only adequate description of that power. Always hold the thought that you can if you think you can.

STRENGTH IN A CRISIS

Take as an example a story which I saw in a newspaper.

A farmer stood in front of his barn watching a light truck move rapidly across his land. His fourteen-year-old son was at the wheel. The boy was too young to get a license but he was car crazy—and seemed plenty capable of handling one. So he had been given permission to drive the pickup truck around the farm, staying strictly off the public road.

But suddenly to his horror the father saw the truck overturn into a ditch. Racing to the spot, he saw there was water standing in the ditch and that the boy, pinned under the truck, was lying with his head partially submerged!

Now this farmer was a small man. According to the newspaper account he stood 5 feet 7 and weighed 155 pounds. But without an instant's hesitation he jumped down into the ditch, put his hands under the truck, and lifted it just enough so that a farmhand who came running up could pull the unconscious boy out from under.

The local doctor came at once, examined the boy, treated him for bruises, and pronounced him otherwise unhurt.

Meanwhile, the father started wondering. He had lifted that truck without stopping to consider if he could. Out of curiosity he tried again. He couldn't budge it. The doctor said it was a miracle. He explained that the physical organism sometimes reacted to an emergency by sending an enormous discharge of adrenalin through the body, giving extra power. That was the only explanation he could offer.

Now of course the capacity to deliver that much adrenalin had to be there in the glands. Nothing could have activated what wasn't there. A person normally has a great deal of latent physical power in reserve.

But experiences of this kind tell us an even more important fact; something happened to the farmer physically to produce that surge of super-normal strength. But it was more than a physical reaction. Mental and spiritual forces were involved. His mind-response, when he saw that his son might die, motivated him to the rescue with no thought but to get that truck off the boy. Such a crisis summons the amazing latent powers with what you might call spiritual adrenalin, and if the situation calls for enhanced physical strength, the mental state produces it.

DARE TO BE HEALTHY AND STRONG

Any number of things can serve to activate these reserves of inner power. It doesn't have to be sudden danger or crisis. William H. Danforth, whom I knew when he headed the Ralston Purina Company, was first made aware of his potential by a dare handed him by a teacher. In his early teens he was a sickly boy, resigned to being a chronic semi-invalid. Then one day this schoolteacher said, "I dare you to be the strongest boy in this class. I dare you to chase those chills and fevers out of your system. I dare you to fill your body with fresh air, pure water, wholesome food, and daily exercise until your cheeks are rosy, your chest full and your limbs sturdy."

Recalling that experience Danforth wrote: "As he talked, something seemed to happen inside me. My blood was up. It answered the dare which surged all through my body into tingling fingertips as itching for battle. I chased the poisons out of my system. I built a body that has equaled the strongest boys in that class and has outlived and outlasted most of them. Since that day I haven't lost any time on account of sickness."

Later in life Bill Danforth, whenever he discerned

unrealized potentials in other men, would challenge them the same way. For example, the young man employed as a mechanic in a company making electric equipment. He had dropped out after high school to go to work. He began to watch other men his age getting into much better jobs—the technically trained college graduates. Danforth writes, "I dared him to leave his job and go back to school. Again I saw that priceless light of battle leap into the eyes of a fighter. He had no money, but somehow he got to college, was graduated with honors, and today the might-have-been-mechanic is a prominent electrical engineer."

Realize that you have reserves of inner force. Let the challenge of your ambitions, of your aspirations, rouse your slumbering and often unused powers into action. Dare to be what your best self knows you ought to be; dare to be a bigger human being than you have ever been. Have great hopes and dare to go all out for them. Have great dreams and dare to live them. Have tremendous expectations and believe in them. The more you venture to live greatly, the more you will find within you what it takes to get on top of things and stay there.

I last saw William H. Danforth when he was eighty-six. It was in the crowded lobby of a St. Louis hotel. "How do you maintain your magnificent physical condition at your age?" I asked. "Let me in on your secret. I'd like to be as strong as you when I'm eighty-six."

He needed no encouragement. "I will show you the exercises I do," he replied, and proceeded right then and there to put himself through a series of calisthenics, unconscious of the numerous bystanders gathered to watch. Everybody knew and loved him. He was an unusual man. Actually, he got all of us to join him in his calisthenics. "But," he said, "the secret is more than physical exercise. It's also to keep exercising your mind. Think health—always think health."

One further story of how this man was always challenging people to activate their latent powers. A salesman once came to his office and said dispiritedly, "Mr. Danforth, I'm going to quit."

"Why? Give me one good reason why," snapped Danforth.

"Because I'm just no salesman," the man answered. "I don't have the ability or the nerve. So I'm quitting."

Danforth looked him long and straight in the eye and said, "If I know how to evaluate, you have all the qualifications of a producing salesman. So I dare you to get out of here right now and come back with more orders than you ever got in a single day. I dare you! Get going!" Instantly he saw in the salesman's eyes a gleam of battle. He turned on his heel and walked out. That night he came back exhilarated. He had done precisely what his boss had dared him to do. He had topped his previous record. He went on to become one of the best producers in the company.

An old saying declares: "When fate throws a dagger at you, there are two ways to catch it: either by the blade or by the handle." Catch the dagger by the blade and it may cut you, perhaps injure you. But if you catch it by the handle you can use it to fight your way through. When faced with a big obstacle, seize it by the handle. In other words, let a challenge rouse your fighting spirit. You can't get anywhere without a good fighting spirit. So get it going. It will draw your latent powers into action.

YOU HAVE WHAT IT TAKES TO MEET OBSTACLES

Always remember that you have spiritual and mental qualities within you which give you what it takes to overcome even the seemingly impossible. Pit that inner resistance power against any obstacle confronting you.

My old friend, George Cullum, Sr., a Dallas, Texas, contractor who often has to drill through solid rock to lay pipes, says it pretty well: "When the rock is hard we get harder than the rock. When the job is tough we get tougher than the job."

Don't let any obstacle stop you. Get right up on top of things and stay there.

Studying people as I have for many years, I have noted with interest that those who do the best in their chosen activity are the people who never take "no" for an answer. I had lunch in Poughkeepsie, New York, the county seat of Dutchess County where my farm is located, with two good friends and successful businessmen. Ronnie Morris is partner in an outstanding store and Elmer Dill is a top producer in insurance.

During the luncheon we got to talking about motivation; teaching people to do good jobs and build creative lives. 1 asked Ronnie Morris how he selected such competent personnel as the people in his store. He replied that they teach positive attitudes toward people and toward the job. A humble, friendly way of meeting people and selling them what they need and will enjoy is the sales training goal. Elmer Dill explained how the training of an insurance man is quite complex, for the agent must be many things. A sort of doctor, for one thing, to size up a prospect's fitness to pass the physical examination. He must also have some of the know-how of a lawyer and tax man to do proper estate planning.

"But," said Elmer, "we teach him a form of deafness; never to hear the word 'no'!" This remark reminded me of another sales expert, Elmer Letterman, whose philosophy is, "The sale begins when the customer says No."

A friend, John Tigrett, and I were talking about a mutual friend, Roy Thomson, better known as Lord Thomson of Fleet, publisher of 240 newspapers in England, Scotland, Canada, and the United States. Roy Thomson, born in Canada, was a poor boy who moved on to a spectacular career.

In reply to my question as to Lord Thomson's motivation, John Tigrett said, "He has a great asset—only twenty percent vision. This causes him to wear thick glasses with a small but strong lens in the center. In reading print he must hold the paper close to his eyes. But the advantage is, he never sees the stone walls which confront him. Hence these barriers to success have no effect upon him." Roy Thomson obviously is a practitioner of the "you can if you think you can" principle.

I asked a sales manager who sat with me on an airplane flight about his method for training his salesmen to overcome their obstacles and get on top of things. "We teach them to be *how* thinkers rather than *if* thinkers," was his response.

BE A HOW THINKER, NOT AN IF THINKER

He pointed out the important distinction between an "if" thinker and a "how" thinker. "The 'if' thinker," he explained, "broods over a difficulty or a setback, saying bitterly to himself, 'If I had done this or that . . . If the circumstances had been different . . . If others had not treated me so unfairly . . .' So it goes from one weak explanation or rationalization to another, round and round, getting nowhere. The world, unfortunately, has a sizeable quota of defeated 'if' thinkers.

"But the 'how' thinker wastes no energy on post-mortems when trouble or even disaster hits him. He immediately looks for the best solution, for he knows there is always a solution. He asks himself, 'How can I use this setback creatively? How can I work something good out of this? How can I stage a comeback?' Not 'if,' but 'how.' That is the success formula we teach our salesmen," he declared.

"The 'how' thinker gets problems solved effectively because he knows that values are always to be found in difficulty. He wastes no time with futile 'ifs' but goes right to work on the creative 'how.' He eliminates destructive thinking; he uses constructive thinking. And he never gives up! Never, no matter what. Believe me," he concluded, "if we had more 'how' thinkers in the world today, imagine what could be accomplished!"

One "how" attitude that really helps in getting on top of things and staying there, is the "Try—really try" principle. Two other principles closely related are: (1) "Believe—really believe," and (2) "Pray—really pray." Taken together, they cancel out the futile "ifs" and underscore the creative "hows". Take for example a letter from Herbert J. Stiefel, New York City advertising agency head who employs all three of these dynamic principles of successful achievement. I am printing his letter here for its effective description of techniques used by him in an important milestone in his business and personal life.

Dear Norman: Here is a testimonial on the power of prayer which is "hot off the press."

Some weeks ago my agency was one of several invited to solicit for a very substantial international advertising account. Actually, it is one of the largest companies in the world, employing some three hundred thousand people and doing a huge annual volume.

We were by far the smallest advertising agency invited to solicit for the account and, frankly, I was fearful that we would lose out because the other agencies had much more big client experience.

This past Tuesday was "Decision Day" and I knew the review meeting would be held in their offices at 10:45 A.M. I was haunted by the nagging fear that we were going to wind up as an also-ran and I had pretty well convinced myself with all of the reasons why we wouldn't get this account.

I was awake most of the night before. I sat in my office and wondered, "What could I do to convince these people that we were the right agency? Should I telephone and put in a final plea? Should I suggest a special fee arrangement which might offer them cash savings?"

Suddenly I realized that I hadn't used the most powerful convincer of all. I closed my office door, opened the Bible and read and prayed. I also took out of my desk drawer and read two of your booklets, *Thought Conditioners* and *Spirit Lifters*.

After a few moments I closed my eyes and concentrated very intently on all of the reasons why we were ideally suited to handle this business. I saw very clearly that I should not do anything more, that it was in God's hands, and that He was working with me.

I opened my eyes and, although the day had

started out as a dull, dreary morning, suddenly the sun came out. I felt very good and confident about the decision which would be forthcoming any minute. An hour went by and I really had to keep a firm thought about the outcome. Then the telephone rang. The caller said, "It was a tough meeting and a very difficult decision. Frankly, we were leaning very heavily in another direction when someone pointed out that a smaller agency could give more personal and dedicated service, which is what the company badly needed. This was the turning point. In just a few minutes we made up our minds to go with your agency and I am happy to tell you that you have our account effective today."

I know that this decision was God-directed and God-inspired. It has helped me in my continuing growth to be more loving and understanding and it has served as an excellent illustration to all of the members of my staff who also realized that a power far greater than human power helped make this decision. It is the biggest account we have ever secured and has opened up an entirely new field for my firm.

Your help, guidance, and friendship have come to mean so much to me in so many ways. Thank you.

Kindest personal regards. Cordially yours, Herb."

Now suppose Herb had not gotten that account. He is too profound a philosopher and positive thinker to have let that faze him. He would have made use of the philosophy my mother taught me so many times. "Norman," she would say, "when a door shuts in your face [and quite a few have] that is the time for you to realize that the Lord let that door shut in order to lead you to another door, an open one, that is the right one for you."

Some might explain that such a letter as the foregoing is materialistic. But in my opinion every one of your personal and business interests needs spiritual thinking for a sure and right outcome.

There has been an effort the past few years to downgrade business, and aspersions are cast on the business community largely from so-called intellectuals unmindful of the fact that they are themselves supported by business.

I can only say that I have been associated with businessmen all my life and by and large they are honest, generous, and participating people who give of their time and intelligence to bettering community life. In fact, some whom I've known have taught me a great deal about how to live with people and be helpful to them. And always the vital element of straightforwardness has been evident.

One instance that I recall vividly concerns Amos Sulka, once a poor immigrant boy, who built a chain of some of the finest men's furnishing shops in the world. We were fellow members of the Rotary Club of New York. He was a strong personality, always thinking straight, fearlessly honest, with a big, loving heart. He was always helping the unfortunate and especially the poor, for he never forgot what it meant to be one of the poor people. He became successful but he never forgot.

One time Amos said to me, "In order to do a good job with anything, you've got to know all there is to know about it. Then do the best you can, continue to study, trust God, be honest, give value received, have good merchandise, treat people right and always have confidence in yourself."

He told me about the day William Randolph Hearst came into his shop. Hearst, who owned a big string of newspapers, was at that time one of the greatest newspaper tycoons in the country. He was said to be sort of a tyrant, an imperious kind of man. Assertive by nature, he tended to issue orders in a way that appeared demanding. He was used to being obeyed.

He came into the shop, according to Amos Sulka, and a clerk, failing to recognize him, asked, "May I help you, sir?"

Hearst snapped, "I want to see Sulka!"

"But," the clerk said, "he does not usually wait on customers."

"I am William Randolph Hearst and I want to see Sulka."

So Sulka came out and politely said, "Welcome, Mr. Hearst, what can I do for you?"

"I want some new collars just like the one I'm wearing," said Mr. Hearst. (This was in the days when men had separate collars that fastened onto the shirt.) "I want two dozen of them."

Sulka saw at once that the collar Hearst was wearing was very out-of-style and didn't suit him at all, and he so advised the publisher courteously. Hearst bridled, "I know what I want. I've worn this collar for years and it's the right collar for me."

Amos quietly replied, "Mr. Hearst, you are the greatest newspaperman in the world. And I am Amos Sulka, the greatest haberdasher in the world. You are an expert on newspapers. I am an expert on collars, and I must tell you that the collar you're wearing doesn't do anything for your great personality. I am sorry, but I just cannot sell you that collar. I cannot mistreat you in that manner."

Hearst bristled some more. "Look here, Sulka, I tell you again; I have worn this type of collar for years and I know what collar to wear. Either you sell me this collar or you don't sell me anything."

"I would rather sell you nothing than that particular collar," Sulka answered softly. "I do not want the great William Randolph Hearst to be seen in an incongruous, out-of-date collar and for people to know he got it from Sulka."

The eyes of the two men met, both of them knowing their business, both strong men, and finally Hearst said, "All right, you old egotist, what collar do you want me to wear?"

"Did you sell him your choice of collar, Amos?" I asked.

"Of course I did," he replied, "and always he came back for the right collar. And we became great friends, too."

HOW TO AVOID THE THREE L'S

Another thing should be mentioned. Many men and women never get what they want from life because they have become conditioned in their thinking to the "three L's." And what are those destructive three L's that stand in the way of a good future for so many? The three L's are—lack, loss, limitation.

Everywhere people are saying, "I lack ability," "I lack opportunity"—"I lack, I lack, I lack." Or again, "I've got a built-in limitation," "I'm handicapped," or

"I'm poor." Thus do people manufacture their own self-limitation. The conscious mind accepts the thought of limitation, then passes it to the unconscious, which makes it determinative.

And then follow the dismal post-mortems: "I lost my chance," "I lost my money," "I tried and I lost out." So runs the depressing recital of all the things that went wrong.

Our country today is being surfeited with the three L's. You can hardly read a newspaper without being bombarded with lack thinking. In fact, practically everything in the newspapers has to do with what we lack, what we have lost or what we are losing and how we are limited. And then if you listen to the news broadcasts you will get even more of it. Most commentators are artists in reporting lack, loss, and limitation.

And of course in reading magazines you will get more of the same. Go to the theater and you will find it there, too. Heaven help us, even some pulpits are filling American minds with the three L's. No matter where we go, all of us are subjected to a barrage of lack, loss, and limitation. Really, and perhaps unconsciously, the American public is actually being made sick by being told what they haven't got, what they have lost, or what they cannot do. Wouldn't it be tremendous if somebody said, "Sure, there is lack, but there is also prosperity. There is loss, but there is also gain. There is limitation, but there is also great possibility." This kind of thinking, this kind of talking will counteract the lack, loss, and limitation psychosis that manifests itself everywhere and destructively.

But the great upbeat fact is that there are some, yes, there are thousands of people who repudiate the three L's and get on top of things to stay there. And one of them was Charles Atlas. I noted with sorrow his passing recently in his eighties. I shall never forget Charles Atlas. When I was a young man he inspired me with the tremendous principle that you can take charge of your weak, shrinking, defeated self and, with God's help, change into a really worthwhile person; that you can if you think you can.

And who was Charles Atlas? Well, I first saw him at Coney Island years ago where he was billed as the world's strongest man. It was said he could bend a spike with his bare hands, though I never saw him do that. There at Coney Island he stood beside a sign offering five hundred dollars to any man who could equal his exploits of physical strength. Admiringly, I stood watching that magnificent physical specimen; those great muscles, that tremendous torso.

He was born in Italy, Angelo Siciliano by name, and early emigrated to Brooklyn with his parents, a far different environment from the grape and olive farm in the old country. And the kids on the street, with the sometimes unmeaning cruelty of children, ridiculed him, for he was undersized, weighing less than a hundred pounds at fourteen years. One day a husky twelve-year-old beat him up. But his worst experience was when he took a girl to the beach at Far Rockaway. He had finally worked up the nerve to ask this girl to go out with him that day. They sat on the sand, Angelo dressed in his best "Sunday suit," as they called dress-up clothes in those days, and a boy came along and kicked sand all over him. The girl, disgusted that he didn't do anything about it, left him cold. He sat, humiliated and frustrated by his weakness.

Then a wonderful thing happened. Someone took him to the Brooklyn Museum, and as he stepped through the door he stopped short in astonishment. There stood great marble statues of heroic men; tall men with rippling muscles, powerful and broad-shouldered. Could it be possible there ever were such men? Then came an audacious thought; he would be like them.

He started by praying to God to make him strong. Prayers receive curious answers. He began to notice his cat, how she tensed her muscles, pitting one against the other. Why couldn't he do the same? He studied many procedures of physical development, and gradually this weak little fellow grew stronger, until came the day when he appeared at Coney Island and was justifiably billed as the world's strongest man. And his boss persuaded him to take the name of Atlas, Charles Atlas. To cap the climax, a sculptor made a statue of him like those old Grecian figures in the museum.

But Charles Atlas, now strong, never forgot those boyhood miseries of weakness. And he knew how many boys were suffering as he had suffered. Accordingly, he devoted his life to helping boys to have new hope, to become strong men, not only physically, but morally and spiritually as well. He taught them how to get on top of things; better still, how to get on top of their weakness.

KNOW WHAT YOU WANT AND BELIEVE YOU CAN HAVE IT

The great secret of getting what you want from life is to know what you want and believe you can have it. And always do something for others, especially the less fortunate. Then ask God to help you and get at it; hit it hard. Give it all you've got. Never give up. Don't be like the batter I saw at a baseball game.

I tuned in to this ball game on television. But I only followed it for about two innings, because I got disgusted. There was one man on base; there was one out. This batter walked up to the plate in a lackadaisical sort of manner, spit on his hands, rubbed them on his legs, pounded the bat on the ground, and acted like he was going to do something! The pitcher wound up and threw him a ball. It was wide and outside, and I didn't blame him for letting it go by. Then the pitcher wound up again and put a fast one right across the plate, right in the strike zone—a beautiful pitch! And he let it go by. I said to myself, "Why didn't he hit at it?"

Anyway, he pounded his bat some more. Then the pitcher wound up and put another strike right across the plate. It was a beauty; just above the knees and as straight as an arrow. What did he do? He let it go by. The next pitch was just wide of the plate, and it was called a ball. Again the pitcher went into a windup and the most beautiful strike came straight across the plate, and what did the batter do? He let it go by! He was called out on strikes. He never struck at a thing. It was incredible!

So I got to thinking about Babe Ruth. There was never anybody like him, a great big fellow. He looked old even when he was young. He was a powerful man. He had more strikeouts than any notable big-league batter. But he also had more home runs, 714 in number, than any player in history. What was the secret of his success? It was simply that he went up to the plate and hit at them! He may have had more strikeouts, but he averaged out spectacularly. "All you've got to do," he said, "is try, always try. Hit at them."

I knew Duke Kahanamoku, the world-famous Hawaiian swimmer who was once a beach boy in Honolulu; one of a dwindling number of pure Hawaiians. His fellow citizens made him sheriff to honor him as one of the greatest Islanders, and I first met him when I addressed the Honolulu Chamber of Commerce.

The Duke was one of the great swimmers of this century. Back in 1912 he won the 100-meter free-style swim in the Olympics, and eight years later he won it again, even though by then he was being crowded by a younger generation. He came close to winning it a third time in 1924, but Johnny Weissmuller beat him by a hair.

Duke Kahanamoku was a quiet, untalkative man, but he had plenty of wisdom. "It is practice, practice, practice," he said. "That is absolutely necessary. But also it is to use all your resources of body, mind and spirit—not part of them, not a fraction of them, but all of them. It is to compete all the way to the finish line, swimming with all your heart, your mind, your spirit. All your resources. You can be an ordinary athlete," he continued, "and get away with less. But if you want to be a great victor, you have to give it all you've got—everything."

The Duke died at the age of seventy-seven. He had asked for a beach boy's funeral. Ten canoes lined up on the beach in the shadow of Diamond Head and put out across the lagoon to the open sea. There they put the Duke's ashes on the bosom of the Pacific, which he loved and in which he learned to swim and from which he came to worldwide fame. Then at a given command the ten canoeists turned around and paddled furiously to shore, grounding their canoes on the beach to demonstrate the unconquerable competitive spirit of this man who said that the way to compete is to employ all your resources.

People who always try are always doing something. They do not let opportunities go by. They do not let themselves get called out on strikes. They hit at life! They hit at injustice; they hit at evils. They make life great for themselves and for others because they are motivated. They try.

So just keep on hitting, keep on trying, keep on helping people, keep on praying and believing—and you will get on top of things—and stay there.

What, then, is our sum-up of the principles suggested in this chapter?

1. *Always keep hope going for you.*
2. *Believe, and never stop believing, that the tide always comes back.*
3. *Realize there is more potential strength built into you than you have ever demonstrated.*
4. *To use an old-fashioned but powerful phrase —dare to be what you want to be and can be.*
5. *Never take no for an answer.*
6. *Do your best and leave the results to God.*
7. *Drop the three L's—lack, loss, limitation— from your vocabulary.*
8. *Hold the image of the life you want and make the image become fact.*
9. *Keep on hitting; keep on trying.*
10. *And don't forget prayer. It releases power.*

—And remember . . . always remember—
YOU CAN IF YOU THINK YOU CAN.